JOHN & YOKO/PLASTIC ONO BAND

BY JOHN LENNON & YOKO ONO

WITH CONTRIBUTIONS FROM
THE PEOPLE WHO WERE THERE

weldon**owen**

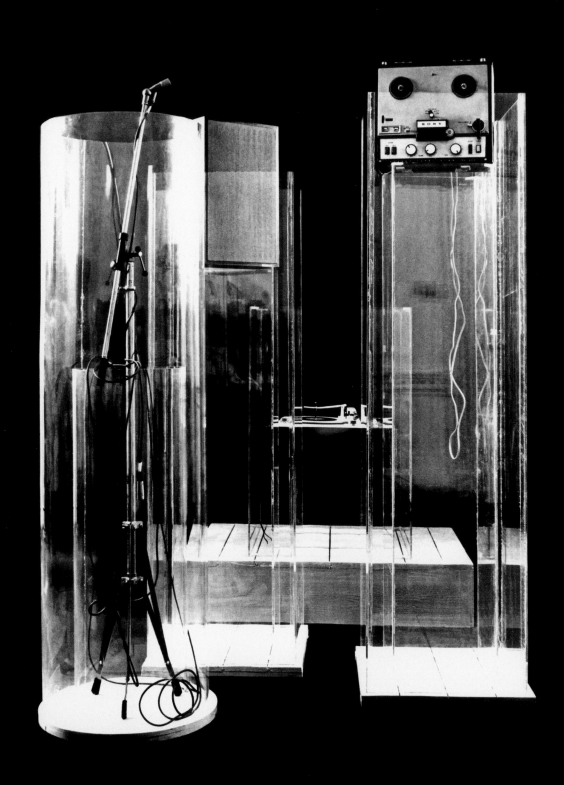

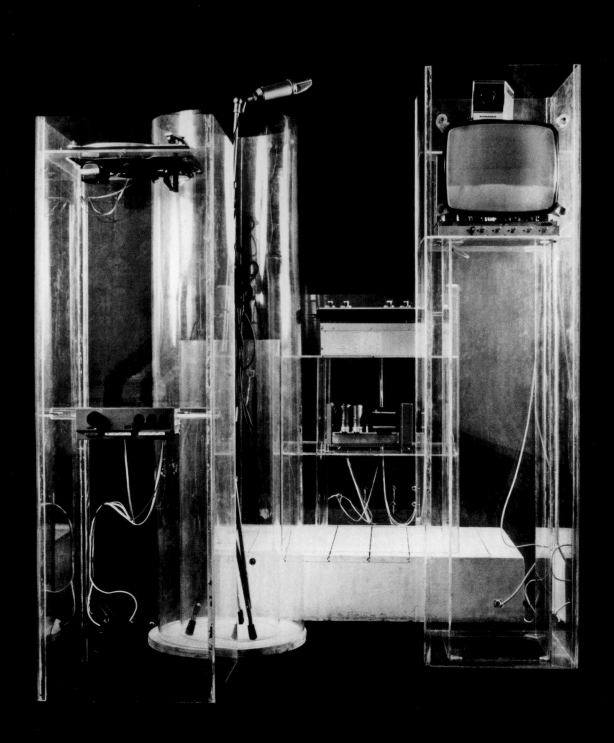

CONTENTS

YOKO ONO / PREFACE

In 1967, before John and I got together, I was invited to do a show in Berlin. I thought it would be great to do a show where on the stage there would be a band, but instead of each member of the band being a human being, there would be plastic boxes with a mechanism or robot inside that would perform or play an instrument or a tape recording.

A year later, when I explained this to John, he immediately got a piece of wood to use as a base and pasted up a band on the stage. He put a few plastic objects together: a cassette box, a paperweight, the tube from a record cleaning cylinder brush, and created a little plastic model and said, 'well, we should call our band Plastic Ono Band'. That was the beginning of Plastic Ono Band.

The following year, when we recorded 'Give Peace A Chance', we thought, let's release it as a Plastic Ono Band single because it wasn't just John & Yoko on the record, it was all the people with us in Montreal and the audience – we wanted everyone in the world to join us and sing the song to create world peace.

The concept of Plastic Ono Band was 'the message is the music'. So everyone on the recording is in it, everyone listening to the recording is in it, everyone who sings the song is in it, you're in it and everyone in the world is in it – making Plastic Ono Band the most musical and imaginative group in the world.

When we played at the Rock 'n' Roll Revival show in Toronto, we were introduced onto the stage as Plastic Ono Band and the name stuck. It was exciting for John because he felt he didn't need to live up to the Beatles mystique. We could be anybody or perform anything and we had total freedom and total communication.

During 1970, we did intensive Primal Scream therapy for six months, which was very beneficial for us and many of the songs were inspired as a result of those sessions. John's songs were a literate expression of his feelings and I was more interested in expressing my feelings using revolutionary vocal sounds.

At one point, John wanted to call his album 'Primal' and my album 'Scream', but I had been screaming long before we started therapy, and we realized the therapy, whatever its title, was just a mirror. John was looking into a mirror at his own soul and soon realized the fundamental truths he discovered for himself was advice needed by everybody: feel your own pain, learn to cry, believe in yourself, love is real, it's gonna be all right.

I was using my vocal training and technique to discover primeval expressions, sounds and rhythms from deep within that could also metaphysically reconnect us with our souls and our collective unconscious.

Everyone was in it. We called the albums *Plastic Ono Band*.

Remember:
A dream you dream alone is only a dream
A dream you dream together is reality

love, yoko

Yoko Ono Lennon
New York City

Opposite: Yoko Ono Lennon portrait with a cut grapefruit, photographed by Matthew Placek at home in the kitchen; The Dakota, 1 West 72nd Street, New York, 17 May 2013.

Who are the Plastic Ono Band?

YOU|ARE|THE|PLASTIC|ONO|BAND

Page 14: 'Who Are The Plastic Ono Band?' advertisement, *New Musical Express*, 28 June 1969.
Page 15: 'You Are The Plastic Ono Band' advertisement for the single 'Give Peace A Chance', featuring the *Plastic*

Ono Band sculpture superimposed on a page from the phone book, doctored to include many familiar names from the Beatles, Apple and friends hidden amongst the listings of the Joneses; original artwork, July 1969.

Plastic ONO Band is a musical group which
believes that "the message is the music".
and the communication of it is the performance.
Whoever has a message is therefore part of the group.

The music is in your mind.
The mind is what we share.
like sunshine and water.

What we can do, is to keep it running, flowing,
and keep it clean - drinkable. For us, there is
no still water. All words are verbs and all
statements are communication. Also imagination
is not a product of a genius. Imagination comes
out of necessity of communication —
and two minds are always better than one

because mind needs recharging and the more
recharged the better.

That is why we believe that the Plastic ONO Band
which includes all minds of the world is the
most imaginative, and the most musical group
in the world.

Plastic ONO is you recharged. And you recharge
the Plastic ONO.

"on Plastic ONO Band"
~~New York~~, New York
y.o. 71

POST CARD. ©COPYRIGHT JOHN&YOKO '70

Opposite: 'On Plastic Ono Band', a manifesto by Yoko Ono in her handwriting, New York, 1971.
Below: Plastic Ono Band original designs and manifesto, illustrated by John Lennon, 1969.

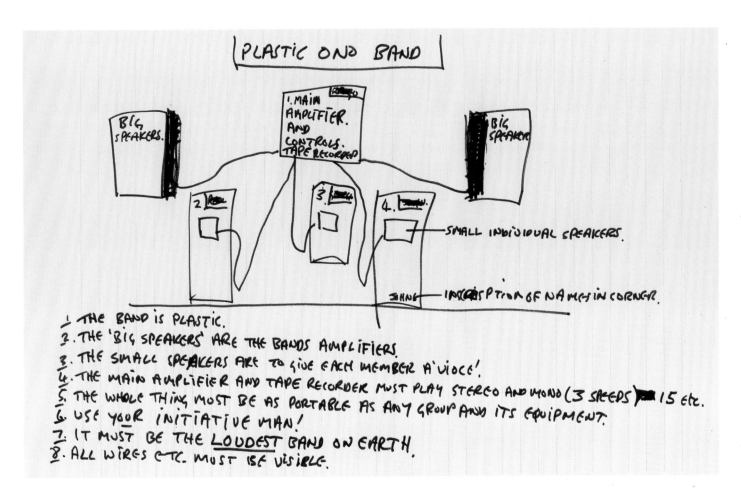

The first incarnation of the *Plastic Ono Band* sculpture, created and assembled by John Lennon using a wooden 'stage', a plastic box, a 'Parostatik Disc Preener' box, a Perspex paperweight and a compact cassette box, photographed above the television in the Sun Room at home (below) and in the garden (opposite).

Also visible are four versions of Yoko's *Painting To Hammer A Nail* (1961), her Indica Gallery catalogue and a collection of idols, tchotchkes and souvenirs that John had accumulated from touring and travelling all over the world; Kenwood, St George's Hill, Weybridge, Surrey, December 1968.

Overleaf: 'PLAY LOUD' and 'PLAY QUIET' labels for Apple's
UK pressing of the single 'Instant Karma! (We All Shine On)' /
'Who Has Seen The Wind?' released on 20 February 1970. It
went to No. 5 in the UK and No. 3 in the US charts, and was
the first solo single by a Beatle to sell over a million copies.

THE PLASTIC ONO BAND 1968

(APPLES.1003A)
APPLES 1003

Produced:
PHIL SPECTOR

Northern Songs Ltd.

℗ 1970

Composed:
Lennon

PLAY LOUD

Mfd. in U.K.

LENNON/ONO
With the Plastic Ono Band

INSTANT KARMA!

Apple Records - All Rights of the Manufacturer and of the Owner of the Recorded Work Reserved

(APPLES.1003B)
APPLES
1003

Produced:
JOHN
LENNON

Ono Music

℗ 1970

Composed:
Ono

PLAY

QUIET
Mfd. in U.K

LENNON/ONO
with the Plastic Ono Band

WHO HAS SEEN THE WIND ?

Unauthorised Public Performance, Broadcasting and Copying of this Record Prohibited

BED PEACE / MONTREAL

John: I always considered myself an artist, musician, or poet. And the so-called pain of the artist was always paid for by the freedom of the artist. And the idea of being a rock 'n' roll musician suited my talents and mentality. And the freedom was great. But then I found I wasn't free. I'd got boxed in. It wasn't just because of a contract. But the contract was a physical manifestation of being in prison. And that I might as well have gone to a nine-to-five job as carry on the way I was carrying on. And there's two ways to go. You either go to Vegas – and singing any great hits if you're lucky – or go to hell, which is where Elvis went; literally dying.

Yoko: When John was in India, I went to this Indian guy in London who read my palm and said, 'You're like a wind which is going around the world very fast, that is almost invisible. You've just met somebody that is going to change your life, who is like a big mountain. He's not going to stop you. He's going to make a connection with you and the world. He's going to make you become physical so that you will be visible to the world. The next four years is going to be something that you never dreamed of.' Very few people have lived this kind of life.

John: She came from this avant-garde field, and I'd come from the straight rock field. We wanted to know what could we do together because we wanted to be together. We wanted to work together. We don't want to just be together on weekends. We want to be together and live and work together.

The first attempt at our being together and producing things together was the *Two Virgins* albums and the events we did – whether they were Bed-Ins or posters, or whatever the events or films we did then. We crossed over into each other's fields, like people do from country to pop. We did it from avant-garde left field, from rock 'n' roll left field. We tried to find a ground that was interesting to both of us and we both got excited and stimulated by each other's experiences.

People still had this idea that the Beatles were some kind of sacred thing that shouldn't step outside of its circle and it was hard for us work together then. It was impossible for a Beatle to be in a bag in Trafalgar Square with a Japanese actress, or say, 'Peace, Brother!' to the newsreel. That's why we ended up doing things like Bed-Ins, because that was, 'how can we do it?' but still do it *à la Ono* – including me, because it was great and I wanted to be part of it. And that's why she ended up doing things like pop music.

We knew that when we got married we would be followed by the press. So we sat down and said: 'What use can we make of the situation that would be entertaining, a nice projection of what can be, that isn't just Vietnam and death-to-the-invader or "Kill a Cop for Peace", or any of the variations that were going on. How can we utilize the situation we are in?' We had a honeymoon in public.

The point of the Bed-In was a commercial for peace, as opposed to a commercial for war, which was on the news every day those days, in the newspapers. Every day it was dismembered bodies and napalm and we thought, 'Well, why don't they have something nice in the newspapers?'

We tried to do it in New York, but the American government wouldn't let us in. They knew we'd done it in Amsterdam; they 'didn't want any peaceniks here'. We ended up doing it in Montreal instead, and broadcast it across the border.

We enjoyed the Bed-Ins and the seven days talking to the reporters was hilarious. Seven days. Ask anything. No secrets, no time limit. Come in as long as you like, until you've got everything you need to know about John & Yoko and what we stand for. They all came charging through the door, thinking we were going to be screwing in bed. And of course, we were just sitting there with peace signs! It didn't matter what the reporters said, because our commercial went out irrespective.

After answering all these questions many, many times, it got down to all we were saying was 'give peace a chance'. Not 'we have a formula', or 'communism or socialism will answer it', or 'any -ism could answer it'. We didn't have a format. We couldn't give you a plan. But just consider the idea of not having this war. Just consider it. So that's what we were saying. We recorded it in the bedroom of the Montreal Hilton.

Petula Clark: I was doing a series of concerts at the Place des Arts in Montreal. I'd previously gone to Montreal as a French performer. But then 'Downtown' became a huge hit everywhere, and they asked me to go back to Montreal, so I thought I could do a bilingual show and do both French and English songs. I was wrong. I sang in French and the English-speaking audience were unhappy and quite vocal, and the French were particularly vocal when I sang in English. It was like open war. It was really very hard, and I was very hurt and I couldn't understand it at all. I really didn't know what to do and I needed to talk to somebody

Drove from Paris to the Amsterdam Hilton
Talking in our beds for a week
The newspapers said
'Say, what you doing in bed?'
I said, 'We're only trying to get us some peace'

'The Ballad of John & Yoko', verse 5

John & Yoko holding a carnation and a rose at their
Bed-In; Room 1742, Queen Elizabeth Hotel, Montreal,
Quebec, photographed by Ivor Sharp, May 1969.

John & Yoko preparing to perform 'Give Peace A Chance' with
Petula Clark, Tommy Smothers, Timothy and Rosemary Leary, Murray
The K and many others during the Montreal Bed-In. John carves the
'Montreal 69' portraits of himself and Yoko onto the body of his 1964
Gibson J-160E, adding to those from the Amsterdam Bed-In; Room
1742, Queen Elizabeth Hotel, Montreal, Quebec, 1 June 1969.

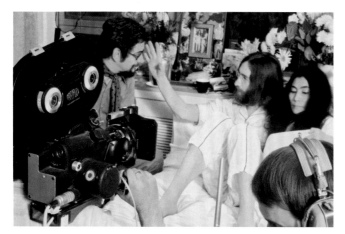

who I had no connection with, and John was in town with Yoko doing a Bed-In for peace. I remember it was pouring with rain, and I walked over to the hotel, a far enough walk to get drenched. I went up, no security whatsoever. The door was open and I walked in and there they were sitting up in bed in white and I arrived like a drowned rat, crying. He said, 'What's up with you?' – and we'd never met before. He put his arms around me and said, 'What's going on?' I told him the story and he was very, very sweet; very funny about the whole thing. And then he said, 'You know what? Fuck 'em!' And I went, 'Oh, OK thank you for that, John.' He said, 'You know what, you need a glass of wine. Go into the living room.' It was a suite and there were a few people I knew in there – one of the Smothers Brothers and Timothy Leary was there. It was very nice, very cool and they had this music playing in the background and somebody handed out this lyric sheet and we all started singing along and it was 'Give Peace A Chance', and it was all being recorded and I am on that record. I can't hear myself, but I'm there!

Tommy Smothers: I was in Montreal and I was invited to show up. They were in bed and Timothy Leary and a whole bunch of radical people were there and [impersonating John] 'We're singing a song, Tom, here's another guitar.' He started playing and singing in D, or some simple chord. So I went up to the next chord inversion, put a little diminished passing chord in – I thought I was showing him all my good stuff. He said, 'Just play it the way I wrote it, Tommy. If I wanted you to play it another way I would have written it like that.' [laughs] It was a beautiful song, wasn't it? And just so simple. I kinda had a feeling it was going to be that kind of song.

Timothy Leary: In the twenty-first century, as we look back at the wild and woolly twentieth century, I think the legend of John & Yoko will stand out as something great. The fusion of an Oriental woman and a Western man; an upper-class woman and a working-class boy. Yoko was Fifties, John was Sixties. That linkage in partnership – my wife Barbara and I hold it as a model. We try to do it too. And I think there are millions of people that are going to benefit from what they did.

John: My rhythm sense has always been a bit wild. If you hear the record, halfway through it, I got on the on-beat instead of the backbeat, so I had to put on a lot of tape echo to double up the beat, to keep a steady beat right through the whole record – so it goes 'Boo-boom, Boo-boom', instead of 'Baa, Baa'.

I didn't write it with Paul. We always had that thing that our names would go on songs even if we didn't write them. It was never a legal deal between Paul and me, just an agreement when we were fifteen or sixteen to put both our names on our songs. I'd put his name on 'Give Peace A Chance', though he had nothing to do with it. It was a silly thing to do, actually. It should have been Lennon/Ono.

As kids, we were all opposed to folk songs because they were so middle class. It was all students with big scarfs and a pint of beer in their hands, singing folk songs in 'la-di-da' voices: 'I worked in a mine in Newcastle', and all that shit. There were very few real folk singers. I liked Dominic Behan a bit and there was some good stuff to be heard in Liverpool. Just occasionally, you would hear very old records on the radio or TV of real workers in Ireland, or somewhere, singing these songs, and the power of them is fantastic. Today's folk song is rock 'n' roll. Although it happened to emanate from America, that's not really important in the end because we wrote our own music and that changed everything.

I was pleased when the movement in America took up 'Give Peace A Chance', because I had written it with that in mind. I hoped that instead of singing 'We Shall Overcome' from 1900 or something, they would have something contemporary. I felt an obligation even then to write a song that people would sing in the pub, or on a demonstration. That is why I would like to compose songs for the revolution now.

Yoko: All those Vietnam protests really changed the world. There was always that element who were really resisting it. That was the saving grace – that people were aware that they were that young generation who were really against it. And so it worked very well for the world. And the Bed-In was just part of it, a definite part of it. It was a statement on a very theatrical level and I think it was very effective. We were artists and did it our own way. We felt very good about it then, and it was such an incredibly strange thing that we were doing. At the time it was a courageous thing to do. John was making the statement in a way that he was looking at the far, far future. I saw it in his eyes. He was saying, 'OK this is what we're going to do together.' And we're going to give peace a chance. To the world.

John: It wasn't like, 'You have to have peace!' Just give it a chance. We ain't giving any gospel here, just saying, 'How about this version for a change?' We think we have the right to have a say in the future. And we think the future is made in your mind.

Everybodies talking bout

Bagism	Ministers	resolution	John + Yoko
Shagism	sinisters	evolution	Timmy Leary
Dragism	bannisters	masturbation	Tommy Smothers
Madism	Cannisters	flagellation	Bobby Dylan
Ragism	Bishop +	regulations	Tommy Cooper
Tagism	Fishops	intergrations	Derek Taylor
This-ism	Rabbies	meditations	Norman Mailer
That-ism	Popeyes	United Nations	Alen Ginsberg
	Bye Byes.	Gongratulations	Hare Krisna
			Hare Krana

All we are saying is give peace a chance.

GIVE PEACE A CHANCE

Two, a one two three four

Everybody's talking 'bout
Bagism, Shagism, Dragism, Madism
Ragism, Tagism, This-ism, That-ism
-ism, -ism, -ism

All we are saying is give peace a chance
(That's all we're saying)
All we are saying is give peace a chance
(Yeah! Come on!)

Everybody's talking 'bout
Ministers, sinisters,
Banisters and canisters
Bishops and fishops and
Rabbis and Popeyes
and bye bye
(Bye bye)

All we are saying is give peace a chance
(What are we saying?
Give peace a chance)
All we are saying is give peace a chance
(Give it a chance, baby,
Give it a try. Right!)

Let me tell you now
Everybody's talking 'bout
Revolution, evolution,
Mass inflation, flagellation
Regulation, integration,
Meditation, United Nations
Congratulations!

All we are saying
(Keep talking)
Is give peace a chance
(Hey! They can't ban this one)
All we are saying
(Let's hear it for the West Coast)
Is give peace a chance
(Oh let's! Listen to this. OK!)

Everybody's talking 'bout
John & Yoko, Timmy Leary, Rosemary,
Tommy Smothers, Bobby Dylan,
Tommy Cooper, Derek Taylor,
Norman Mailer, Alan Ginsberg,
Hare Krishna, Hare, Hare Krishna

All we are saying is give peace a chance
(Come on, come on, come on)
All we are saying is give peace a chance
(Let's hear it for the squares)
All we are saying is give peace a chance
(Let's hear it for the hippies
And the yippies. Yay!)
All we are saying *(Come on!)*
Is give peace a chance
(Let's hear it for people now. Yeah!)

All we are saying is give peace a chance
(Let's hear it for Hare Krishna! Yay!)
All we are saying is give peace a chance
(Everybody now, come on)
All we are saying is give peace a chance
(What are we saying, let me hear it)
All we are saying is give peace a chance
(Everybody now, come on)

All we are saying
(You won't get it unless you want it
And we want it now)
Is give peace a chance *(Yeah, now!)*
All we are saying *(Come together)*
Is give peace a chance
(Come together, all together)
All we are saying is give peace a chance
(Can anybody hear me? Yeah!)
All we are saying
(We can get it tomorrow, today)
Is give peace a chance
(If you really want it, now. OK! Now)
All we are saying is give peace a chance
(Yes. Yeah!)
All we are saying is give peace a chance
OK, beautiful! Yeah, we made it!

Previous pages: John & Yoko and Tommy Smothers rehearse 'Give Peace A Chance'.
Opposite: John & Yoko perform 'Give Peace A Chance' accompanied by Murray The K, Timothy and Rosemary Leary, Antony Fawcett, Tommy Smothers, Petula Clark, Derek Taylor, Kyoko Cox and many others, recorded by André Perry; Room 1742, Queen Elizabeth Hotel, Montreal, Quebec, 1 June 1969.

Below: Original single sleeve for Apple's UK release of the Plastic Ono Band's 'Give Peace A Chance' / 'Remember Love', featuring a black-and-white photograph of one of the *Plastic Ono Band* sculptures. Released on 4 July (UK) and 7 July (USA) 1969, the single reached No. 2 in the UK and No. 14 in the US charts.

The cover of the sheet music for 'Give Peace A Chance' by Plastic Ono Band, featuring a photo collage of the *Plastic Ono Band* sculptures and cut-outs of Ethan Russell's photographs of the launch party at Chelsea Town Hall, London, on 3 July 1969.

DEREK TAYLOR / WHAT IS THE PLASTIC ONO BAND?

Congratulations on a hit, everybody!

The ad said 'YOU are the Plastic Ono Band' and that is the truth. You are and I am and the Beatles are, any of them, or none at all. Anyone. The first record was 'Give Peace A Chance' and it is a good thing that this is so because it is nice to launch a band with a Number One record, but it wasn't necessarily the first release; it just happened that way; it just happened. It could have been a song written against a track recorded for *Sgt. Pepper* and not used in that most wonderful of all albums. It could have been a track recorded by Swinging George Harrison and his All stars – a beautiful thing he recorded especially for the Plastic Ono Band – recorded expressly by George and his friends because they love John and will do his bidding. It was 'Give Peace A Chance' because it happened. And all its other releases will happen as they happen.

The band was made in Perspex in Hoylake, in Cheshire (where Selwyn Lloyd and I were brought up separately) by an inventor I know called Charles Melling. It was Yoko's idea, with John, made to her specifications; four pieces – like John, Paul, George and Ringo, three taller and one shorter. Two rectangular, one cylindrical and a cube. One column holds a tape-recorder and amplifier, another a closed circuit TV set with live camera, a third a record player with amplifier, and the fourth has a miniature light show and a loud speaker. But they could hold anything, they're as adaptable as the Beatles. The Perspex columns were fitted with their equipment by Apple Electronics under the direction of (Magic) Alexis Mardas and here ends the first and last technological press release you will have from me. To other details of the Plastic Ono Band....

The band may be the property of Apple, but it also belongs to everyone because what it represents is freedom, freedom for performers to be themselves, taking no heed of who they are, or what they look like, or where they have been, or what their music is supposed to be. It could be children in a playground screaming their release from the bondage of the classroom, or it could be John & Yoko screaming their love one for another. It could be anything.

The band will tour – the British band will tour here, and in the US another band is to be built, built to withstand the long hauls across that amazing continent and maybe beyond, maybe far beyond one day. Who knows, any more?

'Give Peace A Chance' was born in Montreal one Saturday night when the mood was right and the moon was full. John had written it maybe for the Beatles, maybe for anyone who turned up and seemed right. That night in Montreal forty or more seemed right and ready: Tim Leary, Tom Smothers, John, Yoko, a few journalists, many friends, a few activists from the peace movement now proliferating in North America (and not without reason) and dare I say there was a member of the CIA there in drag.

I don't know what the Plastic Ono Band is; the more I think about it, the more I don't know what to say it is. But I know it's right and I know it's good. I know it works. You only have to feel it to know it's good and right and workable.

I just phoned John to ask him what he would say the Plastic Ono Band was. He wouldn't know what to say except to repeat the ad, the ad that says it all.

YOU are the Plastic Ono Band, And because you are you, you understand. Don't you?

Derek Taylor, *Disc and Music Echo*, 26 July 1969

It is nice to be, as Derek Taylor pointed out last week, a member of the Plastic Ono Band. If you remember, you are too – our first hit record and it is a good feeling. Play it somewhere friendly, and sing along and it does feel right. Sometimes you must read the papers or hear the radio or even watch the degrading spectacle of television (remember when television had a capital 't'?) and feel sad at the cruelty, the stupidity and the selfishness of a great number of those with whom we share this planet. They will take it from us if we don't stop them. Then think, when you are saddened, about some of the good people who breathe the same air you do, who walk the same land you do and who see the same sunshine and feel the same rain as you. Most of them you'll never see or meet or know – but they're there and you'd like them, love them if you did meet them. John Lennon and Yoko are two of them. I don't know the other Beatles – I've only met John and his lady twice and briefly: however, I honestly feel as close to Yoko and John as I do to any other people on earth. To talk to the two of them is to talk to one person which sounds daft but isn't. The chances are good, that you'll never meet them and I probably won't again. It doesn't matter much anyway because it is a joy to know that they are alive somewhere. It is a joy to know that so many good and thoughtful people are alive somewhere – and some are no longer alive in the very narrowness of the idea of 'living'. It is good to know that YOU are alive. Perhaps it's just another record. Apple IS just another company, John & Yoko are just other people. To me it's a magic record and they are magic people.

John Peel, *Disc and Music Echo*, 2 August 1969

The Plastic Ono Band's launch party for 'Give Peace A Chance' at Chelsea Town Hall, London, on 3 July 1969. The sculptures were exhibited onstage with a camera pointing at the audience that showed the viewer as part of the band ('You are the Plastic Ono Band') on the television screen in the sculpture. Behind them is a large photo collage by designer Christine Marsh, featuring portraits of influential people. The compère for the evening was friend and DJ Kenny Everett.

LIVE PEACE IN TORONTO / VARSITY STADIUM, TORONTO

John: We got this phone call from Toronto on a Friday night that there was a Rock 'n' Roll Revival show, with a hundred thousand audience and that Chuck Berry, Jerry Lee Lewis, Bo Diddley, all the great rockers, were going to be there – and The Doors were top of the bill.

Kim Fowley (MC, Rock 'n' Roll Revival show): We had a problem. We only sold 2,000 tickets and no one was interested in coming to Canada from America via Detroit and the other cities. Halfway through the week I met with the promoters – John Brower, Ken Walker and Thor Eaton of Eaton's Department Store who financed the thing. It was my idea to bring John Lennon over and act as an MC. So John Brower called Apple Records. John Lennon got on the phone and heard the pitch in two minutes. And he replied he would rather join in and be a part of it and didn't require any money. But Lennon did require film rights and recording rights. John Lennon was in the music business. He was in show business. Allen Klein showed up and D. A. Pennebaker showed up with the film unit and this whole thing was recorded and a gold album came out of it.

John: We didn't have a band then. We didn't even have a group that had played with us for more than half a minute. I called Eric.

Eric Clapton: When John phoned, I was really excited and very pleased. It sounded like such a good idea, even though none of us had played together on a stage before.

Klaus Voormann: John said, 'Klaus, I want to put a band together, called the Plastic Ono Band. Do you want to play the bass?' I didn't know Yoko and I had no idea what they were going to do. Were they going to be in underpants on stage? What were we going to do? I had no idea. Maybe no pants at all! And he said, 'No, no, no! I want to have a band that tours and records. Eric Clapton already said yes and now I'm asking you.' So I said, 'Yeah, OK, let's do it. Who's the drummer?' 'No idea, no drummer yet.' And he called Alan White.

Alan White: I said, 'Absolutely!' The limo came in the morning, and there I was in the VIP lounge at London Airport and there was John & Yoko and Klaus Voormann and I sat down and introduced myself and John said, 'Oh, I forgot to tell you, Eric Clapton's playing!' He walked out of the bathroom right then. And I went 'Oh my god, this is incredible!' I was only twenty.

John: We didn't know what to play – we'd never played together before. And on the airplane we were running through these oldies with electric guitars, so you couldn't hear… saying, 'Are we doing the Elvis version of "Blue Suede Shoes", or the Carl Perkins with the different break at the beginning, "ta-jing-jing" instead of "De…"' whatever.

Alan White: I remember John being really adamant that we were going to play the Carl Perkins version of 'Blue Suede Shoes' because it had an extra beat in it and he was really worried somebody was going to make a mistake. We eventually got it right and that was my first introduction to working with him – going through the songs in the back of an aircraft!

John: I hadn't got the words to any of the songs. I knew 'Dizzy Miss Lizzy', 'Blue Suede Shoes' and a couple I hadn't done since The Cavern, and that's all we could do.

Klaus Voormann: The flight was over in no time and then we were at the airport. There were these big limousines standing there picking us up and it was all new to me. It was just incredible. When we hit the highway, in came all these great people on motorbikes, escorting us down to the stadium.

Mal Evans: Immediately we arrived at the stadium, I began to feel all the tremendous excitement of the old touring days. I don't know what it is but whenever the Beatles used to near a theatre or stadium, you could feel the tension, and when the 20,000 audience in Toronto sensed that John was there, there was an incredible feeling of excitement in the air.

Eric Clapton: John stood in the dressing room, which was admittedly rather tatty, beforehand saying, 'What am I doing here? I could have gone to Brighton!' After all, it was a long way to go for just one concert.

Mal Evans: They quickly gathered together backstage and plugged all their guitars into one small amp and started running through the numbers they were going to perform.

Finally, at midnight, the compère Kim Fowley went onstage to announce the Plastic Ono Band. He did a really great thing. He had all the lights in the stadium turned right down and then asked everyone to strike a match. It was a really unbelievable sight when thousands of little flickering lights suddenly shone all over the huge arena.

Poster advertising the Toronto Rock 'n' Roll Revival 1969 concert for an audience of over 20,000 people, featuring The Doors, Bo Diddley, Chicago, Alice Cooper, Chuck Berry, Jerry Lee Lewis, Gene Vincent, Little Richard and many others, with Kim Fowley as MC. John & Yoko appeared as the Plastic Ono Band with Eric Clapton, Klaus Voormann and Alan White. The performance was released as their album *Live Peace in Toronto 1969*, the first live album by any member of the Beatles; Varsity Stadium, Toronto, 13 September 1969.

Illustration by Klaus Voormann featuring Yoko, Dan Richter (assistant), Alan White (drums), Klaus Voormann (bass), Eric Clapton (guitar) and John (guitar) rehearsing for the first time the songs they would all play that evening; on board the plane to Toronto, 13 September 1969.

Illustration by Klaus Voormann featuring the Plastic Ono Band: Alan White (drums), John (guitar), Klaus Voormann (bass), Eric Clapton (guitar), Yoko (vocals); rehearsing in the dressing room at Varsity Stadium, Toronto, 13 September 1969.

In limousines organized by manager Allen Klein, the
Plastic Ono Band speed from Toronto airport towards
Varsity Stadium, escorted by a motorcade of eighty bikes
from the Toronto Vagabonds Motorcycle Club led by
founder Ed 'Edjo' Leslie; Toronto, 13 September 1969.

Above: The Plastic Ono Band: Klaus Voormann (bass), Eric Clapton (guitar), Alan White (drums), Yoko Ono (vocals), John Lennon (guitar) performing Yoko's 'Don't Worry Kyoko (Mummy's only looking for her hand in the snow)'; Varsity Stadium, Toronto, 13 September 1969.

Below: Fans and security congregate outside the backstage area entrance on Bloor Street as the Plastic Ono Band are about to take to the stage; Varsity Stadium, Toronto, 13 September 1969.

Kim Fowley: *Get your matches ready. Ladies and gentlemen, the Plastic Ono Band! Toronto welcomes the Plastic Ono Band! Toronto! Brower and Walker present the Plastic Ono Band! Give Peace A Chance! Give Peace A Chance!*

John: I'd never seen it anywhere else. I think it was the first time it happened. The sun was just going down and all these candles lit up and it was really beautiful.

Alan White: I remember walking out into the middle of the stage and there was a drum riser there and I went and sat on the stool. I had no drums and I was going, 'Excuse me guys, there's no drums here!' John and Eric were tuning their guitars and doing all that kind of stuff and then finally a whole bunch of guys came out of nowhere with one drum each and they put a drum kit together in two minutes, thrust a pair of sticks in my hand and then John went 'one, two, three, four' and that was it!

John: *Hello and good evening! OK, we're just gonna do numbers that we know, you know, because we've never played together before.*

John: The buzz was incredible. I never felt so good in my life. Everybody was with us and leaping up and down doing the peace sign, because they knew most of the numbers anyway. When we did 'Money' and 'Dizzy' I just made up the words as I went along. The band was bashing it out like hell behind me. Then after 'Money' there was a stop, and I turned to Eric and said 'What's next?' He just shrugged, so I screamed 'C'mon!' and started into something else ('Dizzy Miss Lizzy'). We did 'Yer Blues' because I've done that with Eric before. It blew our minds. And we did a number called 'Cold Turkey' we'd never done before and they dug it like mad.

Eric Clapton: It was really refreshing to do these songs because they are very simple and uncomplicated. John and I really love that music. That's the kind of music that turned John on initially and it's the same for me. In fact, I could go on playing 'Money' and 'Dizzy Miss Lizzy' for the rest of my life.

Mal Evans: Finally, came John's last number 'Give Peace A Chance'. Before he sang it, John said, 'This is what we came for really, so sing along,' and the audience did. I think every one of the 20,000 people there must have joined in. It was a wonderful sight because they all thrust their arms above their heads and swayed in time to the music. Then John said, 'Now Yoko is going to do her thing all over you.'

Yoko had been inside a bag howling away during John's numbers. She sang two songs, 'Don't Worry Kyoko' and 'John, John (Let's Hope for Peace)'.

Alan White: I had my monitors on stage and I thought the monitors were feeding back and Klaus said 'No it's Yoko! Look!' and I looked over the drums and there was a white bag writhing around there on the floor. And I went, 'Oh, OK!'

Klaus Voormann: We never rehearsed for Yoko. We had no idea what was going to come out of her throat, not the faintest idea. John just said, 'Oh, play this Bo Diddley riff, just on E and open tuning and you just play along.' And then suddenly Yoko came out of this bag and she started screaming. 'Christ! What is it?' And this went on for a while and then this amazing feeling came across me that soldiers were lying dead next to you, tanks were rolling across…. Yoko was screaming these things and the shivers went down my back. I felt so much for Yoko. I thought, 'What a great thing to do. To go out there and just do this.' I couldn't believe it. I really warmed towards her so much. I was standing behind her. I saw her from the back. She was screaming like mad. Everybody can hear the record. She's really just screaming. It was incredible.

John: I said, 'Look, at the end of the show, when she's finished doing whatever she's doing, just lean your guitars on the amps and let it keep howling and we can get off like that.' Because you can't very well go 'ji-jing!' like the Beatles and bow at the end of screaming and fifty watts of feedback. So we all left our amps on, going like the clappers and had a smoke on the stage. Then, when they stopped, the whole crowd was chanting 'Give Peace A Chance'. We didn't know what the reaction would be. Something magical happened that night and it affected Eric and Klaus and Alan. They really got turned on by that night's experience, so that of course turned us on even more!

Mal Evans: After that, the boys gave a ten-minute press conference. When it was over we all piled into four big cars and drove for two hours to a huge estate owned by a Mr Eaton, who is one of the richest men in Canada. His son had actually picked us up after the show so that we could stay overnight at his house. The next day we got into golf carts and went all over the estate. It really is a wonderful country. Miles and miles of trees, hills, lakes and green frogs. The whole show was recorded for a special album which should be out pretty soon and you will hear all this on the LP.

John & Yoko and the Plastic Ono Band perform
'Cold Turkey' at the Toronto Rock 'n' Roll Revival 1969
concert; Varsity Stadium, Toronto, 13 September 1969.

John & Yoko and the Plastic Ono Band perform at the
Toronto Rock 'n' Roll Revival 1969 concert; Varsity Stadium,
Toronto, 13 September 1969.

Overleaf: Alan White, Eric Clapton, Klaus Voormann and John & Yoko, the morning after the show, relaxing by the swimming pool on the estate of concert promoters and department store dynasty heirs, George and Thor Eaton; Eaton Hall, King City, Ontario, 14 September 1969.

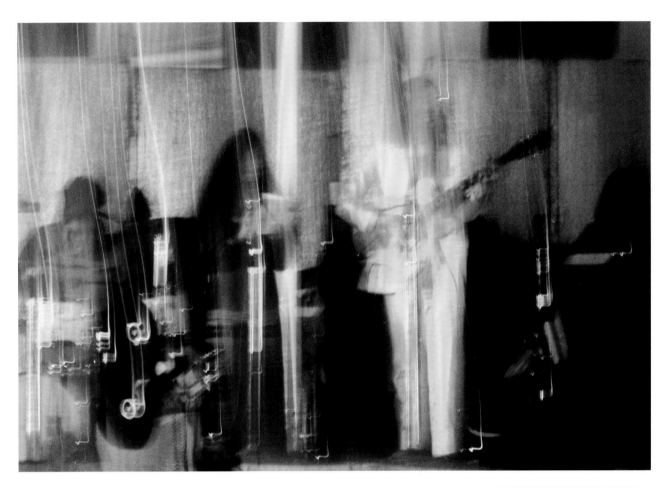

Advertisement for the album *Live Peace In Toronto 1969* by Plastic Ono Band, featuring a photograph of John & Yoko backstage at Varsity Stadium, Toronto, the *Plastic Ono Band* sculptures and a passing cloud; *Cashbox* magazine, 20 December 1969.

The album *Live Peace In Toronto 1969* by Plastic Ono Band, with cover artwork by Yoko Ono; music recorded live at Varsity Stadium, Toronto, on 13 September 1969 and released worldwide on 12 December 1969.

BLUE SUEDE SHOES
MONEY
DIZZY MISS LIZZIE
YER BLUES
COLD TURKEY
GIVE PEACE A CHANCE

DONT WORRY KYOKO
(Mummy's only looking
for her hand in the snow)
JOHN, JOHN
(Let's hope for peace)

JOHN LENNON / Guitar, Vocals
YOKO ONO / Vocals
ERIC CLAPTON / Guitar (by courtesy
of Polydor Records)
KLAUS VOORMANN / Bass Guitar
ALAN WHITE / Drums

PRODUCED BY JOHN AND YOKO
(BAG PRODUCTIONS)
'BEING BORN IN SCOTLAND CARRIES
WITH IT CERTAIN RESPONSIBILITIES'
– DEREK TAYLOR

My temperatures rising   My body is aching.
fever is high   ~~Sweat is my body~~ goose pimple
can't see no future   can't see nobody   bone
can't see no sky   leave me alone
they ~~broke~~ gave to hang   my eyes are wide open
and so is my head.   ~~not eyes are too wide open~~ can't go
I wish I was a baby   ~~I stick my tongue out~~   to sleep
I wish I was dead.   one thing I'm sure of
                               ~~I know this is hell~~.
                                ~~the~~ I'm in at the deep freeze

COLD TURKEY

Temperature's rising
Fever is high
Can't see no future
Can't see no sky

My feet are so heavy
So is my head
I wish I was a baby
I wish I was dead

Cold turkey has got me on the run

My body is aching
Goose-pimple bone
Can't see no body
Leave me alone

My eyes are wide open
Can't get to sleep
One thing I'm sure of
I'm in at the deep freeze

Cold turkey has got me on the run
Cold turkey has got me on the run

Thirty-six hours
Rolling in pain
Praying to someone
Free me again

Oh, I'll be a good boy
Please make me well
I promise you anything
Get me out of this hell

Cold turkey has got me on the run

COLD TURKEY

John: 'Cold Turkey' is self-explanatory. It was the result of experiencing cold turkey withdrawals from heroin. Everybody goes through a bit of agony some time or another in their lives, whatever it is. 'Cold Turkey' is just an expression that I would have thought is suitable to explain the other side of life. I'm always thinking about love and peace and now I'm thinking about agony to remind people that I'm human and that we suffer like everybody else. This is the after effects.

Heroin. It just was not too much fun. I never injected it or anything. We sniffed a little when we were in real pain. People were giving us such a hard time. I've had so much shit thrown at me and especially at Yoko. We get in so much pain that we have to do something about it. And we got out of it.

Yoko: I didn't like marijuana, so I didn't constantly take it like most people. Acid was not bad, but acid is very strong, so you don't take it every day. George says it was me who put John on heroin, but that wasn't true. John wouldn't take anything he didn't want to take. John was very curious. He asked if I had ever tried it. I told him that while he was in India with the Maharishi, I had a sniff of it in a party situation. I didn't know what it was. They just gave me something and I said, 'What was that?' It was a beautiful feeling.

John was talking about heroin one day and he said, 'Did you ever take it?' And I told him about Paris – I said it wasn't bad. Because the amount was small, I didn't even get sick; it was just a nice feeling. When you do a little more, you get sick right away if you're not used to it. Luckily we never injected, because both of us were totally scared about needles. So that probably saved us. And the other thing that saved us was our connection was not very good.

Then somebody gave us the wrong information that there was a new drug called methadone that gives you the same high as smack, but you don't get hooked on it, and so, 'whoopee!', you know, and at that time we were totally dry. Most people take methadone because they want to withdraw from smack and we weren't taking smack. We weren't taking anything. So it was the silliest thing to do. So we got hooked on methadone. Coming off methadone was the hardest thing that I've ever done and I'm sure that's true for John too. After that, we couldn't get hooked on anything.

It's a myth that we went into the hospital to withdraw. We were so totally scared. We thought it's an illegal thing, we can't openly go to hospital, they might arrest us.

So we never even dreamt of going to hospital. We just cold turkey-ed.

After the 'Lost Weekend', we both went on a juice fast for forty days in 1975, just drinking fruit juice, and we cleaned ourselves. John had incredible will and once he decided to do something, he did it. Those forty days were very hard, but we were totally clean. When we were on it, we were both on it, so it wasn't like we alienated each other. But it was self-destructive and unhealthy.

John: I've always expressed what I've been feeling or thinking at the time, however badly or not, from early Beatles records on. It became more conscious later. So I was just writing the experience I'd had of withdrawing from heroin and saying, you know, this is what I thought when I was withdrawing.

I offered 'Cold Turkey' to the Beatles, but they weren't ready to record a single. I went to the other three Beatles and said, 'Hey lads, I think I've written a single.' But they all said, 'Umm… err… well…' because it was going to be my project. So, I thought, 'Bugger you, I'll put it out myself.' So I did it as the Plastic Ono Band. I don't care what it goes out as, as long as it goes out.

If 'Cold Turkey' had the name 'Beatles' on it, it probably would have made the Number One position. 'Cold Turkey' has got Ringo and me on it and yet on half of the tracks on *Abbey Road*, I'm not on them. I'm not even on half of the tracks on the double album [*The Beatles*, a.k.a. the 'White Album']. Even way back then, sometimes there might only be two Beatles on a track. Eric Clapton was on that too.

Yoko: Yes. And also we did attempt a few musically advanced, interesting things.

John: When it came out, Marc Bolan said it was the only new thing that had happened since the original Beatles. But I wasn't thinking, 'I'm going to make a new sound' – it was pretty much what they call minimal now – just bass, drums and guitars.

It was banned again all over the American radio, so it never got off the ground. It was banned because it referred to drugs. To me it was a rock 'n' roll version of *The Man with the Golden Arm*, which showed Frank Sinatra suffering from drug withdrawal. To ban the record is the same thing. It's like banning the movie. Because it shows reality.

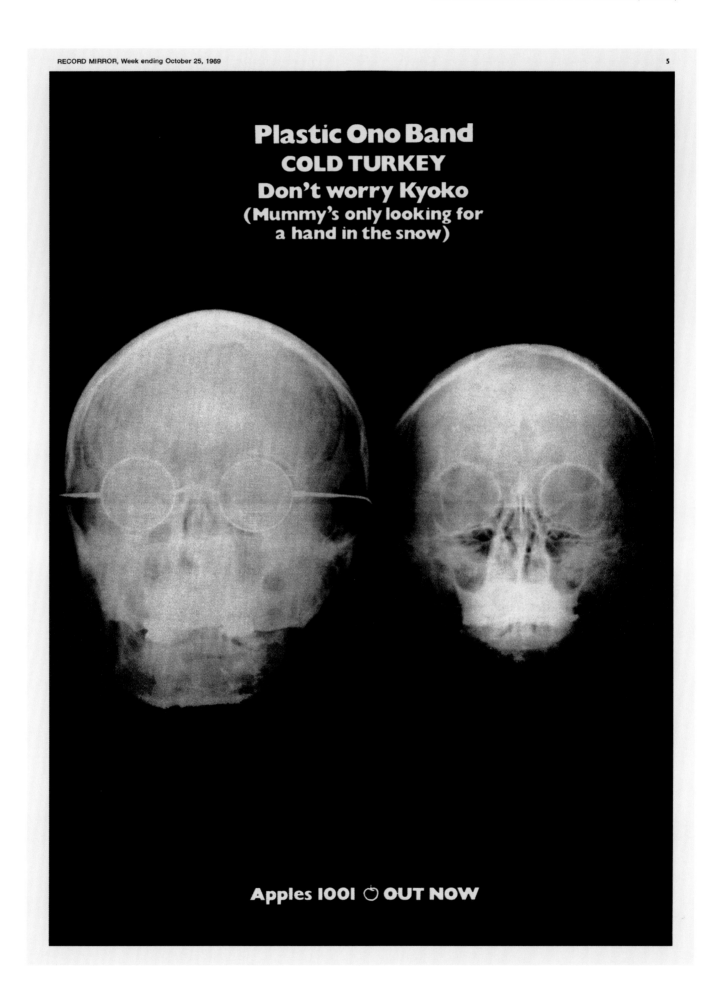

John & Yoko in the Bag Productions office on the
ground floor of the Apple offices; 3 Savile Row,
London, 25 November 1969.

Yoko: They say that a blind man has an honest face because he doesn't know how to express himself using the muscles on his face – because he can't see his face. It's almost like that. As an artist if you get truly inspired and something comes through you, like songs or poetry or whatever, then it's part of your experience. So you can't lie in your work. 'Cold Turkey' was something that reflected our life. And that's the kind of thing that always brings you trouble. So, from around 'Cold Turkey', we started to really pay our dues for being honest.

John: They're so stupid about drugs. They are always looking at some peripheral manifestation of it, like the guy on the corner selling dope, or a student with a few joints in his pocket. They never face the reality. They're not really trying to solve the drug problem because they're not looking at the solution. Why is everybody taking drugs? To escape from what? Is life so terrible? Do we live in such a terrible situation that we can't do anything about it without reinforcement from alcohol or tobacco included, aspirins, sleeping pills? They are always absolutely missing the point. Why we take them is important, not who's selling it to whom on the corner. That's why the drug problem will never be solved.

We were planted. I have a record for life because the cop who bust me and Yoko, and also bust Brian Jones and the Stones – he was scalp-hunting and making a name for himself. I have problems getting in countries because this guy bust me.

There was a question raised in the Houses of Parliament, 'Why do they need forty cops to arrest John & Yoko?' That thing was set up. The *Daily Mail* and the *Daily Express* were there before the cops came. He'd called the press. In fact, Don Short had told us 'they're coming to get you' three weeks before. So, believe me, I'd cleaned the house out, because Jimi Hendrix had lived there before in this apartment, and I'm not stupid. I went through the whole damn house.

The Statute of Appeals ran out. I don't have a legal mind and I went to find out about it because I wanted to get this thing off my record. And they told me, 'Oh you should have applied within the first two years.' The only reason I pleaded guilty was because I thought they'd send Yoko away because we weren't married and throw her out of the country.

Your Majesty, I am returning my MBE in protest against Britain's involvement in the Nigeria-Biafra thing, against our support of America in Vietnam and against 'Cold Turkey' slipping down the charts. With love, John Lennon.

I began to feel ashamed I was British. I wanted to send it back maybe a year ago and was thinking about doing it privately. If I had sent it back privately, it would have gotten back to the press anyway. The Biafran public relations people thought it was good for their cause, and I'd accept their opinion over yours any day. I'm not worried about what other people think I should be doing. The people of Biafra thanked me for doing that event, and that's enough. They want all the publicity they can get. If I gave every penny I've got, then I've got nothing and I've got to start again. Those people need money for advertisements to bring the attention of the public to the problem. They don't care how you do it, as long as you get them some attention, and that's what it's all about. If I'm going to get myself on the front page, I might as well get myself there with the word 'peace'. Everybody in this century uses advertising, including politicians, the Biafrans, the Vietnamese, everybody. I use advertising to promote what I think. And I think 'peace'.

I don't believe people believe politicians, especially the youth. They've had enough of short hair and suits saying this, as if every priest is a holy man just because he's got a dog collar on. Nobody believes that any more. And we do this intuitively. But after we've done it for a few times, we always had some irrelevancy, or something in the campaign, you know.

I've learned from being in the public eye that if the castle falls, it falls from within. Yoko was telling me how this ancient Chinese book [*The Art of War* by Sun Tzu] advises how to fight a battle. You never close all the doors because the enemy will attack in vast concentration, but if you leave one door open, you know where the enemy is going to come in. We leave many doors open, like irrelevant comments about 'Cold Turkey', long hair and nakedness. While people are so busy attacking; while they're bothering with how long my hair is, or the irrelevancy of 'Cold Turkey', we can go on protesting for peace. That's the purpose of leaving the door open. It doesn't interfere with the campaign. Nobody attacks peace.

Most journalists wrote about how my aunty felt about my MBE rather than peace in Biafra. That's their whole game: prejudice and fear. They were frightened of committing themselves, and rather than being conned by the entertainer, they'd sooner divert their attention to something irrelevant. But what's important: the MBE, Biafra, Vietnam or Aunt Mimi's feelings?

John returns his MBE (Member of the Order of the British Empire) to the Queen, Prime Minister Harold Wilson and the Central Chancery of the Orders of Knighthood, from Bag Productions at the Apple offices; 3 Savile Row, London, 25 November 1969.

BAG PRODUCTIONS 3, SAVILE ROW, LONDON W.1. 734 8232

PEACE  TO

Her Majesty The Queen

Yours Majesty

I am returning this MBE in protest against
Britain's involvement in the Nigeria-Biafra
thing, against our support of America in
Vietnam and against Cold Turkey slipping
down the charts.

with love John Lennon.

John Lennon of Bag

Poster advertising *Peace And Love For Christmas*,
a concert in aid of UNICEF, secretly headlined
by John & Yoko and the Plastic Ono Supergroup;
Lyceum Ballroom, London, 15 December 1969.

PEACE AND LOVE FOR CHRISTMAS / LYCEUM BALLROOM, LONDON

John: I announced 'Cold Turkey' at the Lyceum saying, 'This song's about pain.' So pain and screaming was before Janov.

I came home from holiday and read I was performing at the Lyceum Ballroom – they said we were coming. Whether or not someone in the office gave them a hint or something, we never said anything. It's a good UNICEF gig, but that's what they'd done.

Alan White: I got a call from Mal Evans and he said, 'Alan put your drum kit in the car; John is going to do a show tonight and he wants you to play at it. Meet us at the Lyceum Ballroom.' So I drove down there with my drum kit, loaded it in, put it on stage and then went to the dressing room and there was John & Yoko and Klaus. I said, 'Well what are we going to play?' And John said, 'Well, I've got this lick and we'll just do that and keep playing it.' We were just about to go onstage and in walks George Harrison and Eric Clapton and they said, 'We've got the whole band outside in the car!'

John: George had been playing invisible man in Delaney and Bonnie's band with Eric – to get the pressure off being the famous Eric and the famous George. They all turned up, and it was like the concert in Toronto. I said, 'Will you come on?' They said, 'Well, what are you going to play?' I said, 'Listen, we're going to do probably a blues', or whatever was current, 'Cold Turkey', which is three chords, and Eric knew that. And 'Don't Worry, Kyoko', which was Yoko's, which was three chords, a riff. I said, 'Once we get onto Yoko's riff, just keep hitting it'.

Alan White: They had Delaney and Bonnie Bramlett, Jim Gordon on drums, Carl Randall on bass, a horn section with Bobby Keys and Jim Price, and also Keith Moon and Billy Preston – they just walked in and said, 'We'll do it!' So we stalled the show for about forty-five minutes and they brought all the equipment in. We had to hustle another couple of drum kits, set it all up, got everything where it needed to go and then we walked onstage, this whole troupe of players. John started playing this riff over and over and over with a billion solos from the horn players. It was a jam forever.

John: As soon as we started, the whole room lifted. The whole ballroom just took off. We really got somewhere new that night. It was a fantastic show. Half the audience walked out, but the ones that stayed, they were in a trance, man. They just all came to the front, because it was one

of the first real heavy rock shows, where we had a good, good band and that John & Yoko did together. And I always think that some of those kids formed those freaky bands later, because there were about 200 kids at the front there, somewhere about thirteen, fourteen, fifteen, who were looking at Yoko and looking at us the way we were playing that 'Don't Worry Kyoko', and it really reached a peak. It really went out there that night. And I often think 'I wonder if…' you know, I hear touches of our early stuff in a lot of the punk new wave stuff. I could hear licks and flicks coming out. And it pleases me; it pleases both of us. I'd love to know, were they in the audience? And did somebody go and form a group in London because it sure as hell sounds like it!

That was some show, I'm telling you. It was a small dance hall of maybe 1,000, 2,000. We blew them away. I don't care what the pop press said, we were sky high – it was an amazing high. A seventeen-piece band. It's great with four musicians grooving, but when you've got seventeen it's something else. Plastic Ono Band plays the unexpected – it could be 'Blue Suede Shoes' or it could be Beethoven's Ninth. With Plastic Ono, anything goes. The day we go on and the audience is the rhythm section, then we're really grooving – that's what I want. So it wouldn't matter whether I was on the stage, or if I got fed up and went down in the audience for a bit. Let's take it in turns to be superstar.

Yoko: The best trend is that everybody does their own thing. To realize that they count. That what they do and think is going to change the world. And it really does. Even if you have nasty thoughts in the corner of the room, that vibration is going to really affect the whole world. And so if everybody starts to think that they're the hope of the world, then that's when something will start to happen.

Alan White: Something I remember about that show is that one song went on for about forty minutes and I realized nobody really knew how to finish it. We were all looking at each other, going, 'How are we going to get out of this, we're gonna explode!' So I just started speeding up and they all looked round at me like 'Alan's speeding up!' By that time Keith Moon was on the stage beating the crap out of my sixteen-inch tom tom with these crazy eyes looking at me going, 'boom' and I was going, 'This is getting out of hand!' So I sped up and I sped and I sped up until it was so fast nobody could play the lick any more and it was just one note going. I did a drum break and looked like I was going to finish and that's how we got out of it.

In front of a giant backdrop proclaiming 'WAR IS OVER! If You Want It, Happy Christmas from John & Yoko', the Plastic Ono Supergroup, comprising John & Yoko, George Harrison, Eric Clapton, Delaney Bramlett and Bonnie Lynn, Klaus Voormann, Bobby Keys, Jim Price, Billy Preston, Jim Gordon, Alan White, Legs Larry Smith and Keith Moon headline the *Peace And Love For Christmas* concert, playing 'Cold Turkey' and 'Don't Worry Kyoko'; Lyceum Ballroom, London, 15 December 1969.

John performing 'Cold Turkey' with Plastic Ono Band, playing his Epiphone Casino ES-230TD hollow body guitar from which he had sanded off the original sunburst finish; Lyceum Ballroom, London, 15 December 1969.

Above: Yoko performs 'Don't Worry Kyoko' with John and the Plastic Ono Supergroup; Lyceum Ballroom, London, 15 December 1969.

Below: John & Yoko and the Plastic Ono Supergroup onstage. The *Plastic Ono Band* sculptures are visible stage left. A cameraman was filming the audience so their faces appeared on the television in the sculpture.

The Plastic Ono Supergroup backstage after the show. Back row: Jim Price (trumpet), Bobby Keys (saxophone), Jim Gordon (drums), Klaus Voormann (bass), Bonnie Lynn (tambourine), Delaney Bramlett (guitar); middle row: George Harrison (guitar), Alan White (drums), Keith Moon (drums), Neil Boland (Keith Moon's chauffeur), Keith Robertson (photographer), Billy Preston (keyboard), Eric Clapton (guitar); front row: Legs Larry Smith (percussion), John (guitar, vocals), Yoko (vocals).

INSTANT KARMA. (we all shine on)

1) Instant Karmas gonna get you!
Gonna knock you on the head.
You better think about it darlin.
Pretty soon your gonna be dead.
What in the world you thinkin· of?
Laughin in the face of love?
What on earth you tryin to do?
- its up to you - yeah!

2) Instant Karmas gonna get you!
gonna look you right in the face
You better get yourself together baby
Come and join the human race
- How in the world you goin to see?
Laughing at the likes of me?
Who on earth you think you are?
Super Star?   Yes you are!

INSTANT KARMA! (WE ALL SHINE ON)

Instant Karma's gonna get you
Gonna knock you right on the head
You better get yourself together
Pretty soon you're gonna be dead

What in the world you thinking of?
Laughing in the face of love
What on earth you trying to do?
It's up to you, yeah you!

Instant Karma's gonna get you
Gonna look you right in the face
Better get yourself together darling
Join the human race

How in the world you gonna see?
Laughing at fools like me
Who on earth d'you think you are?
A superstar? Well, right you are!

Well we all shine on
Like the moon and the stars and the sun
Well we all shine on
Everyone, come on!

Instant Karma's gonna get you
Gonna knock you off your feet
Better recognise your brothers
Everyone you meet

Why in the world are we here?
Surely not to live in pain and fear
Why on earth are you there?
When you're everywhere
Come and get your share

Well we all shine on
Like the moons and the stars and the sun
Yeah, we all shine on
Come on and on and on, on, on

Yeah, yeah, alright, uh huh, ahh

Well we all shine on
Like the moon and the stars and the sun
Yeah, we all shine on
On and on and on, on and on

Well we all shine on
Like the moon and the stars and the sun
Well we all shine on
Like the moon and the stars and the sun

Well we all shine on
Like the moons and the stars and the sun
Yeah we all shine on
Like the moon and the stars and the sun
Well we all shine on

John & Yoko travelled to Denmark, to spend
New Year with Yoko's daughter Kyoko, and improve
relations with Yoko's ex-husband Tony Cox and
his new wife Melinde at a farmhouse near Vust.
John: We went there to talk to Kyoko, and it was
really a case of 'brother, brother, brother' and all that.

After a week free from being hassled by the press,
they granted interviews to the press, including
an ELSK film crew; 6 January 1970.

John plays a Guild F30 acoustic guitar, sitting with Yoko
on mattresses on the floor, Yoko's tama (talking drum)
in the corner; Ellidsbølvej 37, 9690 Fjerritslev, Denmark,
13 January 1970.

Photographed by roadie Mal Evans, John runs through
'Instant Karma! (We All Shine On)' on George Harrison's
Gibson Jumbo J-200 sunburst acoustic guitar; EMI
Studio 3, 3 Abbey Road, London, 27 January 1970.

INSTANT KARMA! (WE ALL SHINE ON)

John: I wrote it for breakfast, recorded it for lunch and we're putting it out for dinner.

George Harrison: John phoned me up one morning in January and said, 'I've written this tune and I'm going to record it tonight and have it pressed up and out tomorrow, that's the whole point – "Instant Karma!" – you know?' So I was in. I said, 'Okay, I'll see you in town.' I was in town with Phil Spector and I said to Phil, 'Why don't you come to the session?' There were just four people: John played piano, I played acoustic guitar, there was Klaus Voormann on bass and Alan White on drums. We recorded the song and brought it out that week, mixed – instantly – by Phil Spector.

John: Recording it was great. I wrote it in the morning on the piano, like I've said many times. I went to the office and sang it. We booked the studio, and Phil came in, and said, 'How do you want it?' I said, 'You know, Fifties, but now.' He said, 'Right.' And 'boom!' I did it in about three goes. And went in and he played it back and there it was. The only argument was I said 'a bit more bass', that's all. And off we went. Phil doesn't fuss about with the stereo or all the bullshit. Just, 'Does it sound all right? Let's have it.' It doesn't matter whether something's prominent or not prominent. If it sounds good to you as a layman or a human, take it. Don't bother whether 'this is like that', or 'the quality of this', just take it and that suits me fine.

Klaus Voormann: This little man came in with his high voice saying, 'Oh can you put this level a little higher?' He was talking and doing things and I thought, well who the fuck is this? I didn't know who it was. He kept on saying really clever things and we got playing and it sounded really good.

Andy Stephens (tape op): John kept trying to pull him to the fore. Spector stood back and didn't volunteer or dictate much at all. Then Lennon really pulled him out: 'C'mon, Phil!' Once he got into his stride, it was like all hell breaking loose. Tape machines, tape loops, tape delays, echo chambers, you name it.

Alan White: I had an idea of what I wanted to do – one of those things where you are playing a rhythm, but when it comes to a drum break, you play in a different meter. It came naturally – and John said, 'Alan, whatever you're doing, keep doing it. It's wonderful.'

Klaus Voormann: Alan White, now I knew he can play. He played wonderful drums. And we thought the tracks

sounded good. And then this Mickey Mouse voice came through the speaker saying, 'Come on, have a listen.' So we went into the control room. We all stood at the back and it started and it was so incredible. The sound was just like we had heard in the headphones but with all these incredible effects. Then I knew it, because I heard that sound and I thought, this is the Phil Spector sound. It's very, very simple. He has got these effects on the pianos and these wavering sounds. The bass and the kick drum were completely clean. The voice was more or less clean. So that was typical for Phil Spector. And I love Phil Spector. I loved him then. From then on, it was incredible. Beautiful. I loved it.

Alan White: I also played piano with a few people. Phil Spector wanted to have everything doubled up and made it sound like one. So it was John and myself on one piano and the other piano had Klaus playing, just layering all these different pianos and then Phil would never put one tambourine on a record; he had to have fifteen of them!

Billy Preston: John wanted some crowd, some people to sing background, so I got in his Rolls Royce with Mal Evans and we went to the clubs and got everybody to 'come on down!' We had a great time.

Alan White: These people must have been drinking all night. They came in and I remember there was Klaus, myself and John conducting. I thought this is going to be a total mess, people are going to be out of tune, out of time, and anyhow we went through one run-through and I went 'Oh my god!' We all looked at each other and we couldn't believe it – they were all singing in time and in tune, we got that done within an hour and we had a huge backing, but no one went back to the club. It was like, that too was very instant about 'Instant Karma!'

John: 'Instant Karma!' was a case of the idea of instant karma coming to me. Everybody was talking about karma all of a sudden, always going on about it, especially in the Sixties but it's still around now and it occurred to me that karma is instant as well as one about this life, which no one really knows about anyway – it influences your past life or your future life, those kind of influences that do or do not exist according to your taste or beliefs – that the actual instant karma, the action-reaction is what that is, what it's about. Also, I'm fascinated by commercials and promotion and I am fascinated by it as an art form. You know the TV commercials and the commercials in newspapers fascinate me because I enjoy them, so instant karma was like

Portraits of John (opposite) & Yoko (below) photographed
by Richard DiLello in matching turtleneck jumpers;
Apple offices, 3 Savile Row, London, 9 February 1970.

instant coffee. Except for presenting it in a new form. It's like they say about karma: you have to come back and go through that thing again if you don't get it right this lifetime. Well, those laws that are sort of 'cosmically' talked about accepted or not accepted, but you know the ones they all talk about, they're all referring to, they apply down to the minutest detail of life, too. It's like, instant karma, which is my way of saying it's right. You know, it happens about a cup of coffee or anything. It's not just some big cosmic thing, it's that as well, but it's also the small things like your life here and your relationship with the person you want to live with and be with, there are laws governing that relationship, too. And you can either give up halfway up the hill, and say 'I don't want to climb this mountain. It's too tough. I'm going to go back to the bottom and start again.' And well, we were lucky enough to go through that, and come back and pick up where we left off, although it took us some kind of energy to get in the same synch again. It took some time.

Yoko: What the so-called leaders don't understand is when they are saying something about 'we should do this', or 'we should do that', actually they are working out their own karma. There might be some need in them to be violent, or something like that, but you can't really push that on other people; it's a very sticky area. People should not get ticked off by a trend, or what they read in a book. They should trust their own instincts.

John: Well there are ones that didn't follow their instincts and went to Vietnam and got crippled and deformed and only woke up afterwards. They are the responsibility of the people who sent them there – who sent them there under an illusion.

Yoko: Even on the level of non-violence because they have a need to be non-violent because of their parents or something. Each person has their own karma in that sense.

John: Ghandi and Martin Luther King are great examples of fantastic non-violents who died violently. I can't ever work that out. We're pacifists, but I'm not sure. What does it mean when you're such a pacifist that you get shot? I can never understand that.

John: Pain is what we're frightened of. We all seem to think we have a secret. The secret is that we hurt because of lots of things that happened to us.

Klaus Voormann: I think we did two BBC *Top Of The Pops* performances. And there was a guy standing there playing with us, who played a bass too.

John: B. P. Fallon playing the bass guitar, that's concept art!

B. P. Fallon: I can't play bass, but it's better than whacking a tambourine into John's left ear and almost putting him off his singing! [laughs]

Alan White: Purely the fact that John & Yoko were doing *Top Of The Pops* became a big spectacle. It was pretty amazing. Yoko was knitting, which was pretty weird. She had a Kotex blindfold on for some of it. He loved her way of expressing her art and it seemed to be part of the music at that time.

John: I enjoyed the 'Instant Karma!' thing because there were the people right there. And we were talking about the fact that she was knitting. Because we did everything together. I'm doing 'Instant Karma!' with a backing tape with live vocal and she's just sitting there knitting this scarf, and there was some review the next day – 'How dare she sit there knitting?' But we wanted to be together, and her contribution to that event, instead of having a smoke bomb or a coloured light, a psychedelic light, Yoko only knitted. You see. And… 'What are they doing?!'

Yoko: Knitting is something very interesting. It's almost like knitting a web of the mind. I was blindfolding myself with a Kotex and knitting something that was going nowhere, while a man symbolizing our future was singing, 'We all shine on'. Yes, we will shine, but for that we have to take the blindfold off and stop knitting, when we don't know what we are knitting. It was my way of showing what we women must free ourselves from. The blindfold means to me everybody in the world is blind and trying their best.

John: The thing is that if 'Instant Karma!' is in the charts and Plastic Ono Band is everyone, you're all in the charts. That's the feeling we want to get over. So Yoko was knitting, there was some guy pretending to play bass, B. P. Fallon and things like that and that anybody can be on the session. In fact, there were all sorts of strange people on the session. The whole of a London discotheque was singing on it and we used doormen and roadies and everybody to make the backing track and just to get that feel that we're all in it together.

The UK and US releases of the single 'Instant Karma! (We All Shine On)' / 'Who Has Seen The Wind?' by Lennon/Ono with the Plastic Ono Band. The single went to No. 3 (USA) and No. 5 (UK).

LENNON
INSTANT KARMA!

APPLES 1003

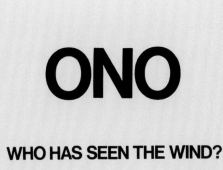

ONO
WHO HAS SEEN THE WIND?

APPLES 1003

JOHN ONO LENNON
INSTANT KARMA!
(WE ALL SHINE ON)

PRODUCED BY
PHIL SPECTOR

APPLE RECORDS 1818

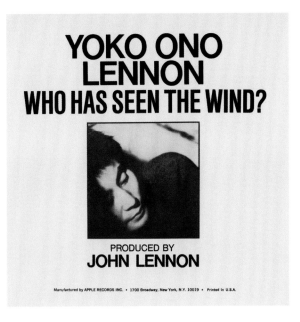

YOKO ONO LENNON
WHO HAS SEEN THE WIND?

PRODUCED BY
JOHN LENNON

Manufactured by APPLE RECORDS INC. • 1700 Broadway, New York, N.Y. 10019 • Printed in U.S.A.

To promote their latest single, John & Yoko announce they are going to auction the hair they had cut off in Denmark to raise funds for Michael X's Black House community centre, a venture they were already financially supporting.

After arriving with chauffeur Les Anthony, they are pictured with Michael X holding their hair and Muhammad Ali's blood-stained boxer shorts, also to be auctioned; the Black House, 95–101 Holloway Road, London, 4 February 1970.

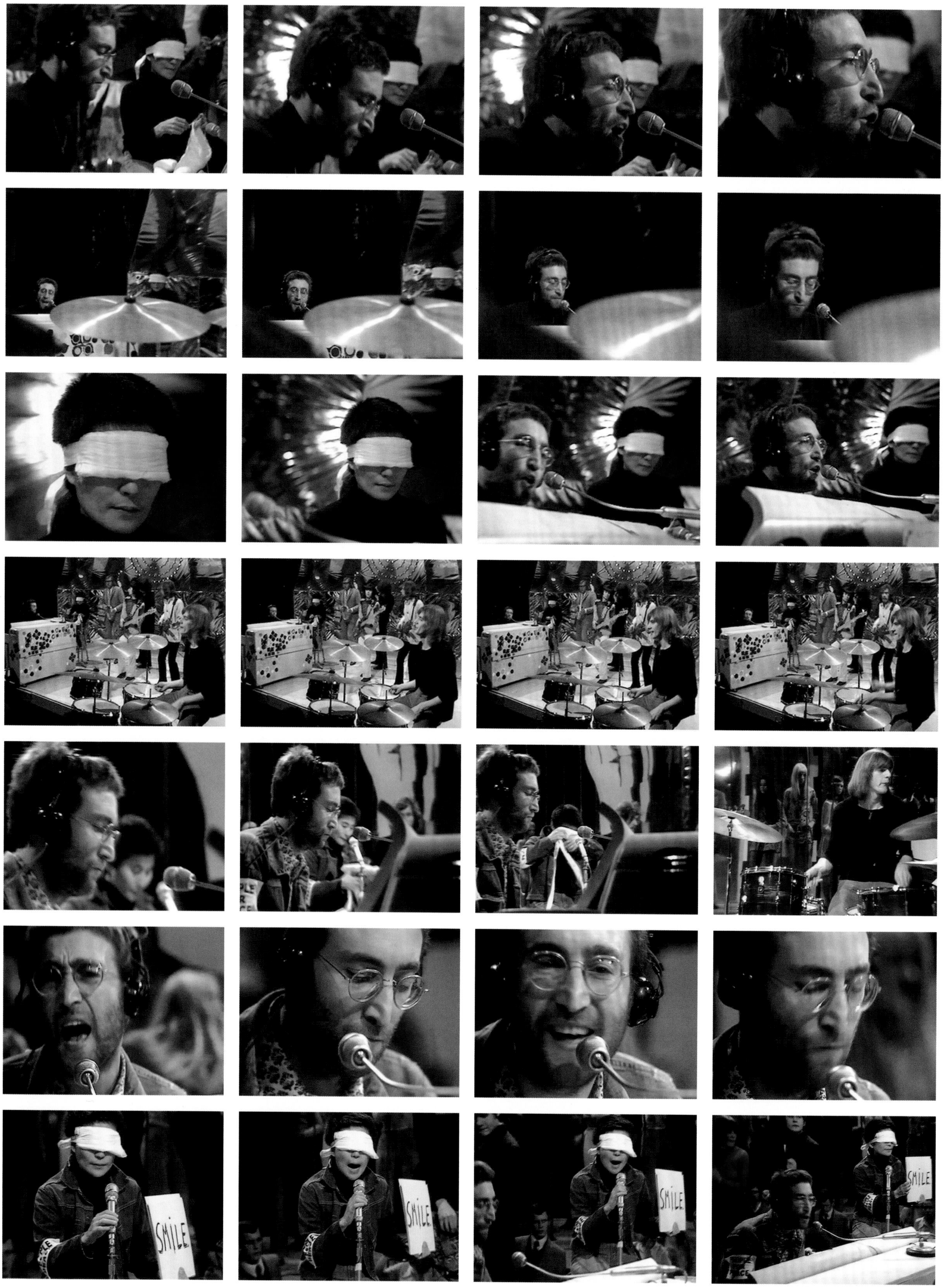
SMILE.

Video stills from two out of four performances of 'Instant Karma! (We All Shine On)' for BBC TV's *Top Of The Pops* show, broadcast on the 12 and 19 February. John & Yoko are joined onstage by Klaus Voormann (bass), Alan White (drums), Mal Evans (tambourine), B. P. Fallon (bass/tambourine) and Richard DiLello (Nikon). Yoko performs, blindfolded by a sanitary towel. In one take she is knitting and in the other she holds up boards that say 'BREATHE', 'SMILE', 'PEACE', 'LOVE' and 'HOPE'; Studio 8, BBC Television Centre, London, 11 February 1970.

Yoko: I was blindfolding myself with a Kotex as
I knitted, to show what women were going through
in the world. Chained to the world, blindfolded
and still working hard, knitting.

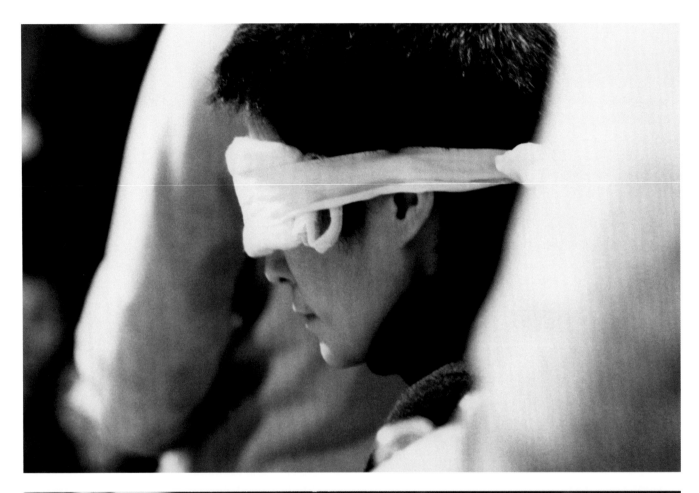

'PEOPLE FOR PEACE': John & Yoko hugging, elated, after their performance. Yoko is still carrying her boards, the top one instructing the audience to 'BREATHE'; Studio 8, BBC Television Centre, London, 11 February 1970.

Overleaf: Photograph of John & Yoko in bed, part of which was used on the cover of the US single release of 'Instant Karma! (We All Shine On)' / 'Who Has Seen The Wind?'; Tittenhurst Park, Ascot, Berkshire, 27 January 1970.

John sent out many copies of Arthur Janov's book, *The Primal Scream*, to his friends. Included here are the dedications to Spike Milligan (above right), Pete Townsend (below left) and Eric Clapton (below right).

ARTHUR JANOV, PhD

THE PRIMAL SCREAM

PRIMAL THERAPY: THE CURE FOR NEUROSIS

Some years ago, I heard something that was to change the course of my professional life and the lives of my patients. What I heard may change the nature of psychotherapy as it is now known—an eerie scream welling up from the depths of a young man lying on the floor during a therapy session. I can liken it only to what one might hear from a person about to be murdered. This book is about that scream and what it means in terms of unlocking the secrets of neurosis.

This book is dedicated to my patients, who were real enough to recognize that they were sick and wanted to end the struggle, and to the youth of the world—the real hope of mankind

Dear Spike
we saw your T.V.
~~thing~~ thing - it
was very REAL.
I think this
book might 'turn you on'
as they say. lots of love
John + Yoko
(Lennon)

This book is dedicated to my patients, who were real enough to recognize that they were sick and wanted to end the struggle, and to the youth of the world—the real hope of mankind

To Peter the Seeker
- I think this is the
last trip - read this and
see if you recognise yourself!
love from
John + Yoko
I'm in L.A. in the middle of it
if you want
to know more
ring Sally or Diane at Apple - they'll
hook you on to me.

This book is dedicated to my patients, who were real enough to recognize that they were sick and wanted to end the struggle, and to the youth of the world—the real hope of mankind

Dear Eric +
'becoming American'
won't stop the Pain.
love to you and yours
from
John + Y.Ko

March 18 70.

'THIS IS IT!' Rough full-page layout design for an advert for the *San Francisco Chronicle* that John enthusiastically showed separately to Arthur Janov and Jann S. Wenner, who both advised him against running it; May 1970.

ARTHUR JANOV / PRIMAL SCREAM THERAPY

Primal Therapy has to do with the traumas you've undergone in the womb, at birth, in infancy and childhood. We have needs that we're all born with, and when those basic needs are not met, we hurt. And when that hurt is big enough, it's imprinted in the system. It changes our whole physiologic system and all those pains are held in storage, causing tension, anxiety and depression.

Most psychotherapy is talk therapy and it's not words that we need to go to. We have to find a way to go to that brain that feels, talk to it in feeling terms and then let it communicate itself to the therapist. We found a way to go step-by-step down the ladder towards deep feeling, re-live those pains, give people access to their feelings and get them out. Once we do that, all of the symptoms that are based on repression fall away – migraines, high blood pressure, epilepsy, all kinds of ailments. Instead of pushing back feelings with tranquillizers and drugs, we let the feelings up and liberate them. That's a big difference.

Each re-living experience I call a 'Primal'. We have seen several hundred birth Primals over the past few years which leave little doubt about the fact that birth can be a significant trauma and contributing factor to the genesis of neuroses. People are a minute or two away from that pain plus many, many others, every minute of their lives. It's not a rebirthing, it's not a plunging down. It's a slow descent into the deepest, deepest pains and it takes months and months. It's predictable and we know what's going to happen with the patient.

A lot of people go to psychoanalysis because they want to get their defences strengthened. We try to take their defences apart, so they can get back to their feelings and recapture some part of themselves. We help them feel. And once they have their feelings, we normalize the system so they're no longer driven by their unconscious feelings and they're able to lead a conscious life exactly as they see fit. And that's so important for everybody.

My publisher at the time of *The Primal Scream* sent them the book. I had no idea. They were supposed to review the book, but instead Yoko called me and asked me to come to London to treat John. He was in bad shape. He couldn't leave his room. I said there's no way I could come there: 'I've got a clinic full of patients and it's impossible', and I hung up. That was the end of it. And my son and daughter, who were eleven and twelve said, 'Who was that?' and I said, 'It was Yoko and John Lennon', and they started screaming and running around the house like maniacs saying, 'What

did you say?' and I said, 'No' and they said, 'Call him back right now and ask if we can go too!' So I did. They said yes, so I took the kids out of school and the kids had the best time of their lives. We went out to Tittenhurst and while we were doing therapy, in the height of Beatlemania, my son was playing frisbee in the park with John.

They were building a recording studio. We had a soundproofed room where they were going to make recordings, but there were people working there, walking by and hammering nails while we were trying to do therapy. I said, 'We have to be alone. We just have to be.' There were an awful lot of calls from a guy named Klein who was his business manager and he said, 'You've got to meet Klein one day because he has all our money.' [laughs]

John was a very good patient. Very cooperative. Did everything I asked. He adhered to the rules and he felt deeply, all the time. He responded very well because he had an enormous amount of pain. I've seen an awful lot, but I don't think I've ever seen the equal. It was terrible and also good because it just drove him and made him what he was – incredibly insightful, very close to his feelings and driven by his feelings.

John was incredibly honest about himself and about everybody else. He had this incredible perception – he could see inside people in a way that I've rarely seen. We'd be walking down the street and he'd say this person that and this. And he always knew. When we were walking in London, the kind of adulation and adoration he got was incredible. People project on famous people whatever they want, whether it's John Lennon, or whoever is the star of the day.

So many people have this dream that somehow something out there is going to transform us and make life beautiful, whether it's fame or riches or whatever. And people find out that there's nothing in life but you. That's all there is. And when you can feel, that's all there is – to feel the life you're living. That's the aim of therapy.

The only thing that is really real in life is love. And it's free. I think a lot of what the therapy did is put him in touch with that need for love and what love was about. He was just yearning for it all the time and he became famous because of his need for love. And then when he got there, he found out: 'Hey, wait a minute, I still don't feel love and I'm taking drugs. Something's wrong. I can't get out of my room. I've got everything anybody could want. I've got fame and fortune

Arthur Janov outside the Primal Institute at 620 North Almont Drive, Los Angeles, California, 1970.

Overleaf: John & Yoko, wearing roll-neck Aran jumpers purchased in Edinburgh during their family driving holiday, standing outside the room that seventeen months later will become the White Room where the iconic 'Imagine' video will be filmed; Tittenhurst Park, Ascot, Berkshire, 31 January 1970.

and everything.' But he didn't have the most precious commodity on earth.

With the actors and rock stars that I've seen, they've almost all been totally rejected in childhood. Most of them are very deprived as children. We all need it and it never goes away. It gets transformed, but it never goes away. It takes an incredible drive to get where John got, to practise every day and tour, and the pressure is enormous. He had a solid core of hostility and anger and cynicism and scepticism that kept all the nonsense away. He had this incredible musical ability and the feeling in John's voice – I don't think it's matched by anybody today. He was loaded with feeling and that's why he moves you and that's why he was great, because he was in touch with this for you.

John had a horrible childhood. He was searching for love from his mother and his father. His aunty raised him, who was very strict and then really cold. I remember once his dad came by. He was a dishwasher. He was drunk and John gave him money and said goodbye and I said, 'Why did you give him money?' and he said, 'Oh, he's a poor old guy.' He was very forgiving of his father who he believed had totally rejected and abandoned him. His mother had been around a bit, so she was a target for his needs, for his love. The father was just totally absent – it didn't matter in his life. But unconsciously he needed his father just as much as he needed his mother. If you don't have a father figure in your life, either you find a substitute and you marry your mother or have creative outlets – which he did – but even creative outlets for his feelings didn't quell his pain, or you take drugs. He did a lot of drugs. He's admitted it, so it's not a secret.

LSD is the most devastating thing for mental health that ever existed. To this day, we see people who've been on LSD, and they have a different brain-wave pattern, as if their defences are totally broken down. I think Timothy Leary destroyed so many people by touting LSD. It's a very, very dangerous drug. It depresses all the controls for feelings and liberates what's down below. It comes up, there's nothing to stop it. It just liberates everything, but out of sequence. It just throws up the whole thing. You have 'cosmic consciousness' and all kinds of things that are nonsense – you've got a release of all this immense pain, but you don't have a chance to feel all the feelings that are coming up. Even heroin wouldn't stop it after that.

It was the time of drugs. Everybody was taking LSD. I took LSD several times. But what we found is that people who

have taken more than ten trips on LSD don't do so well afterwards. They have a hard time sleeping. They have Attention Deficit Disorder – a hard time concentrating and focusing. They seem scattered and they can't relax. We've seen patients ten, fifteen years after their LSD trip and we can still see signs in their electroencephalograph of that. It's a very dangerous drug. Even ecstasy is very dangerous because it liberates an awful lot of stuff that should not be liberated unless you're ready to feel it and integrate it.

Before all the drugs he was incredibly repressive, but then they were doing hallucinogens and all kinds of drugs and his defences blew. He was stripped naked in front of his fame and it was right there, all the time, and he had to deal with it. Some people deal with it by drink. He dealt with it by writing songs, luckily for all of us. I have a feeling the methadone medication didn't help. It crushed a lot of his defences. So he had ended up in pain and his level of pain was unbelievable.

I couldn't stay in London for more than a month, so then they came to LA and we continued there. He rented a house in Bel Air, which is a very ritzy area and I spent some time with him there. He talked about life and human beings and the human condition. He used to finish a session and just feel incredibly good, but it's a process and you open up slowly and you can't go too fast with it. That's why it can take a year or eighteen months.

It's very different than any other therapy. We don't see eight patients a day, we see one and that's the patient for the month. I never tell people when to come. I don't give them an hour or a day or anything. They have individual therapy every day and then they do group therapy which John did a lot, too – and you see the pain in other people. It's done in a soundproof, darkened room and they just get to the feeling slowly. The therapist is there all the time. They can last two or three hours and then only the feelings of the patient end the session. I never say, 'John we're through for the day.' When John's had enough pain, he feels really good, he would say, 'OK, I've had enough' and we'd stop. The therapy is quite miraculous. You really do get down to your zone of the interior.

The world is divided between people who feel, which is right brain, and those that do not feel, who are defended and way off somewhere in the left brain. They see the world differently and they relate differently to each other. With people who are in a lot of pain, the feelings that are on the right brain go up to the top and then they go over to the left

John & Yoko on top of the damaged Austin Maxi in which they, Kyoko and Julian had been injured in the remote Scottish Highlands; Tittenhurst Park, Ascot, Berkshire, 31 January 1970.

Overleaf: John & Yoko photographed in the arboretorial gardens at Tittenhurst Park, Ascot, Berkshire, 31 January 1970.

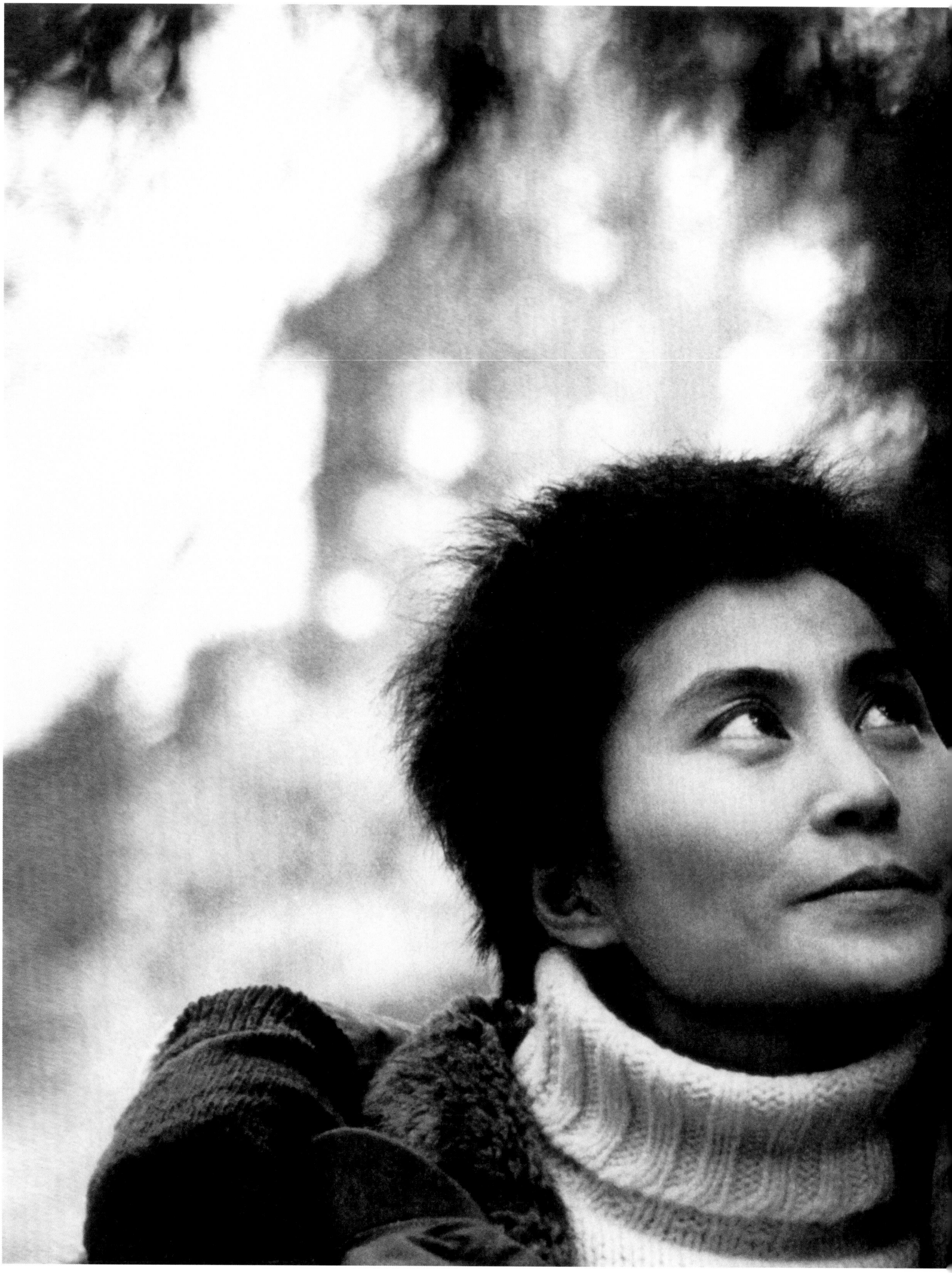

Richard DiLello: These photographs at Tittenhurst were all shot in one session, John & Yoko's first portraits at home after their new haircuts. They were very photogenic and not at all self-conscious about being photographed, which made it really enjoyable.

John & Yoko standing in front of the statue of Diana and amongst the weeping cedar trees, photographed by Richard DiLello; Tittenhurst Park, Ascot, Berkshire, 31 January 1970.

side (that symbolizes), and they get into religion and lots of belief systems. Marx said, 'Religion is the opiate of the masses.' It's true. The belief systems are designed to strengthen your defences against feelings. People get into tremendous pain in their therapy and then they'll come out of it and start to believe certain mystical things. Once we get them deeper into their feelings, it goes away. So we see how it works in the brain. The less pain they have, the less they believe. I think some belief systems tend to be institutionalized madness.

John said, 'God is a concept by which we measure our pain.' That was what John could do. He could take a very profound, philosophical concept and make it simple. And make the words and the music simple. The elegance of his simplicity was so great, he could cut through everything. Little by little, all the veils were being pulled away. All of the idolatry, all the people he felt were just incredible. And he realized when all is said and done, you only have yourself and that's just the truth. And he came to that conclusion very quickly in therapy.

I have a lot of people who are not even religious who beg, that will say, 'Dear God, love me' and then they get down to the feeling of 'Mama, love me'. He did a lot of that. He would lie on the floor all day screaming, 'Mummy, don't go. Love me, Mummy. Where are you? Come back!' He could only say goodbye to her after he had felt his need for her and it finally dawned on him through his feelings that he was never going to get it from anybody, especially from his mother.

He was really into Yoko. There's no question about it. They were like two peas in a pod. They were never separated. Never. They were just together – twins. Yoko was seven years older – a mother figure in some respects. I think that half of the world are mother and father for each other. You symbolize and marry substitutes. I think that's what you do. If you need it, you need it and you're going to make it where you can find it.

Everything he had to say about Cynthia was good. He hardly ever saw Julian, but I had never known him to be hostile to her. I think what happened in the last few years of his life is he realized how important it was to be a father. That love from the father is important – which was not the case before therapy. Certainly not with Julian. I think Julian was very angry about that. John had been too involved with his own pain to even think about Julian. One of the things he got out of therapy was then becoming a decent parent. It seemed

to be a natural evolution of being a human being – loving the people around you.

John came to me after four months of the therapy. He said. 'I'm taking out a full-page ad in the *San Francisco Chronicle*. It will say "This is It!"' And I asked him not to do that. It's a dangerous thing to associate a very important therapy that saves lives with John Lennon. It's far more important than the Beatles in the long run. Also he wasn't halfway through and he could easily have turned around and said, 'This Isn't It!'

His mentality and music was revolutionary. He defined what we were all about and what we were all seeking and no other group could do that. The Rolling Stones did a lot of great stuff, but they didn't come close to that kind of intimacy and simplicity. That's what genius is – all that simplicity, that directness.

'Imagine' is an extension of 'God'. He told us when he didn't believe in anything and then a year or two later when he made 'Imagine' he told us what life could be. He went to the future and that's what I think 'Imagine' is all about. It's one of his greatest songs and he's so down on belief systems and religion and all, I think it's pretty amazing. The lyrics of 'Imagine' are brilliant. He's imagining the world it could be if we all got along, if everything was in peace and no war and that kind of thing, and he's right, isn't he?

Our therapy is very effective, but you have to do the whole thing and he couldn't. He would have stuck with it longer had he not been harassed out of the country by Nixon. When he left, I think he understood the power of feelings and the power of the unconscious that drove him. He didn't know what to do about it, because after he left, he didn't come back. He went to New York and he should have come back but he didn't. It wasn't my job to tell him to come back. That was up to him.

Before he finished the album, he sent me a copy. I had group therapy that night and I played it and there were about fifty people in a heap, bawling and crying – and it was incredibly moving. He touched them enormously. There is an idea that you lose your creativity when you lose your neurosis and that's just nonsense. The more you have of yourself, the more you have to draw on for creativity. That album was amazing. I just loved it. If you're in touch with your feelings, it'll move you. It paved a new way for music and for the honesty of rock artists and art.

Julian (above) and Julian and John (below) riding
a Honda Z50A Mini-Trail 'monkey' motorbike XUC 91H;
Tittenhurst Park, Ascot, Berkshire, 31 January 1970.

JOHN LENNON/PLASTIC ONO BAND ●

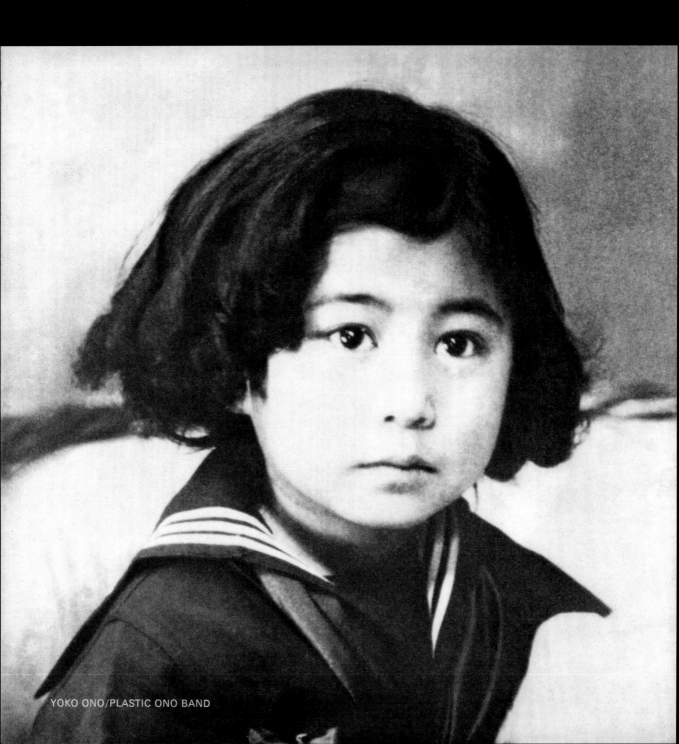

YOKO ONO/PLASTIC ONO BAND

Mother

① Mother, you had me
but 9 never had you
oh 9 wanted you -but you didn't want me,
So 9 got to tell you
Goodbye - goodbye

② Father you left me
but 9 never left you
oh 9 needed you , but you didn't need me,
so 9 just got to tell you
Goodbye - Goodbye.

        Mama don't go
        Daddy come home - repeat

③ Children don't do what 9 have done
oh 9 couldn't walk and 9 tried to run
So 9 got to tell you
Goodbyo - goodbye .

MOTHER

Mother
You had me
But I never had you
I wanted you
You didn't want me

So I
I just got to tell you
Goodbye, goodbye

Father
You left me
But I never left you
I needed you
You didn't need me

So I
I just got to tell you
Goodbye, goodbye

Children
Don't do
What I have done
I couldn't walk
And I tried to run

So I
I just got to tell you
Goodbye, goodbye

Mama don't go
Daddy come home
Mama don't go
Daddy come home

Mama don't go
Daddy come home
Mama don't go
Daddy come home

Mama don't go
Daddy come home
Mama don't go
Daddy come home

Mama don't go
Daddy come home
Mama don't go
Daddy come home

Mama don't go
Daddy come home
Mama don't go
Daddy come home

MOTHER

John: Penny Lane is a suburban district (in Liverpool) where, up until age four, I lived with my mother and father (although my father was always at sea) and my grandfather, in one of those row houses like they always picture the early Beatles life in – in *Yellow Submarine* and other dreamy versions of the poor, working-class lads.

There were five women that were my family. Five strong, intelligent, beautiful women. Five sisters. Those women were fantastic. They dominated the situation in the family. The men were invisible. I was always with the women. I always heard them talk about men and talk about life, and they always knew what was going on. The men never ever knew. That was my first feminist education.

Julia was my mother. A housewife, I suppose. She was a comedienne and a singer. Not professional, but she used to get up in pubs and things like that. She had a good voice. She could do Kay Starr. She used to do this little tune when I was just a one- or two-year-old, from the Disney movie [*Snow White and the Seven Dwarfs*], 'Want to know a secret? Promise not to tell? We are standing by a wishing well.'

My mother and father split when I was four. Then my father split. He was a merchant seaman and it was the Forties in the war and I guess she couldn't live without somebody. She was the youngest and she couldn't cope with me and I ended up living with her elder sister.

Mimi told me my parents had fallen out of love. She never said anything directly against my father and mother. I soon forgot my father. It was like he was dead. But I did see my mother now and again and my feeling never died off for her. I often thought about her, though I never realized for a long time that she was living no more than five or ten miles away.

I moved in with my aunty who lived in the suburbs in a nice semi-detached place [251 Menlove Avenue, Woolton] with a small garden, and doctors and lawyers and that ilk living around. I was a nice clean-cut suburban boy and in the class system I was about a half an inch in a higher class than Paul, George and Ringo who lived in government-subsidized houses. We owned our own house, had our own garden and they didn't have anything like that. I was well protected by my aunty and my uncle and they looked after me very well. My mother was alive and lived a fifteen-minute walk away from me and I saw her sporadically, all the time. I just didn't live with her.

I re-established a relationship with my mother for about four years. She gave me my first coloured shirt. I started going to visit her at her house. Julia became a sort of young aunt to me, or a big sister. As I got bigger and had more rows with Mimi, I used to go and live with Julia for a weekend. I met her new bloke and didn't think much of him. I called him 'Twitchy'. Bobby Dykins – a sleazy little waiter with a nervous cough and thinning margarine-coated hair. Used to always push his hand in the margarine and grease his hair with it before he left. Used to keep his tips in a big tin on top of a cupboard in the kitchen and I used to always steal them.

She taught me music. She first taught me how to play banjo chords – that's why in very early photos of the group I'm playing funny chords – and from that I progressed to guitar. I used to borrow a guitar at first. I couldn't play, but my mother bought me one from one of those mail-order firms. It was a bit crummy, but I played it all the time and got a lot of practice. The first song I learned was 'Ain't That A Shame' – an old rock hit by Fats Domino – and it has a lot of memories for me. Then I learnt 'That'll Be The Day'. I learned the solos on 'Johnny B. Goode' and 'Carol', but I couldn't play the one on 'Blue Suede Shoes'.

And then unfortunately, she was run over – by an off-duty policeman who was drunk – after visiting my aunty's house where I lived, but I wasn't there at the time. That was another big trauma for me. I lost her twice. Once as a five-year-old, when I was moved in with my aunty, and once again where she actually physically died. I was at art school. So I must have been seventeen.

I was staying with Julia and Twitchy that weekend. The copper came to the door to tell us. It was just like it's supposed to be, the way it is in the films, asking if I was her son and all that. Then he told us, and we both went white. It was the worst-ever thing that happened to me. We'd caught up so much, me and Julia, in just a few years. We could communicate. We got on. She was great. I thought, 'Fuck it! Fuck it! Fuck it! That's really fucked everything. I've no responsibility to anyone now!'

Twitchy took it worse than me. Then he said, 'Who's going to look after the kids?' And I hated him. Bloody selfishness. We got a taxi over to Sefton General where she was lying dead. I didn't want to see her. I talked hysterically to the taxi driver all the way, ranted on and on, the way you do.

John Lennon, aged eight, being tickled by his mother
Julia in the garden of her sister, Anne 'Nanny' Cadwallader;
Ardmore, 486 Old Chester Road, Birkenhead, Cheshire,
summer 1949.

Top row, left to right: John's aunt Mary 'Mimi' Smith; cousin Liela Birch (age ten), aunt Harriet, mother Julia 'Judy' Lennon and aunt Anne 'Nanny' Cadwallader; second row: cousin David Birch (three), John (eight), cousin Michael Cadwallader (eighteen months), Liela and half-sister Julia Dykins (two and a half); 'Nanny'; third row: aunt Elizabeth 'Mater' Parkes; cousins David, Liela and Michael, half-sister Julia and John; Ardmore, 486 Old Chester Road, Birkenhead, Cheshire, summer 1949.

The taxi driver just grunted now and again. I refused to go in, but Twitchy did. He broke down.

That was a really hard time for me and it just absolutely made me very, very bitter. And the underlying chip on my shoulder that I had as a youth was really big then. Being a teenager and rock 'n' roller, and mother being killed just when I was re-establishing a relationship with her. It was very traumatic for me. I was in a blind rage for two years. I was either drunk or fighting. I was a troublemaker.

It's hard for me to speak about death. I have had so much death around me. My uncle [George] died right around the same period as my mother, within a few years of each other. Stuart Sutcliffe died of a brain tumour. So did Len Gray, another guy in one of our groups. Buddy Holly died when I was in art school. They all affected me, but I can't find a way to put the feeling into words. It's like you lose a piece of yourself each time it happens.

The next verse says 'Father, you left me but I never left you.' I never knew my father. I saw him twice in my life till I was twenty-four. He turned up after I was famous. I didn't want to see him. I was too upset about what he'd done to me and to my mother, and that he would turn up when I was rich and famous and not bother turning up before. He knew where I was all my life. I'd lived in the same house in the same place for most of my childhood. I thought it was a bit suspicious, but I gave him the benefit of the doubt after he'd put a lot of pressure on me in the press. I opened the *Daily Express* and there he was, washing dishes in a small hotel, very near where I was living, in the stockbroker belt outside London. The front-page news was: 'John's dad is washing dishes, why isn't John looking after him?' I said, 'Because he never looked after me.'

I started supporting him, then I went to therapy and remembered how furious I was in the depths of my soul about being left as a child. So I came out of the therapy and told him to get the hell out, and he did get the hell out, and I wish I hadn't really, because everyone has their problems – including wayward fathers. I'm a bit older now and I understand the pressure of having children or divorces and reasons why people can't cope with their responsibility, or whatever happens when you're feeling your own misery.

He died a few years later of cancer. But at sixty-five he married a twenty-two-year-old secretary that had been working for the Beatles, and had a child, which I thought

was hopeful for a man who had lived a life of a drunk and almost a Bowery bum.

Freddie Lennon (from the foreword of the autobiography he arranged to be sent to John after his death in 1975): *Dear John, By the time you read this I will already be dead, but I hope it will not be too late to fill the gaps in your knowledge of your old man which have caused you distress throughout your life. Of course, your only source of information has been your aunt Mimi who for reasons best known to herself refrained from telling you anything about me. Perhaps the revelations in my life story may bring you a clearer picture of how fate and circumstance control so much of our lives and therefore must be considered in our judgment of one another. Until we meet again, some time, some place, your father, Freddie Lennon.*

John: You know, all he wanted was for me to hear his side of the story, which I hadn't heard. Why he wasn't there. And there's this incredible manuscript of every detail of his life. It's a wild adventure. He was a sailor and he was always in trouble all around the world. He was in prison in Africa during the war and running around New York and boxing in Bali, going to bars, this incredible trip. He said (on the phone), 'Read the book, read the book, read the book.' I said, 'OK, I'll read it.' And then he died and left me this book, which has filled a big hole in my life. I said, 'Oh, that's why he couldn't make it.'

A lot of people thought 'Mother' was just about my parents, but it can apply to anyone. It doesn't have to be someone who lost them. Fathers do leave their children – not physically, but mentally. They never need the child the way the child needs the father.

The mother I had, 'I never had you' – meaning my mother left me or my mother died. Lots of people, say Yoko for instance, had their mother with them all their life, but literally didn't have enough love from them. Well, lots of us suffer that because parents have got their own hang-ups.

I've got the security of Yoko and it's like having a mother. I was never relaxed before, I was always in a state of uptightness, and therefore the cynical Lennon image came out.

Yoko: John used to call me 'Mother' – that started around 1980. I think part of him was thinking, 'I'm going to make her a mother, because she's so not'. I started thinking 'Maybe John's right, maybe we are going to live together forever and this is getting all right. Now I can see it – that a couple and a family can work.'

A sheet of Polyfoto portraits of schoolboy John in his
grey school uniform with cap, taken at Lewis's Department
Store, Ranelagh Street, Liverpool, on a Christmas trip
with Aunt Mimi and Uncle George; December 1946.

John's home between 1945 and 1963 was with his
uncle and aunt, George and Mimi Smith, seen here in
the garden with Sally the dog; Mendips, 251 Menlove
Avenue, Liverpool, 1947.

John: As a kid I had a dream – I wanted to own my own bicycle. When I got the bike I must have been the happiest boy in Liverpool, maybe the world. I lived for that bike.

Above left: John with bicycle, 1947.
Above right: John with cousin David Birch and aunt Anne 'Nanny' Cadwallader, outside Mendips, 1948.
Below left: John leaning on the gate, 1948.
Below right: view of Mendips from the back garden, 1948.

Above left: John's father Alfred 'Freddie' Lennon washing dishes at the Greyhound hotel, Hampton Court, Middlesex, when the *Daily Express* found him and put him on the cover, intimating he had been abandoned by John.
Above right: Freddie with the single he co-wrote with manager and guitarist Tony Cartwright, 'That's My Life (My Love and My Home)' on Piccadilly Records, 31 December 1965. Below left: Freddie Lennon arriving at Schiphol airport, Netherlands, on 18 March 1966 where he will perform the song on *Voor de Vuist Weg*. Below right: Freddie, 55, with his fiancée Pauline Jones, 19, announce their engagement on 5 January 1968.

Kennwood.
Cavendish Rd
Weybridge
Surrey.

Dear Alf Fred Dad Peter whatever,

Yours the first of your letters I've read without feeling strange - so here I am answering it - ok? As you know I'm pretty tied up at the moment. I've a hell of a lot to do - if I get time I'll give Uncle? Charles a ring - but anyway I'll get in touch with you before a month has passed - after all I'm going to India a couple of months so I'll try and make sure we meet before then. I know it will be a bit awkward when we first meet and maybe for a few meetings but there's hope for us yet! I'm glad you didn't land yourself with a bloody big family - it's put me off seeing you a little more - I've enough families to last me a few life times - write if you feel like

Love
John

P.S. Don't spread it (press I mean). I don't want Mimi cracking up.

Hold on John

intro ...

① Hold on John, John hold on
it's going to be alright
you gonna win the fight.

② Hold on Yoko, Yoko hold on
it's gonna be alright
you gonna make it fly

Ⓜ when your by yourself
and there's no-one else
you just have yourself
and you tell yourself to hold on ...

③ Hold on world, world hold on
its gonna be alright
you gonna see the light

when your one
really one
you get things done
like they never been done
So hold on.

HOLD ON

Hold on John
John hold on
It's gonna be alright
You're gonna win the fight

Hold on Yoko
Yoko hold on
It's gonna be alright
You're gonna make the flight

When you're by yourself
And there's no-one else
You just have yourself
And you tell yourself
Just to hold on

Cookie!

Hold on world
World hold on
It's gonna be alright
You're gonna see the light

Oh and when you're one
Really one
Well you get things done
Like they've never been done
So hold on

HOLD ON

John: 'Hold On John' was just about holding on. Even though it's not all that hot, let's hold on. It's only going to be all right. it's now, this moment. That's all right, this moment. And hold on, now. We might have a cup of tea, or we might get a moment's happiness any minute now. So that's what it's all about, just moment by moment. That's how we're living – cherishing each day and dreading it, too. It might be your last day – you might get run over by a car.

When the Beatles were depressed, thinking, 'the group is going nowhere', and 'this is a shitty deal', and 'we're in a shitty dressing room', I'd say, 'Where are we going, fellas?' They'd go, 'To the top, Johnny!' And I'd say, 'Where's that, fellas?' And they'd say, 'To the Toppermost of the Poppermost!' And I'd say, 'Right!' Then we'd all cheer up.

I go through despair and hopefulness. I try and hang on to the hopeful bit. Otherwise, there's just no point at all.

When I made 'Revolution' and 'Revolution 9', I wanted to put out as a single what I felt about revolution. I'd been thinking about it up in the hills in India. And I still had this 'God will save us' feeling about it: 'it's going to be… alright'. But even now I'm saying, 'Hold on, John, it's going to be alright'. Otherwise, I won't hold on.

There's no such thing as just happiness, pure, like that. I think you can reach a state of consciousness. I don't know whether you can make it in this life. All the Buddhas and the Jesus-es, all the great ones that were pretty hip, conscious-wise, I don't think they had complete happiness. I think complete happiness is when you are a bit of electricity, when you've made the absolute. And then the concept of what we think of happiness, of just being, which is what happiness will be for all of us – is not to. And I've had that through meditation. Just a state where you are not aware of anything. So there you'll be and that's complete happiness. You just are. And that is the peace we're looking for – is just to be. And nothing affects you, and you affect nothing, literally. You just are. The happiest people are the people that are 'being' more times a week than anybody else. And it's just down to that.

The bit about 'being' is the same as when you're playing a groove. Every time there's a good session, you watch musicians and they're really playing well, they're out of it. And that's when you are just 'being'. There's nothing hassling you, or not hassling, or anything. And that's it. And you get it writing, and you can get it daydreaming, or I remember

having it as a kid on a desk, or in the grass in the sun, just for a moment.

I believe that meditation is a kind of 'found truth'. Don't run on this path but walk on it. The only way is to recover space in your mind. All you need is mind control. You have nothing to lose to try it. It will not make you crazy, you don't have to be more smart to do it.

Even when you're meditating and doing these things with the whole expressed purpose of getting into that state, you've got to practise it like you'd practise anything. You have got to stop being frightened when you get to the different levels you get to on meditation. You get to a plane thing and whoop! You're fighting it all the time. The whole time is spent stopping yourself from being frightened of nothing.

I think the world is on a trip. As humans, we've been through the tribal bit, childlike. And then we're suddenly becoming aware of something and becoming self-conscious and going through all the hassles you go through being self-conscious where you're so self-conscious you can't do anything. And then to come out of that is the next stage, which I think we're going into, of being self-conscious but realizing that you can handle it. And that's the breakthrough. We've become too self-conscious of it and now we've got to put it in perspective. And we can have cars and tellies and that, but still get back to the spiritual bit, which is the bit we've missed out on. Becoming unselfconscious.

I believe the universe is in your head. Literally in your head. Physically we're insignificant when you look around to the size of it, but the physical bit is a load of crap. It's like you're worrying about your car and talking about it as if there's no driver. The driver's the bit, and the car is nothing. The car just happens to be the thing you are driving. But the driver's the bit and the driver's your soul. And that's universal, omnipresent, and all the rest of it. And it is. And you can realize it. If you realized it once, you remember when you've realized it before – as a child or any time in your life – and it's there.

I was 100 per cent saying meditation could do it. I still believe it. People can become aware of this with acid, meditation and a macrobiotic diet. So that's what I'm doing now. And the combination of everything is the best thing I've come across so far. You know the day that you're OK, you are at 100 per cent potential and you can handle whatever the situation is.

John practising the clawhammer, finger-picking guitar style he had learned from Donovan on Donovan's own cherry sunburst Gibson 1965 J-45 acoustic guitar while in India with Maharishi Mahesh Yogi; Swarg Ashram, Rishikesh, Uttarakhand, India, spring 1968.

Dear Christine,

The only way to answer your question is to meditate yourself and experience it – you can only find out so much reading. A guru is "teacher – thats what the word means – hes certainly a teacher. His idea of helping the world is to help everyone – its no good feeding people who are just going to be hungry again in a few months – the point is change the situation which causes starvation disease etc – the cause is people – governments politics – you – me – everything must be changed so that the less fortunate aren't. Theres enough food etc for everyone in the world – so where is it? People destroy it for "economical reasons."

I believe Maharishi wants publicity – why shouldn't he? The only way to get a message over to everyone is to publicise it – thats the 20th century. If Jesus was here now don't you think he'd be on t.v.?

You ask me to try God – thats what meditation is about – experiencing God.

'The Kingdom of Heaven is within' said
Jesus — and he meant within which is where
the mantra takes your mind. Sure the system
is scorned in India and elsewhere so is God
so is everything scorned by someone or other
— it doesn't mean it's bad does it!
         Anyway as I said — try it
— it can't harm you — you do not
have to be rich to do it — you do not
have to go to India to do it — you just
DO iT.
              with love
              John Lennon.

P.S   excuse paper I don't seem to have
                anything else.

Letters to Mr Miller from John at Kenwood, St George's Hill, Weybridge, Surrey, and to Mr Bulla from John at Swarg Ashram, Rishikesh, defending Maharishi Mahesh Yogi and recommending transcendental meditation.

Kenwood
Cavendish Rd.
St George's Hill
Weybridge
Surrey.

DZ

Dear Mr Miller

Thank you for your letter. We are not making "long denunciations" to mysticism — and we are well aware of the state of India. Transcendental Meditation is not mystic if anything it is scientific. Its purpose is for the use of householders — and that is what we intend trying to put across to people (India included). The Maharishi also has full knowledge of the truth and this is why we are with him — as there is only one truth there are also many paths — the one we are taking now seems natural so — — . "The Kingdom of Heaven is within you" — that's where we're going — Transcendental Meditation ⚌ simple enough for a child and children are the people we must aim at. Maybe we will work somewhere or other, but please do not condemn the 'Maharishi' with no knowledge of him.

love
John Lennon

Overleaf: Fifteen Dance Instruction cards mailed to John from Yoko in 1967 between September and 9 October (his birthday). John: She did a thing called *Dance Event*, where different cards kept coming through the door every day saying 'Breathe' and 'Dance' and 'Watch all the lights until dawn', and they upset me or made me happy, depending on how I felt.

SPIRITUAL REGENERATION MOVEMENT FOUNDATION OF INDIA

Under the Divine Guidance of His Holiness Maharishi Mahesh Yogi of Uttar Kashi

TELEPHONE:
RISHIKESH 121
CABLE: MEDITATION, DELHI

SHANKARACHARYA NAGAR
P. O.   SWARGASHRAM
RISHIKESH, U.P., INDIA

Our Guiding Light

*His Divinity
Swami Brahmanand Saraswati Jagad-Guru Shankaracharya Jyotir-Math
Himalayas, India.*

THE SPIRITUAL REGENERATION MOVEMENT FOUNDATION is dedicated to offering peace, harmony and happiness to everyone in all walks of life through a simple system of Transcendental Deep Meditation.

His Holiness Maharishi Mahesh Yogi has developed and promoted a simple system of meditation whereby every normal man can easily reach the deeper levels of consciousness, unfold latent faculties and realise more complete happiness.

The main aim of this world-wide movement is to establish meditation centres everywhere and infuse Maharishi's simple system of deep meditation in the daily routine of every individual.

The S.R.M. Foundation aims at world peace through harmony and happiness in the life of each individual.

WORLD CENTRES

INDIA, AFGHANISTAN, BURMA,
WEST INDIES, MALAYSIA,
HONGKONG, JAPAN,
ENGLAND, SCOTLAND, ICELAND,
FINLAND, SWEDEN, NORWAY,
DENMARK, HOLLAND, FRANCE,
GERMANY, AUSTRIA, ITALY,
SWITZERLAND, GREECE, TURKEY,
IRAN, U. A. R., EAST AFRICA,
SOUTH AFRICA, CANADA,
U.S.A., PERU, CHILE,
ARGENTINA, COLUMBIA,
URUGUAY, BRAZIL, AUSTRALIA,
NEWZEALAND.

Dear MR Bulla,

Thank for your letter. — If every request like yours was granted — there would be no 'huge treasure' as you call it. You say 'peace of mind minus all other things on earth is equal to nothing' — this doesn't make sense. To have peace of mind one would have to have all that one desires — otherwise what is the peace of mind?

Even a 'poor' clerk can travel the world — as many 'people' do — including friends of mine some of whom are at His academy now, all equally 'poor'. All you need is initiative — if you don't have this I suggest you try transcendental meditation through which all things are possible.

with love

John Lennon,

jai guru dev.

REGISTERED UNDER THE SOCIETIES ACT 1860, AND TAX-EXEMPTED

John: When I was a student, the days were rare when I could say, 'It's OK, I can handle it'. But when I got onto acid, I thought, 'Aha! It is OK and I can handle it.' The percentage of good days was just a bit better but still a lot of hassling. Then meditation came along and that worked all right and I could handle each day better than I could handle it before. Then the India thing came, and I had some great experiences over there, because I was meditating eight hours a day. And it was really some trip, like acid was nowhere. Just sitting there muttering some word in a room, and it was the biggest trip I've ever had in my life. You just sit there and let your mind go. It doesn't matter what you're thinking about, just let it go. And then you introduce the mantra, the vibration, to take over from the thought. You don't will it or use your will power. There's none of this sitting in the lotus position or standing on your head. You just do it as long as you like.

Yoko's trying to turn me onto this macrobiotic scene. And I can tell you, folks, that the effect on you is – in three days' time, you're in a completely different scene. Every day is a better day – just cleaning out your system, mentally and physically – and it works. We did ten days rice diet, pure, and you think 'you can't do that, you can't do that'. But it's not like giving up cigarettes or anything that you're hooked on. Just to check what you're eating is astonishing! When you really start looking, every bloody thing you shove in your mouth has got some kind of crap in it! And even the things that you think have got no crap in it, the hens were fed crap. It's all completely unnatural. And if you come to think that you are what you eat, then you know the result of everything that happens to you is karma. If you're shoving all this crap into you, how can you expect your system to work?

Ringo Starr (lyrics from his song 'Early 1970'): *Laying in bed, watching TV. 'Cookie!' – with his mama by his side, she's Japanese. They screamed and they cried, now they're free. And when he comes to town, I know he's gonna play with me.*

Yoko: Love is the energy that is really moving the whole world. Love is the creative energy and prayer is the poor man's weapon. With prayer and love we can really create the world. Please send out the strongest energy of love, peace and belief to the world.

Keep on spreading peace without fear. Make sure you keep your head straight. Believe in yourself that if you want to stay sane, you will. Negative thinking blocks, delays and slows down world peace, harmony and love.

You have to be peaceful to get peace. If you are angry and combative, well, that is not going to help. Our heads are the source to think how to get peace. Our hearts are the source of courage to act. When you have peace in your mind, you will get peace. If just enough people are really peaceful, we will get the peace of togetherness.

Love is the only energy we can rely on. And all of us have known it since birth, because it is the only energy and protection that kept us going. Breathing is one of the ways we give ourselves that energy, and to others, too. Happiness and success are all in our minds. You can be happy just looking at a beautiful sky. You can think you were successful when you baked a great loaf of bread.

Think of something that is beautiful around you. Hold on to that beauty until you feel like smiling. Keep breathing deeply and keep smiling. Build your own dream life. Don't concentrate your mind on fear and doubt about the future. You will then be attracting fear and doubt. Look at yourself in the mirror and you will see that you are the one that is shining the truth for all of us to see. Love is a feeling we all have unless we block it, for no reason except fear. It's great to feel love for everything around you and afar. Everything you think, say and do affects the whole world, land and sea. Imagine what you want, and that will be shared by the world.

Don't bottle love, because then it will just sit in the bottle, or escape from the bottle one breath at the time, and pretty soon you will see an empty bottle in your hand. Anything that is at odds with one other should be forgotten. Just hold on to what we agree on. That is where the power is.

Relax. Breathe in and out. It is important to have time when you are just relaxing. You are in the present moment. The present moment seems like a little dot. But that dot carries the human history of past, present and future and all of the people and things you love. Don't waste your time worrying about things. Whatever will be, will be. And know that everything is a blessing if you let it be. A daydream, given the time, always comes true.

We are all people who are into being entertained, day and night. Once it was just kings and queens who asked to have a life of being entertained. Stop being entertained. Feel love for cleaning up your life. You will feel better and be healthy as well. Start there.

1st day

midnight

breathe

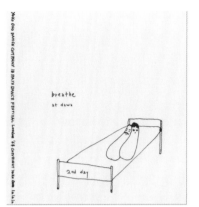

breathe
at dawn

2nd day

3rd day
in the evening

breathe together

watch

draw a large circle in the sky
let us know the diameter of the
circle (guess), direction and the
colour of the sky you were watching and the duration of your
watching experience

4 th day
in the afternoon

watch

go to the nearest fountain
and watch the water dance

afternoon

5th day

6th day   evening

watch

have you seen a horizon lately?
go see a horizon. measure it
from where you stand and let us
know the length.

7th day
evening

watch

have you seen a horizon lately?
go see a horizon. measure it
from where you stand and let us
know the length.

Harold

count

count the clouds
name them

8th day (afternoon)

shake

go shake hands with as many
persons as possible. write
down their names. try in the
elevator, tube, escalator,
street, toilet, on top of a
mountain, in the dark, daydream,
on the clouds, etc. make it a
nice handshake by holding a
flower in your hand, perfume or
wash your hand, etc.

9th day
afternoon

10th day morning

find

go find a clover and send us
measurements weight of all
possible parts of the clover.

send

send something you can't count

11 th day
daylight

12th day
dreamtime

SWIM

SWIM IN YOUR DREAM AS FAR AS
YOU CAN UNTIL YOU FIND AN
ISLAND. TELL US RESULTS.

13 th day
future noo

Colour yourself
wait for the spring to come
let us know when it comes

Dance Report - On Hiding

hide in the cupboard
a) until your family starts to wonder
b) until your family forgets you
(make choice)

Dance Report - On Facing

face the wall throughout the year
and imagine banging your head
against it: a) slowly until the
wall collapses and you see the sky.
b) violently until your head is
gone.

consider if it is such a catastrophy
to live without your head or if it
shouldn't be easier for you to go
around since your body would be much
lighter.

I found out.

i told you before stay away from my door
don't give me that brother. brother. brother
                       -brother
the kids on the phone. won't leave me alone
so don't give me that brother brother brother -
                           brother.
no!   <u>i found out!</u>

① now that i showed you what i been thru
don't take nobodies word-what you can do
there ain't no jesus gonna come from the sky
now that i found out i know i can cry
               <u>i found out</u>

② some of you sitting there with your cock in your hand
don't get you nowhere -don't make you a man
i heard something bout my ma and my pa
they didn't want me so they made me a star

③ old hare krishna got nothing on you
just keep you crazy with nothing to do
just keep you occupied with pie in the sky
there ain't no guru who can <u>see thru your eyes</u>

④ i seen thru junkies -i been thru them all
i seen religion from Jesus to Paul
don't let them fool you with dope and cocaine
can't do you no harm if you feel your own pain.
          <u>i found out.</u>

I FOUND OUT

I told you before, stay away from my door
Don't give me that brother, brother, brother, brother
The freaks on the phone won't leave me alone
So don't give me that brother, brother, brother, brother, no!

I, I found out
I, I found out

Now that I showed you what I been through
Don't take nobody's word what you can do
There ain't no Jesus gonna come from the sky
Now that I found out I know I can cry

I, I found out
I, I found out

Some of you sitting there with your cock in your hand
Don't get you nowhere, don't make you a man
I heard something 'bout my Ma and my Pa
They didn't want me so they made me a star

I, I found out
I, I found out

Old Hare Krishna got nothing on you
Just keep you crazy with nothing to do
Keep you occupied with pie in the sky
There ain't no guru who can see through your eyes

I, I found out
I, I found out

I seen through junkies, I been through it all
I've seen religion from Jesus to Paul
Don't let them fool you with dope and cocaine
No-one can harm you; feel your own pain

I, I found out
I, I found this out
I, I found out

I FOUND OUT

John: I read an article today that said, 'If they'd had psychiatrists, we wouldn't have had Gauguin's great pictures'. Those fucking bastards are just sucking us to death. That's about all that we can do, is do it like circus animals. I resent being an artist in that respect. I resent performing for fucking idiots who don't know anything. They can't feel. I'm the one that's feeling, because I'm the one that is expressing. They live vicariously through me and other artists.

I'm sick of all these aggressive hippies – the 'Now Generation' – being very uptight with me; either on the street or on the phone, demanding my attention as if I owed them something. I'm not their fucking parents. They come to the door with a fucking peace symbol and expect to just march around the house like an old Beatle fan. They're under a delusion of awareness by having long hair, and that's what I'm sick of. I'm sick of them. They frighten me. A lot of uptight maniacs going around, wearing fucking peace symbols.

The only friends I've got are the Beatles and Derek, Neil and Peter Brown, who have been with us over the years, and a few more people we picked up here and there. I've had hangers-on that have been friends that have dropped off because we didn't have enough to give each other. We picked up a few more from Yoko's life, who are determined not to be hangers-on, which is a relief. They pretend the Beatles don't exist!

Apple was a manifestation of Beatle naivety, collective naivety, and we said we're going to do this and help everybody and all that. And we got conned on the subtlest and grossest level. We had to quickly build up another wall round us to protect us, from all the beggars and lepers in Britain and America that came up to us, and the vibes were getting insane.

When we were at Wigmore Street, I saw everyone, day in day out; like we said: 'You don't have to get down on your knees.' There wasn't anybody with anything to offer to society, or me, or anything. There was just 'I want, I want', and why not? Terrible scenes going on in the office with different people getting very wild with me. Even the peace campaign we had a lot of that too, but once you've opened the door it's hard.

George Harrison: I think we didn't really realize the extent to which John was screwed up. For instance, you wouldn't think he could get bitter, because he was so friendly and loving; but he could also be really nasty and scathing.

As a kid, I didn't think, 'Oh well, it's because his dad left home and his mother died', which in reality probably did leave an incredible scar. It wasn't until he made that album about Janov, primal screaming, that I realized he was even more screwed up than I thought.

John: The book came through the post and the thing said *Primal Scream*. Now you know Yoko's been screaming a long time, right? And we were pretty under pressure then. It was early days together and we were living in Ascot in the big house, and there was still a lot of shit coming down on us, and we were getting really wired about it all. And I just particularly was more wanting it than Yoko. But the very name, *Primal Scream*, got me. I didn't have to read the book, just the title was enough. It registered something inside me, it made my heart flutter. I got nervous reading it.

I didn't read anything that Janov said. I just read, 'Charlie so-and-so went in and this is what happened to him.' I thought, 'that's me, that's me'. And so what is it? They get to this thing and then they scream and feel better? OK, it's something other than taking a tab of acid and feeling better. So I thought, 'let's try it'. And we called him and he came over. And they do this thing where they mess around with you until you reach a point where you hit this scream thing, and you go with it and they encourage you to go with it, and you kind of make a kind of physical, mental, cosmic breakthrough through the scream itself. After that, it's up to you.

Therapy made me feel my own pain. I had to really kill off all the religious myths. In the therapy you really feel every painful moment of your life. It's excruciating. You are forced to realize that your pain, the kind that makes you wake up afraid with your heart pounding, is really yours and not the result of somebody up in the sky. It's the result of your parents and your environment.

Your mind blocks off memories from childhood. When you're a child, you can only take so much pain, so when something happens you tend to block it off and not feel it. It's like not wanting to know about going to the toilet, or having a bath. If you don't do it for a long time, it accumulates. As I realized this, it all started to fall into place. All of us growing up have come to terms with too much pain. Although we repress it, it's still there. You are not your emotions. You have emotions and you can master them. Janov doesn't just talk to you about this, but makes you feel it.

John in the office, with his circular artwork *You Are Here* in the background behind his head; Apple offices, 3 Savile Row, London, March 1969.

Above left: The Apple Music press advertisement and poster campaign from 20 April 1968 featuring Apple office manager Alistair Taylor dressed as a one-man-band. It prompted an avalanche of tapes, creatives and hangers-on arriving at the Apple Music offices.

Above right: John's illustration of himself and Yoko sitting happily on a cloud in the sunshine above the businessmen at Apple, who are busy working around a table below; May 1969.
Below: A production meeting in Ron Kass's office; Apple Offices, 3 Savile Row, London, February 1969.

John: Emotions are the same and you accumulate them over the years. And they come out in other forms – violence, baldness or short-sightedness. That's part of his theory. It's pretty revolutionary but from the experience I had there, it seemed pretty valid. You find a way of going back to these emotions that you've blocked off. And you remember things you didn't remember, and experience that emotion, because it's still there. It's like taking a diarrhoea pill, and it all comes out baby!

Once you've allowed yourself to feel again, you do most of the work yourself. When you wake up and your heart is going like the clappers or your back feels strained, or you develop some other hang-up, let your mind go to the pain and the pain itself will regurgitate the memory which originally caused you to suppress it in your body. In this way, the pain goes to the right channel instead of being repressed again as it is if you take a pill or a bath saying, 'well, I'll get over it'. Most people channel their pain into God or masturbation or some dream of making it.

I read some guy saying about the sexual fantasies and urges that he had all his life. When he was twenty, and then when he was thirty, he thought they'd cool down a bit. Then when he got in his forties he thought they'd cool down, but they didn't, they went on: sixty, seventy… until he was still dribbling in his mind when he couldn't possibly do anything about it. I thought, 'Shit!' because I was always waiting for them to lessen, but I suppose it's going to go on forever.

Most of us have been through things with mothers and fathers; most of us have been through something with religion; most of us have been isolated or been in love; most of us remembered things and most of us have wondered what love is, you know [sings] 'love is real, real is love'.

The worst pain is that of not being wanted. Of realizing your parents do not need you in the way you need them. When I was a child, I experienced moments of not wanting to see the ugliness, not wanting to see 'not being wanted'. This lack of love went into my eyes and into my mind. The only reason I am a star is because of my repression. Nothing would have driven me through all that if I was 'normal'. The only reason I went for that goal is that I wanted to say: 'Now, Mummy, Daddy, will you love me?'

The therapy is like a very slow acid trip which happens naturally in your body. It is hard to talk about because you feel 'I am pain' and pain to me now has a different meaning because of having physically felt all these extraordinary repressions. It was like taking gloves off, and feeling your own skin for the first time. I don't think you can understand this unless you've gone through it. I try to put some of it over on the album. But for me at any rate it was all part of dissolving the God trip or father-figure trip. Facing up to reality instead of always looking for some kind of heaven.

When you're born, you're in the pram and you smile when you feel like smiling. But normally the first game that you learn is to smile before you get touched. Most mothers actually torture the kid in the pram – make it smile when it doesn't want to smile – smile and you get fed. That isn't joy.

Those people that go around saying, 'Well let's sing Hare Krishna and let's be joyful.' You cannot be joyful unless you feel joyful, otherwise it's phoney. Mummy makes you smile, or say 'Hare Krishna' before you feel good – then you've gone through a process of falsification of your feelings. If you feel good, you feel good. If you feel bad, you feel bad. There's no way out. It's like you can take drugs or get drunk or you can do whatever, but you're just suppressing the feelings.

I wonder how happy George is, or any of the people that are chanting and meditating. It might help them from cracking completely. I haven't met anybody full of joy – the Maharishi nor any Swami or any Hare Krishna singer. I haven't actually seen somebody full of joy. This dream of constant joy is bullshit as far as I'm concerned. If you're only feeling what you think is joy, you're not living. Life is made up of pain and pleasure. Living is feeling and that entails feeling all sorts of things. There's no constant. I think we're all in pain. Every day is the same isn't it? There's some heaven and some hell. There's no complete joyful day, is there? There's better days, worse days. Every day contains both.

If you know how to feel good, you could tell everybody how to do it. You don't do it, it happens. It expresses itself in your face or in your body. Pain and joy go into your body and unless you feel it or express it, it remains there like constipation. It'll come out in your nerves, or how many cigarettes you smoke or what you do.

If somebody gives me a joint, I might smoke it but I don't go after it. I've had cocaine but I don't like it. I mean, I had lots of it in my day. But it's a dumb drug because you immediately have to have another one, twenty minutes later. Then your whole concentration goes on getting the next fix. Really, you know, I find caffeine is easier to deal with.

Opposite: John & Yoko, George Harrison and Patti Boyd enjoying prasadam with ISKCON founders and devotees of Indian spiritual revolutionary Swami Prabhupada who were all staying at the cottages at Tittenhurst; the Temple, Tittenhurst Park, Ascot, Berkshire, 11 September 1969.

Below: Postcards printed 'LOVE & PEACE JOHN and YOKO' with additional ink stamps relating to ISKCON, Krishna and the Kirtan (Hare Krishna mantra), given to Brazilian Beatles fan Lizzie Bravo outside Apple's offices; 3 Savile Row, London, 1969.

LOVE & PEACE

JOHN and YOKO

Printed by : TEMPLERING LTD. Mitcham Surrey.

WORKING CLASS HERO

1) As soon as your born they make you feel small
by giving you no time instead of it all
till the pain so big you feel nothing at all
— — working class etc =

2) they hurt you at home and they hit you at school
they hate you if your clever and they despise a fool
til your so fuckin crazy you can't falow their rules.
— working class etc. — —

3) Keep you doped with religion and sex and t.v.
and you think your all clever and classless and free
but your still fucking peasants as far as I can see.
working class etc
—

4) when they've tortured and scared you for 20 odd years
then they expect you to pick a career
when you can't really function your so full of fear

5) there's room at the top they are telling you still
but first you must learn how to smile as you kill
if you want to be like the folks on the hill
a working class hero is something to be
yes " " " " " " " "
if you want to be a hero well just follow me
" " " " " " " " " "

WORKING CLASS HERO

As soon as you're born they make you feel small
By giving you no time instead of it all
Till the pain is so big you feel nothing at all
A working-class hero is something to be
A working-class hero is something to be

They hurt you at home and they hit you at school
They hate you if you're clever and they despise a fool
Till you're so fucking crazy you can't follow their rules
A working-class hero is something to be
A working-class hero is something to be

When they've tortured and scared you for twenty odd years
Then they expect you to pick a career
When you can't really function you're so full of fear
A working-class hero is something to be
A working-class hero is something to be

Keep you doped with religion and sex and TV
And you think you're so clever and classless and free
But you're still fucking peasants as far as I can see
A working-class hero is something to be
A working-class hero is something to be

'There's room at the top' they are telling you still
But first you must learn how to smile as you kill
If you want to be like the folks on the hill
A working-class hero is something to be

Yes, a working-class hero is something to be
If you want to be a hero, well just follow me
If you want to be a hero, well just follow me

WORKING CLASS HERO

John: I like 'Working Class Hero' – as a song, or a poem or whatever it is. I think its concept is revolutionary. It's for the people like me who are working class, who are supposed to be processed into the middle classes, or into the machinery. It's my experience, and I hope it's just a warning to people.

The thing about the song that nobody ever got right was that it was supposed to be sardonic. It had nothing to do with socialism, it had to do with: if you want to go through that trip, you'll get up to where I am, and this is what you'll be – some guy whining on a record, all right? If you want to do it, do it. I'm not recommending it, I'm just saying it's something to be, like a lawyer.

Yoko: The Beatles were just saying to people, 'It's gonna be OK' and then suddenly John comes out with this *Plastic Ono Band* album – 'Working Class Hero' and 'God' and all that, saying, 'It's not OK. There are these problems.' Obviously that makes him less popular because people don't want to know about that. People want somebody to always tell them it's OK. And so it's gonna be a little bit less popular, but it shouldn't be if the world gets more mature. They should understand that that's more important somehow.

John: I've been successful as an artist and have been happy and unhappy, and I've been unknown in Liverpool or Hamburg and been happy and unhappy. But what Yoko's taught me is what real success is – the success of my personality, the success of my relationship with her, my relationship with our child, my relationship with the world – and to be happy when I wake up. It has nothing to do with rock machinery or not rock machinery.

I put 'fucking' in because it does fit. I didn't even realize there were two in, until somebody pointed it out. And actually when I sang it, I missed a bloody verse. I had to edit it in. But you do say 'fucking crazy' don't you? That's how I speak. I was very near to it many times in the past, but I would deliberately not put it in, which is the real hypocrisy, the real stupidity. I would deliberately not say things, because it might upset somebody, or whatever I was frightened of.

People like me are aware of their so-called genius at ten, eight, nine…. I always wondered, 'Why has nobody discovered me?' In school, didn't they see that I'm cleverer than anybody in this school? That the teachers are stupid, too? That all they had was information that I didn't need. I got lost at school.

A couple of teachers would notice me, encourage me to be something or other, to draw or to paint – express myself. But most of the time they were trying to beat me into being a dentist or a teacher. And then the fans tried to beat me into being a Beatle or an Engelbert Humperdinck, and the critics tried to beat me into being Paul McCartney.

The establishment irritates you – pulls your beard, flicks your face – to make you fight because once they've got you violent, they know how to handle you. The only thing they don't know how to handle is non-violence and humour.

What am I supposed to be, some kind of martyr that's not supposed to be rich? Did they criticize me when I was a Beatle for making money? In retrospect, a lot of money came our way, and I spent a lot of it, I sure as hell had a lot of fun with it. Through ignorance I lost a lot of it and gave a lot of it away through maybe a misplaced charitable heart. So why are they suddenly attacking me for making money now? Because we were associated with radical causes, feminism and the anti-war movement? To be anti-war you have to be poor? There's many a socialist in the House of Lords, what are they talking about? I mean, if they want a poor man, they can follow Jesus. And he's not only poor, he's dead!

I just like TV. To me it replaced the fireplace when I was a child. They took the fire away, and they put a TV in instead, and I got hooked on it. Yoko was an intellectual, and she thought TV was something you didn't bother with. I've met a lot of people like that. But TV is what everybody in the world watches, and TV is what everyone talks about the next day at work. And if you want to know what everybody, twenty million Americans or twenty million Britons are talking about on Saturday night, it's what they saw on Friday night on TV. Well, it's nice to know what other people are thinking.

TV is a window on the world. Whatever it is, that's that image of ourselves that we're portraying. I was a great one as a kid for standing and just looking out of windows for hours and hours and hours. The TV does that for me, except the view changes immensely. One minute it's *The Saint*, the next minute it's a rocket in Vietnam, and it's very surreal. I leave it on whether I have the sound on or not.

We went to America a few times and Epstein always tried to waffle on at us about saying nothing about Vietnam. So there came a time when George and I said 'Listen, when they ask next time, we're going to say that we don't like that war and we think they should get right out.'

John sitting on the fender of a Land Bulldog truck holding his recently acquired 1958 Rickenbacker 325; Hamburger Dom Funfair, Heiligengeistfeld ('the field of the Holy Spirit'), Feldstrasse, St Pauli, Hamburg, November 1960.

Photographer and close friend Astrid Kirchherr: I liked the rough surrounding of the rusty steel and bits of iron and lorries. It fits with the Beatles' scruffiness, but when you look in their faces, compared to the rough surrounding, that's the contrast I was after.

Below: John, aged twenty-two, making tea at the McCartney family home, 20 Forthlin Road, Liverpool, 25 March 1963. Opposite, top row: the Beatles play the Royal Variety Performance and meet Her Majesty Queen Elizabeth, the Queen Mother, Prince of Wales Theatre, London, 4 November 1963; second row: the Beatles debut on *The Ed Sullivan Show*, watched by a record-breaking 73 million viewers, 9 February 1964; third row: the Beatles presented with Variety Club Silver Heart awards by Labour party leader Harold Wilson, London, 19 March 1964; bottom row: the Beatles receive MBEs from HRH Queen Elizabeth II, Buckingham Palace, London, 26 October 1965.

Previous pages: On their debut 1964 US tour, the Beatles
played thirty-two shows in twenty-four cities in thirty-three
days. The amplification was so insufficient that the band
could not hear themselves play above the noise of the
screaming fans. At the Las Vegas Convention Center
there were bomb threats; Las Vegas, 20 August 1964.

Below: An American Beatles fan holding a banner saying
'John, I Love You' ahead of two Beatles concerts at the
16,000-seater Forest Hills Stadium, Queens, New York,
28 August 1964.

In the summer of 1966, American magazine *Datebook* published out-of-context quotes from Maureen Cleave's *Evening Standard* interviews with Paul McCartney appalled at racial insults in America: 'It's a lousy country where anyone black is a dirty n****r!' and John on religion: 'I don't know which will go first – rock 'n' roll or Christianity.'

American Christian fundamentalists reacted with ire and loathing. Tommy Charles and Doug Layton, DJs at WAQY Birmingham, Alabama, organized a boycott of Beatles' music, and encouraged fans to burn their Beatles records. This provoked a backlash of hatred, and fear and death threats for the band. They never toured again.

John: That's what we did. Up to then there was this unspoken policy of not answering delicate questions, though I always read the papers, you know, the political bits. The continual awareness of what was going on made me feel ashamed I wasn't saying anything. I burst out because I could no longer play that game any more, it was just too much for me. Of course, going to America increased the build up on me, especially as the war was going on there.

> Tokyo, 30 June 1966: Well, we think about it [Vietnam] every day, and we don't agree with it and we think it's wrong. That's how much interest we take. That's all we can do about it… and say that we don't like it.

> Toronto, 17 August, 1966: I mean, we all just don't agree with war for any reason whatsoever. There's no reason on earth why anybody should kill anybody else. Somebody would shoot us for saying it. We're not allowed to have opinions. You might have noticed, you know?

> Memphis, 19 August 1966: It seems a bit silly to be in America and for none of them to mention Vietnam as if nothing was happening. Americans always ask showbiz people what they think, and so do the British. It doesn't matter about people not liking our records, or not liking the way we look, or what we say. They're entitled to not like us. And we're entitled not to have anything to do with them if we don't want to, or not to regard them. We've all got our rights, you know, Harold.

> New York, 22 August, 1966: We don't like it. I've elaborated enough. We just don't like it. We don't like war.

At that time this was a pretty radical thing to do, especially for the 'Fab Four'. It was the first opportunity I personally took to wave the flag a bit. But you've got to remember that I'd always felt repressed. We were all so pressurized that there was hardly any chance of expressing ourselves, especially working at that rate, touring continually and always kept in a cocoon of myths and dreams. It's pretty hard when you are Caesar and everyone is saying how wonderful you are and they are giving you all the goodies and the girls, it's pretty hard to break out of that to say, 'Well, I don't want to be king, I want to be real.'

> Interview with Maureen Cleave, *Evening Standard*, 4 March 1966: Christianity will go. It will vanish and shrink. I needn't argue about that; I'm right and I will be proved right. We're more popular than Jesus now; I don't know which will go first – rock 'n' roll or Christianity. Jesus was all right but his disciples were thick and ordinary. It's them twisting it that ruins it for me.

'The Beatles are bigger than Jesus.' That really broke the scene. I nearly got shot in America for that. The Ku Klux Klan were burning Beatles records and I was held up as a satanist. It was a big trauma for all the kids that were following us.

> Chicago Press Conference, 11 August 1966: If I'd have said, 'television is more popular than Jesus', I might have got away with it. Originally, I was pointing out that fact in reference to England – that we meant more to kids than Jesus did, or religion, at that time. I wasn't knocking it or putting it down, I was just saying it as a fact. And it's sort of… it is true, especially more for England than here. I'm not saying that we're better, or greater, or comparing us with Jesus Christ as a person or God as a thing or whatever it is, you know. I just said what I said and it was wrong, or was taken wrong. And now it's all this.

In a way we'd turned out to be a Trojan Horse. The Fab Four moved right to the top and then sang about drugs and sex, and then I got more and more into the heavy stuff and that's when they started dropping us. There you are up on the stage like an Aunt Sally waiting to have things thrown at you. It's like always putting yourself on trial to see if you're good enough for Mummy and Daddy. You know, 'Now will you love me if I stand on my head and fart and play guitar and dance and blow balloons and get an MBE and sing "She Loves You"? Now will you love me?' [laughs]

One night, on a show in the South [Memphis], somebody let off a firecracker while we were on stage. There had been threats to shoot us, the Klan were burning Beatles records outside and a lot of the crew-cut kids were joining in with them. Somebody let off a firecracker and every one of us looked at each other, because each thought it was the other that had been shot. It was that bad. The music wasn't being heard. It was just a sort of freak show: the Beatles were the show, and the music had nothing to do with it.

Then we decided, no more touring; that's enough of that. I'm not going to put up with it. I was really too scared to walk away. I was thinking 'Well, this is like the end, really.' There's going to be a blank space in the future. That's when I really started considering life without the Beatles – what would it be? What am I going to do? Am I going to be doing Vegas? I mean, where do you go?

At the first press conference of their US and Canada tour in 1966, a dejected and persecuted John was forced by the American press, the Beatles and Brian Epstein to publicly apologise for his misquoted comment about Jesus that provoked anger, death threats and burnings of Beatles records by the so-called Christian community.

The Ku Klux Klan, a far-right white supremacist terrorist organization was picketing shows and threatening vengeance. At the Memphis show, a firecracker was set off in the audience and everyone thought John had been shot; Astor Towers Hotel, Chicago, 11 August 1966.

John: The music wasn't being heard and it wasn't doing anything, it was just a sort of freak show. The Beatles were the show and the music had nothing to do with it. And as we were musicians, we felt there was no enjoyment in it.

Below: John in a pensive mood before going onstage for what would be the Beatles' final stadium concert; Candlestick Park, San Francisco, 29 August 1966.

John and Paul singing 'Day Tripper', whilst chaos reigns with runaway fans escaping the stands and being chased and caught by the police on the pitch as they try to get to the band. The Beatles played their eleven-song, thirty-three-minute set from behind a cage of chain-link fencing to an audience that were screaming too hard to listen.

Richard DiLello: Between 1964 and 1965, the whole culture rapidly changed. Everyone wanted to be a Beatle or Beatle-esque – write their own songs, be creative. The Beatles' great gift to the world was opening people up to the realization that they could believe in themselves, lead their own lives, follow their dreams and not be told what to do.

isolation

① People say we got it made
don't they know we're so afraid, isolation.
we're afraid to be alone
everybody got to have a home, isolation.

② Just a boy and a little girl
trying to change the whole wide world,
the world is just a little town   - isolation
everybody trying to put us down, isolation.

I don't expect you to understand
after you caused so much pain,
but then again, you're not to blame,
your just a human, a victim of the insane.

③ We're afraid of every one
afraid of the sun, isolation
the sun will never disappear
but the world may not have many years
isolation.

ISOLATION

People say we got it made
Don't they know we're so afraid?
Isolation

We're afraid to be alone
Everybody got to have a home
Isolation

Just a boy and a little girl
Trying to change the whole wide world
Isolation

The world is just a little town
Everybody trying to put us down
Isolation

I don't expect you to understand
After you've caused so much pain
But then again you're not to blame
You're just a human, a victim of the insane

We're afraid of everyone
Afraid of the sun
Isolation

The sun will never disappear
But the world may not have many years
Isolation

ISOLATION

John: I remember walking in the mountains of Scotland, up in the north. I was with an aunty, who had a house up there, and I remember this feeling coming over me. I thought, 'This is what they call poetic.' When I looked back, I realized I was kind of hallucinating. You know, when you're walking along and the ground starts going beneath you and the heather, and I could see this mountain in the distance, and this feeling came over me. I thought, 'This is something; what is this? Is this that one they're always talking about, the one that makes you paint or write?' Because it's so overwhelming that you want to tell somebody, and you can't describe it, you can't say 'there's this feeling that I'm having and the world looks like it's sort of glowing', so you have to try and paint it or put it into poetry or something like that.

Everybody has it, but most people just won't allow it to come in. Daydreaming is forbidden in school. I daydreamed my way through the whole of school. I just absolutely was in a trance for twenty years because it was absolutely boring. If I wasn't in a trance, I wasn't there – I was at the movies, or running around.

I wrote 'Isolation' in England on the piano. George said it should have been a single – he liked it best. I had to isolate, using 'being famous' as an immense excuse for never facing anything. Because I was famous – therefore I can't go to the movies, I can't go to the theatre, I can't do anything. Every time I got nervous, I took a bath. I'm free of the Beatles because I took time to free myself mentally from it, and look at what it is. And now I know. So here I am, right? That's it! It's beautiful, you know, it's just like walking those hills.

Yoko: I'm amazed about how resilient people are. They're born with no assurance that they're going to survive. They come in between these parents that are so insecure; they themselves are like children and they survive all that. From the age of three or four, it's 'don't do this', 'don't do that', 'use the spoon properly', or 'you're not supposed to say this and that' – always getting these double messages – 'it's all right to do this, but it's terrible to do this' – and it's amazing how we survived, and we're still beautiful.

We have beautiful emotions and it's such a short life and then around ten it's, 'Well, you're ten now, so you're not five, so you better behave yourself', and when you're eighteen everyone's asking you, 'What are you going to be?' and you have to be nervous about that. There's so many exams that you go through, already creating a lot of inferiority complexes. And then there's all these images that you're supposed to be – you're either too fat or too thin and then you go into who you get together with, and then by end of the twenties, you have to be worried about being old, and have not accomplished anything yet: 'What are you doing?' You know, it's really a hard life, and so I sympathize with everybody.

How are you going to relax? Jealousy and possessiveness come naturally. But the difference is it's all right to have all that. Life is so hard anyway, so we have to be kind to each other. And we all of us hate ourselves for not being that ideal image. I think life is beautiful, and I am enjoying it. I'm an endless optimist.

If you're afraid of losing, you're going to lose. We're so afraid that we don't even want to propagate. If you're not afraid of love, it's always there. Society makes people split, because there are so many different conventions. Like if you're married to somebody, then you shouldn't be loving somebody else. Even once you formally separate or divorce, you're not supposed to even know each other.

The world is so lovely – because there is love, everybody's got love, and that's why they want to know how to make love last. Because everybody wants to be happy, and everybody's been taught that that's the way to be happy. Love really makes everything work. Love makes everything grow, even plants.

Sometimes you feel possessive and that's fine. We shouldn't be ashamed of all the feelings we have. It's fine. And we should go ahead with feeling all these feelings. We're so ashamed of being jealous, we're so afraid of being possessive, we're so afraid of having hatred and all of that, and we shouldn't. It's just all different forms of energy.

Nothing that we possess is ugly. Everything that comes out of us is beautiful. And we're taught that singing a song is beautiful, but if you sing out of tune it's not beautiful, and you have to sing in a certain way. And going to the toilet is ugly, and there's all sorts of labels on what is beautiful and what is ugly. I think that everything that comes out of us is beautiful, because we're human. And so when somebody is shouting or screaming, or somebody's in fear or something like that, I look at these people, and I really think they're beautiful, just because they're human,

Below: An out-take from the *Two Virgins* album cover shoot; 34 Montagu Square, London, 3 August 1968. Overleaf: John & Yoko leaving court surrounded by police, press and public. The previous day they had been arrested for possession of hashish by seven police officers and two dogs. John claimed he only pleaded guilty because he was threatened that Yoko would be deported. The stress sent pregnant Yoko into hospital and the criminal record caused John six years of massive legal fees fighting the US immigration authorities to get his Green Card; Marylebone Magistrates' Court, 181 Marylebone Road, London, 19 October 1968.

Below and opposite: After the drama with the police, Yoko suffers some complications with the pregnancy and is admitted to hospital accompanied by John, who remains at her side throughout her stay. She is typing next to a recent Durrant's press clipping about their situation, with the headline 'No Bed for Beatle John' that will become the title and content of the eponymous song on John & Yoko's album, *Unfinished Music No. 2: Life With The Lions*; Queen Charlotte's Hospital, Room 1, Second West Ward, London, 4–24 November 1968.

Overleaf: John & Yoko surround themselves with taped-up photographs, notes, press clippings and drawings on the walls of their room at Queen Charlotte's Hospital; Room 1, Second West Ward, London, 4–24 November 1968.

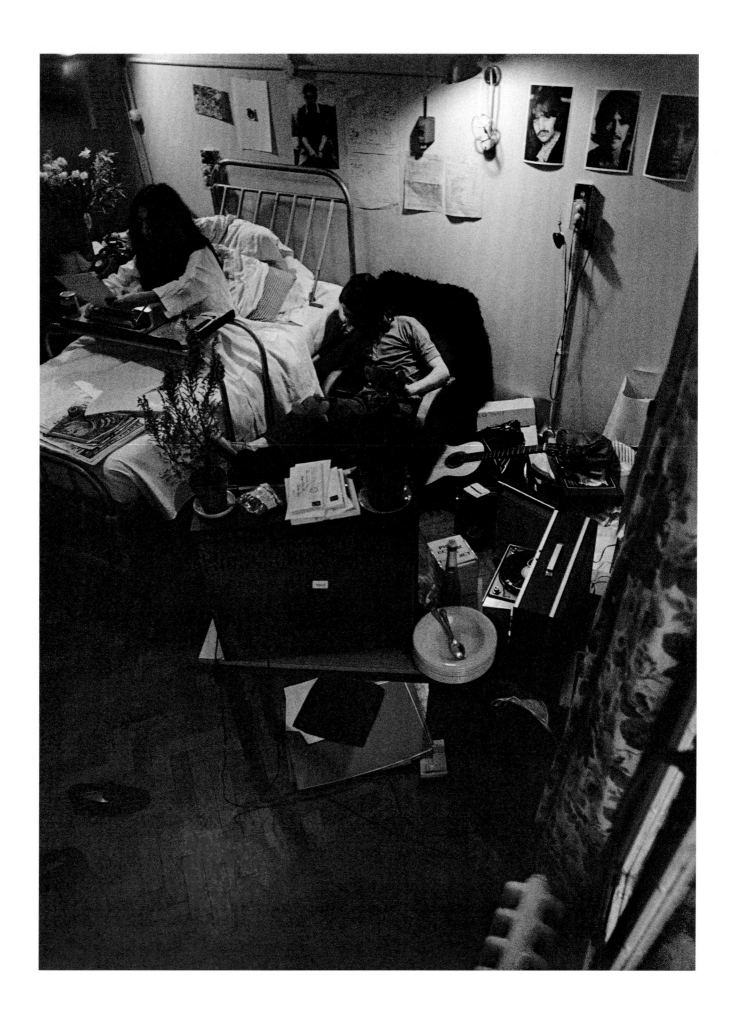

just because they're alive. So in that sense, I think we should have more understanding for each other, and we should give more approval to each other. It's all right to be afraid.

Yoko: John and I had so much in common, which was odd because he was from Liverpool and I was from Tokyo. We simply thought the same way about things. Love won. We were always having a dialogue and we were always inspired by each other, and that kept us going, and also we were always giggling.

John: As soon as we got together, she allowed me to express myself in her medium and vice versa. Although she was doing songs anyway and I was only doing drawings and paintings. I wasn't doing conceptual work. So let's face it, I learned a damn sight more from her then she did from me. I expressed myself in galleries with her.

Yoko: When I met John, he was so different from the idea that I had about men at the time. That they could be very talented but so stiff in their ideas, but John wasn't. He went with anything that came to him that he thought was interesting, and we hit it off. For me, as a woman, being supportive of him was a normal thing. Most women do that for their husbands or partners. But for men to support their woman in her endeavours, like John did for me, was very unusual at the time.

John: People just attacked her all the time. Just for being with me. It had nothing to do with the work she put out. And I got the same slacking with her ilk. 'What does that pop star think he is doing putting up a blank canvas on the wall at his *You Are Here* show?'

When she would say to an engineer, even though it was a freeform jam, 'I'd like a little more treble', 'a little more bass' or, 'There's too much of that, whatever you're putting on that', they'd say, 'What did you say, John?' Now, women are conscious of that now and it's talked about a lot, but those days I didn't even notice it myself and she'd say, 'Didn't you notice that when I talked to them, they answer you as if I hadn't spoken!' Now I know what she's talking about especially as it's happened to me in Japan, too. Because in Japan, even though I'm well known there, she's the queen of Japan, you know? When they talk in Japan and I say, 'A cup of tea, please,' in Japanese. They say: 'He wants a cup of tea?' to her in Japanese [laughs] and so I really understand it now, not only as

a feminist issue, but as a being the 'other'. And no more of the 'other' now. So when she talks, they listen.

Yoko: And also, I have to go, 'This big ego of mine where is it taking me?' Even when I met John, I think I was getting to be like: 'All right, I'm doing all these things, everybody in the avant-garde knows my name,' and in fact I was getting very lonely.

I hated being blamed for the break-up of the Beatles. I wasn't responsible. It was John's decision after Ringo and then George told him they wanted to leave. He persuaded them to change their minds and then he changed his mind. He wanted to say, 'I started the group and I broke it up.' In the end, though, it was Paul who announced the break. John was angry about that because Paul had a new album out at the time and John thought he did it to attract publicity.

John: If we hadn't taken some of it with a pinch of salt, I think we would have both gone under. It was pretty hard. Usually one could sustain and support the other, but there were times when we both would go down. It's very hard because the tendency is to go to drink or drugs, and it's very hard to get out then. But you can't when you're involved with legal court cases or immigration problems. One has to be right on the ball. It might have done a lot of good; it might have done me harm. I can't really tell yet. We seem to just go ploughing on anyway, producing it, but still I wonder how it would have been had we not been harassed. But one cannot always blame everything on the outside.

Whatever happened to us was also partly our creation. And it was probably to do with complete self-involvement and not really taking care of business on an outside level, or looking where we were going. Instead of looking down the road, we were always looking into each other's eyes. So we're not taking the position that society did everything to us. And we take responsibility as well. I mean accidents happen and things do happen to you, but we do take some responsibility for the situation.

Yoko: So many things that have happened to us are so incredible that we just couldn't help. I mean we just had to say to each other, 'Isn't this amazing?' and just laugh about it. There's nothing we can do about it.

John: It was like a Pinter play, only we were in it; never ending.

Eighteen months before Robert Fraser acquired the Magritte painting *Le jeu de mourre* in 1968, John had taken a bite out of Yoko's artwork, *Apple*, at his private view of her Indica Gallery exhibition on 7 November 1966.

The artwork and plexiglas plinth are seen here with Yoko at her London home, 25 Hanover Gate Mansions. Upon opening in 1968, Yoko's artwork was proudly displayed at the offices of the Beatles' new business venture, Apple.

Nic Knowland: I met John & Yoko at Queen Charlotte's Hospital while Yoko was a patient there. They asked me to help them make a film called *"RAPE"* that was a direct experience of being chased by the press and paparazzi. Above: Cameraman Nic Knowland and sound recordist Christian Wrangler pursue Eva Majlata while filming *"RAPE"*;

Lower Sloane Street, Chelsea, London, 22 January 1969. Below: John & Yoko editing *"RAPE"* with Toni Trow (later Toni Myers), observed by Nic Knowland and his son Dan; *Tattooist International*, 13 Greek Street, London, 5 February 1969. Opposite: Stills from the film *"RAPE"* that premiered on ORF TV in Austria, 31 March 1969.

Remember.

① Remember when you were young
how the hero was never hung,
always got away
Remember how the man
used to leave you empty handed
always, always, let you down
if you ever change your mind
about leaving it all behind,
remember, remember. today.

(chorus.)

② Remember when you were small
how people seemed so tall
always had their way
remember ma and pa
just wishing for movie stardom
always, always playing a part
if you ever feel too sad
and the whole world is driving you mad
remember, remember today.

(ch.) don't feel sorry
       the way its gone
       don't you worry
       about what you've done

REMEMBER

Remember when you were young
How the hero was never hung
Always got away

Remember how the man
Used to leave you empty-handed
Always, always let you down

If you ever change your mind
About leaving it all behind
Remember, remember, today
Heh heh hey

And don't feel sorry
The way it's gone
And don't you worry
'Bout what you've done

Just remember when you were small
How people seemed so tall
Always had their way
Heh heh hey

Do you remember your Ma and Pa
Just wishing for movie stardom
Always, always playing a part

If you ever feel so sad
And the whole world is driving you mad
Remember, remember today
Heh heh hey

And don't feel sorry
'Bout the way it's gone
And don't you worry
'Bout what you've done

No, no
Remember, Remember
The fifth of November

REMEMBER

Yoko: I was totally in love with snow all my life. My mother told me that it snowed all night, and then I was born. She had the window open and was surprised that it was snow-covered to the way, way distance. She had me in her arms and prayed that I would have a good life. I remember how bright the snow was. I know you'd think I couldn't possibly see on the first day; well, I did.

I was born in the Yasuda family home in Kamakura, Tokyo, on the eighteenth of February, 1933. That means Aquarius. I'm an air sign and I'm interested in communication. I was the first child. I have a younger brother, Keisuke, and a younger sister, Setsuko. My name means 'ocean child' in Japanese.

My mother, Isoko, was a beautiful, wealthy Japanese heiress. Her grandfather, my great-grandfather, Zenjirō Yasuda, founded one of the fourth largest zaibatsu (financial conglomerates) in Japan, the Yasuda Financial Group, which included the Yasuda Bank (then the largest in Japan, now Fuji Bank) and many companies that handled insurance, mining, textiles, real estate, railways, shipping, warehouses, manufacturing and philanthropy. My mother used to say to me, 'Your father was only president of a bank, but my father owned one.' [laughs]

My father, Eisuke, was a very handsome man, the most handsome of all the Onos. The Onos had been Samurai and were gentry and highly intellectual – most of them spoke three or four languages. Eisuke was famous at Tokyo University for being a genius mathematician. He wanted to pursue a career as a professional concert pianist. His father, Eijirō Ono, who had been awarded a PhD in America, was the president of the Industrial Bank of Japan, a governmental bank. His dying wish was that my father went into banking, and so he then had to give up his dreams of being a musician.

Then he met my mother. She was beautiful and intelligent and a famous Yasuda, and even though my father was above all that fame – he found all the cooks and chauffeurs and staff a little embarrassing and suffocating – they fell in love and got married, which was unusual at the time because Japanese aristocratic society nearly always involved arranged marriages. She was twenty or twenty-one and had me at twenty-two. She was very young, sweet, pure and very intelligent. She was kind of destroyed by the Ono family because the Ono family was so jealous that she was an heiress.

Just two weeks before I was born, my father was transferred from Tokyo to the San Francisco branch of the Yokohama

Specie Bank. My mother was very upset about it. I heard from relatives that my mother cried. I was probably upset too, in her tummy. From when I was born to when I was two and a half, I only knew my father as a photograph. My mother would show me his picture before bedtime and tell me, 'Say goodnight to Father'.

My father was always in foreign countries. He lived for a very long time in New York and Paris. I don't know what kind of freedom he had, really. My mother and I were in Tokyo; not always with him. She was always going shopping and dressing very well and holding dance parties and things like that, and had nothing very much to do with me. She had her own life. She was beautiful and looked very young. It was like having a film star in the house. She used to say, 'You should be happy that your mother looks so young.' But I wanted a mother who made lunch and didn't wear cosmetics. I was never able to get hold of my mother without touching her manicure and fur.

John: She was a very typical woman of that age, she thought only of dancing and being Zelda Fitzgerald and having make-up on – wannabe movie stars.

Yoko: She didn't want to take the responsibility. She didn't have those feelings. She didn't really want to admit that she was a mother. She was always saying things like, 'Today I met so-and-so and these people and they found out that I have children and they were so surprised! They couldn't believe it!' – that kind of thing.

I remember being surrounded by about four or five beautifully kimono-ed servants and she was saying, 'Oh, what shall we do?' She arranged to have me and her filmed, and had the film sent to my father to say, 'Remember us?' The toy dog in the film was one my father sent me. She never spent so much time with me as she did when she was being filmed.

When I was two-and-a-half years old, we left Japan on an ocean liner, to meet my father for the first time. I was standing on the ship's deck with my mother. My dad came up to the deck, and stood in front of us. He kissed mum, and I was wondering if he would kiss me too. I kept looking up to see him since he was so tall. And the San Francisco hill was in a fog behind him. I will never forget that view. It was beautiful. I remember later when they opened the Golden Gate Bridge for the very first time, the 'San Francisco' song they sang, and visiting The World's Fair.

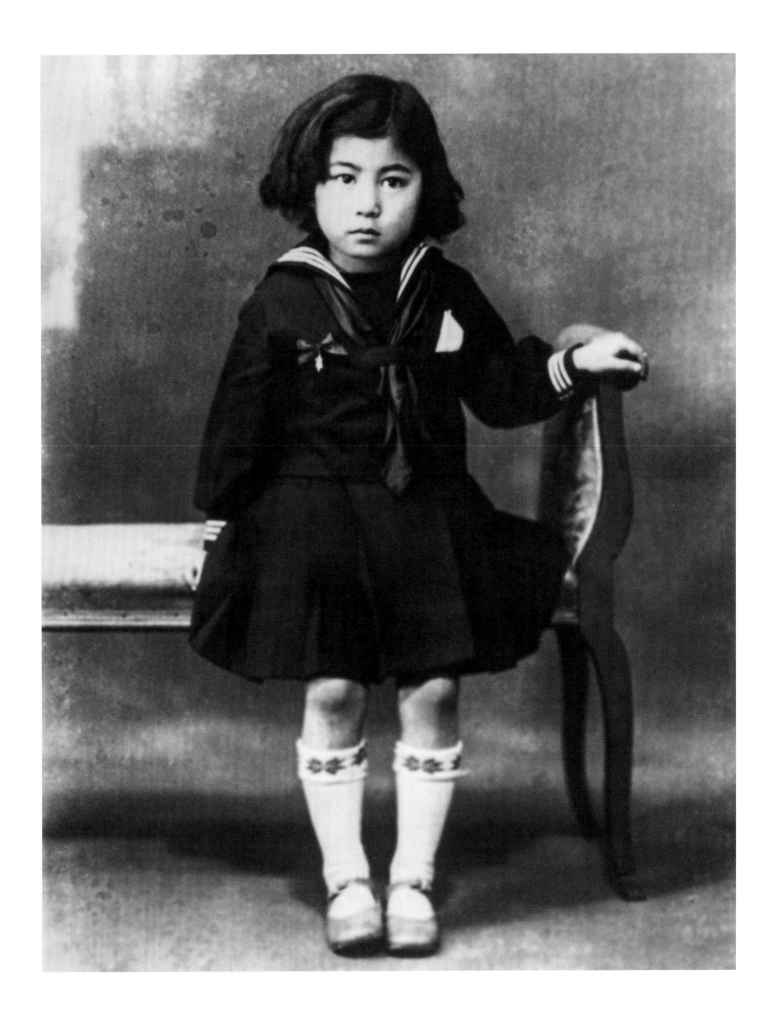

Opposite: The wedding day of Yoko's parents Eisuke Ono and Isoko Yasuda; Eisuke in white tie, holding white gloves, Isoko in traditional Hikifurisode wedding kimono with Sensu folding fan; Tokyo, 3 November 1931.
Above, top left: Yoko's maternal great-grandfather Zenjirō Yasuda (1838–1921); top right: Thanksgiving dinner party for employees of the Yokohama Specie Bank and their families, 28 November 1935; below: magazine feature about Isoko Ono and Yoko at home at the Yasuda Mansion, (Kudan House), 1-1-1 Fujimi, Chiyoda-ku, Tokyo, 1938.
Overleaf: Yoko's parents' family home movies, Kudan House, Tokyo, San Francisco, Chicago, 1933–1940.

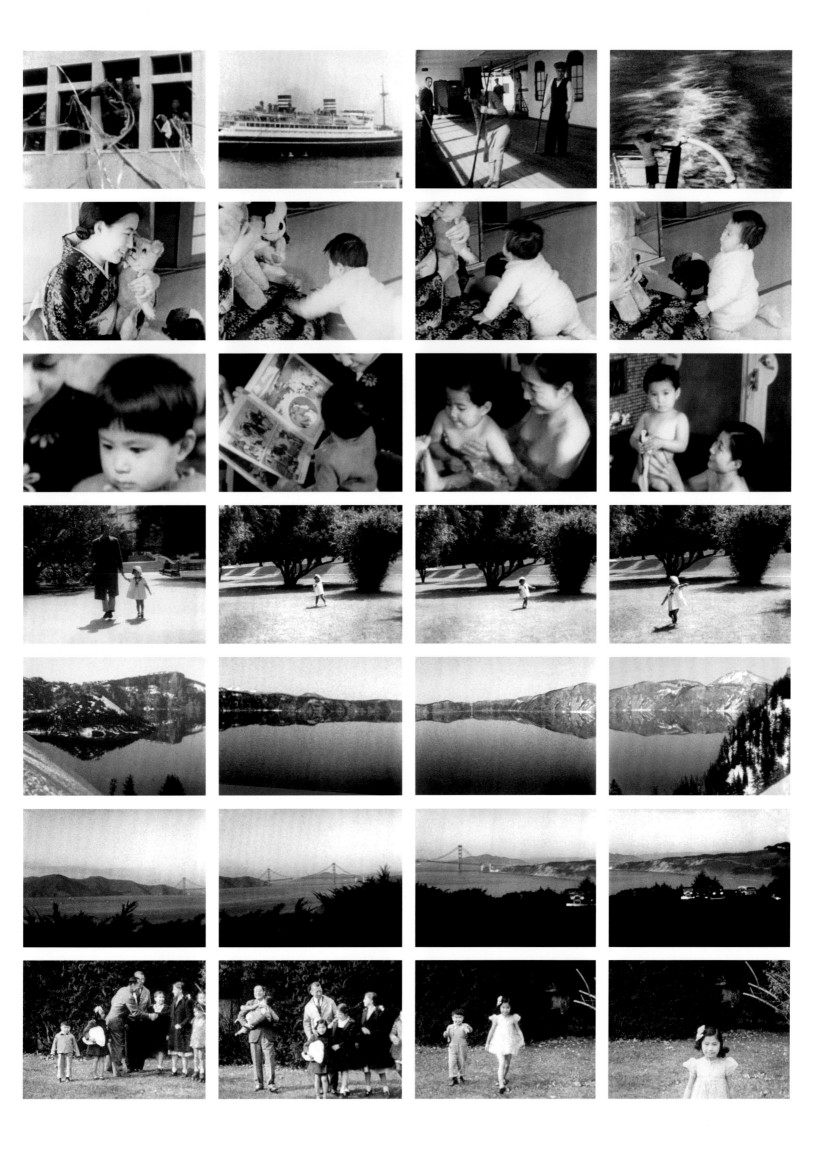

Previous pages: Yoko was twelve when she survived Operation Meetinghouse, the most destructive bombing raid in human history. 1,665 tonnes of American napalm-filled cluster firebombs killed over 100,000 civilians and destroyed over 10,000 acres of property, making over a million people homeless. Tokyo, 9–10 March 1945.

Ono family portraits: above: father Eisuke, mother Isoko, and Yoko, 1937; below: Eisuke, brother Keisuke, Yoko and sister Setsuko on Isoko's lap, 1945.

Yoko: When he met me for the first time, my father said, 'OK, let's see your hands.' I showed him and he said, 'Your hands have to be much longer to play the piano.' And I think my hands actually shrunk when he said it! I remember the feeling. My father was a good pianist and would make comments to me like, 'When you play the piano, you have to continue playing until you finish the work.' And he would not say much else to me. He was the one that first taught me about Schoenberg and Berg and Webern. He was the first person to introduce Kazimir Malevich's artwork to Japan. But for his daughter, he was hoping that I would not be avant-garde. He and my mother never showed their disappointment. The way I knew was that they never came to any of my concerts. And when John and I got married, I knew they wouldn't come to that either.

My father had a huge desk in front of him that separated us permanently. There was always such a space around me. I would play sitting in the deep gaps between tall and fat chairs. I never liked ringing the service bell because it often made me realize that there was nobody at the other end. When it was time to eat, I was told the meal was ready and went into the dining room, where there was a long table for me to eat at. My private tutor watched me silently, sitting on the chair beside me. I was terribly lonely. They were pretend parents, in a way. I didn't see them so often. The maids took care of us and I was frightened all the time, because they tended to be very tough towards children and take it out on you.

When I was five, Japan went to war with China, and my mother, brother and I returned to Tokyo and my mother gave birth to my sister. When I was seven, we all went to live with my father in New York, and returned to Tokyo again in 1941, when I was eight. My father was moved to Hanoi in Vietnam.

When I was twelve, the Tokyo air raids were very heavy and we were immediately evacuated to a farmhouse in the Japanese countryside where we were surrounded by farmers. I was there with my brother and sister, who were very young then, and a maid. My mother wasn't there. The maid was constantly trying to run away and the farmers were terribly nasty to us because we were Tokyo people. And we were starving. I was pushed into being an adult because I had to take care of the household, like getting food for my brother and sister, which meant I had to go to different farmhouses and beg for it. I had to pay a lot, but no money would do, because money meant nothing in those days.

There was this huge, beautiful German antique sewing machine which had all sorts of carvings on it, which had come from my grandfather. I had to exchange it for a 60-kilo bag of rice. It was so ridiculous. They could get away with murder because we needed rice and they didn't need those things.

Towards the end of the Second World War, I looked like a little ghost because of the food shortage. I was hungry. It was getting easier to just lie down and watch the sky. That's when I fell in love with the sky, I think. Since then, all my life, I have been in love with the sky. Even when everything was falling apart around me, the sky was always there for me. It was the only constant factor in my life, which kept changing with the speed of light and lightening. As I told myself then, I could never give up on life as long as the sky was there.

I'm glad that my mother was that way rather than sitting around saying 'My whole life was for you' and 'What did you do to me?' because that would have been a burden. I don't have that kind of sense of owing to her and she did pretty well for herself. She looks beautiful now, still, and so in that sense, I admire her strength and intelligence. I had learned from my mother to be independent so I could survive as a person in the very high pressure Yasuda-Ono family situation.

But at times I was thinking when I went to school and when it was raining and other parents were coming with umbrellas to meet the child, my mother never would think of that, or children bringing lunch boxes with something that mother had made home-made. My mother used to say, 'You should be very proud and thankful that your mother is not one of those plain old mothers; that your mother is beautiful and cares about beauty.' It's better that she was like that. It's also very strange that people become like how they were treated – they repeat the same patterns.

John: We were in danger of being Zelda and F. Scott Fitzgerald. I mean we were happy and we were close, but we were both barmy people, like we all are, and we would've just pushed each other. We couldn't have kept up the pace we were going at.

Nostalgia is all right when you feel like it and I'm sure they were nostalgic in the Fifties for the Forties and the Forties for the Thirties. It's just the human condition to spend a lot of time in the past and a lot of time in the future and hardly any time in the present. So we all go through that danger and it's hard to remember, as A-Wop-Bop-A-Luma, the great guru said, 'Be Here, Now!'

love is real, real is love
love is feeling, feeling love
love is willing to be loved

love is touch, touch is love
love is reaching, reaching love
love is asking to be touched

love is free, free is love
love is giving, giving love
love is needing to be loved.

LOVE

Love is real
Real is love
Love is feeling
Feeling love
Love is wanting
To be loved

Love is touch
Touch is love
Love is reaching
Reaching love
Love is asking
To be loved

Love is you
You and me
Love is knowing
We can be

Love is free
Free is love
Love is living
Living love
Love is needing
To be loved

LOVE

John: I had this dream of this woman coming. I knew it wouldn't be someone buying the Beatles records. The way it was with Cyn was she got pregnant, we got married. We never had much to say to each other. But the vibrations didn't upset me because she was quiet and I was away all the time. I'd get fed up every now and then, and start thinking this 'Where Is She?' bit. I'd hope that The One would come. Everybody's got that 'thinking of The One'. The one what? Well, I suppose I was hoping for a woman who would give me what I got from a man intellectually. I wanted someone I could be myself with.

Yoko: I went to London from New York in 1966, and I met all these English men. And most of them were very feminine. And I thought, 'Oh, is it going to be all like this?' And then there was this guy who looked like a guy and we understood each other. He had a very intelligent side that appealed to me, and also a kind of sensitivity. I thought, 'he understands me'. That's rare. Most men really don't. He was awake, but he was a bit unfocused, like a lost soul. And then when we met, he suddenly had a clear vision like he used to have when he was a boy.

John: I went to the Maharishi. Yoko stayed in England. The meditation was fantastic. It was as big as acid trips and changing my whole thing. Suddenly I was tapping this source of power inside myself and vast vistas of creativity, if I could just hold it and get back. While I was in India, she wrote me these letters – 'I'm a cloud. Watch for me in the sky.' I'd get so excited about her letters. There was nothing in them that wives or mother-in-laws could have understood.

When I got back from India, we were talking to each other on the phone. I called her over. It was the middle of the night and Cyn was away, and I thought well now's the time if I'm gonna get to know her any more. She came to the house and I didn't know what to do; so we went upstairs to my studio and I played her all the tapes that I'd made, all this far out stuff, some comedy stuff, and some electronic music. She was suitably impressed and then she said, 'Well, let's make one ourselves', so we made *Two Virgins*. It was midnight when we started *Two Virgins*, it was dawn when we finished, and then we made love at dawn. It was very beautiful.

I had never known love like this before, and it hit me so hard that I had to halt my marriage to Cyn. And don't think that was a reckless decision, because I felt very deeply about it and all the implications that would be involved. Some may say my decision was selfish. Well, I don't think it is.

Are your children going to thank you when they are eighteen? There is something else to consider, too – isn't it better to avoid rearing children in the atmosphere of a strained relationship? My marriage to Cyn was not unhappy. But it was just a normal marital state where nothing happened and which we continued to sustain. You sustain it until you meet someone who suddenly sets you alight.

With Yoko I really knew love for the first time. Our first attraction was a mental one, but it happened physically too. Both are essential in the union – but I never thought I would marry again. Now the thought of it seems so easy. We never planned our relationship, it just happened and it ended up that we're always together. Freedom is in the mind you know, like they say. It seems that as soon as a couple gets together, the man's supposed to go somewhere and work and the woman's supposed to be somewhere else, but I don't think that's very good for a relationship. It just so happens that that's the way we all live. Maybe in the past they worked together, or within sight of each other, like she'd be digging the potatoes and he'd be cutting the hay or something, or they split for hunting – something like that. I don't see why we should be apart, especially as we can work together and have the same interests. It's not like I'm a mountain climber and she's an archaeologist. Our interests are the same, so that helps.

Nothing is more important than what goes on between two people, because it's two people that produce children, two people that fall in love. You don't generally fall in love with two people at once, I've never experienced it anyway. I'm in love and that's the end of it. She's now fifty per cent of me. So every time I pick up the guitar I sing about Yoko and that's how I'm influenced. I am obviously influenced by her ideas and her coming from that other field, the so-called avant-garde or underground, or wherever she came from. She came in through the bathroom window. She encouraged the freak in me. We're a pretty horny couple and we're artistic and neurotic like everybody else, the kind of people who express themselves sexually a lot. But we've both been through the mill and we've done it all, so what the hell, now we've decided this is what we want. We so satisfy each other that that's enough.

I'm more myself now than I was then because I've got the security of Yoko. That's what's done it and it's like having a mother and everything. That's it. So I'm secure in my relationship with her, so then I can afford to relax. I was never relaxed before, I was always uptight.

Finally made the plane into Paris
Honeymooning down by the Seine
Peter Brown called to say
'You can make it OK
You can get married in Gibraltar near Spain'

'The Ballad of John & Yoko', verse 3

John & Yoko honeymooning down by the Seine,
four days before their wedding in Gibraltar, in
front of the Eiffel Tower, Paris, 16 March 1969.

John & Yoko travelling to their wedding in Gibraltar
by car, plane and walkway, 20 March 1969.

The wedding of John & Yoko with best man Peter Brown at the office of registrar Cecil Wheeler during a ten-minute ceremony in Gibraltar, 20 March 1969. Yoko wears a miniskirt twinset, Linda Farrow sunglasses and floppy white felt hat, tennis shoes and knee-high socks. John wears a white corduroy Pierre Cardin suit with turtleneck sweater. John drew a wedding ring on Yoko's finger with a pen as her ring was being resized.

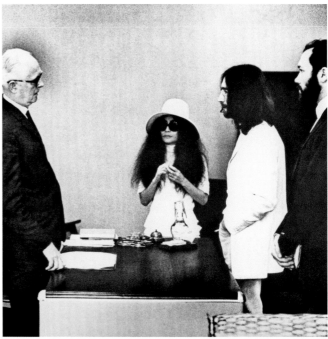

John & Yoko holding up their wedding certificate in front
of the Rock of Gibraltar on their wedding day, Gibraltar,
20 March 1969.

The me that you see now was in there, but it only came out at a very intimate party, or with somebody who knew me very well. I could never relax in these kinds of situations, very seldom anyway. I was always in a state of uptightness and the cynical Lennon image came out and the remarks and all that 'bit'.

I'm not uptight so much these days. I still get uptight but less so, because I'm not hiding anything. I'm trying to break away from that 'what have you got to hide' thing because when you get down to it, I've got nothing to hide. I have fear and paranoia and happiness and joy. I'm just like everyone else and I know everybody has the same problems that I have and they're not something I carry alone.

Yoko and I have clashed artistically. Our egos have smashed once or twice. But if I know what I'm doing as an artist, then I can see if I'm being hypocritical in my reactions. I sometimes am overawed by her talent. I think, fuck, I better watch out, she is taking over, I better get myself in here. And I say, 'Are you taking over?' And then say 'all right, all right', and I relax again. I mean, she's going to haul 365 legs and make a bloody film about a fly crawling over some woman's body? What is it? But it's all right, I know her.

Yoko: An artist couple is the most difficult thing. On the David Frost programme, some guy was saying, 'I like to write music and my fiancée likes to write poetry.' The fact is that we both paint, compose and write poetry, and on that basis I think we're doing pretty well. I think it's a miracle that we're doing all right. But we are doing all right, don't you think, John?

John: It's just handy to fuck your best friend. That's what it is. And once I resolved the fact that it was a woman as well, it's all right. We go through the trauma of life and death every day, so it's not so much of a worry about what sex we are any more. I'm living with an artist who's inspiring me to work. And, you know, Yoko is the most famous unknown artist. Everybody knows her name, but nobody knows what she does. No matter what artistic gains I get, or how many gold records, if I can't make a success out of my relationship with the people I supposedly love, then everything else is bullshit.

I had the early relationship with Sean and it was fantastic. With Julian, I'd come back from Australia and he'd be a different size; there'd be a twelve-year-old boy there, who I had no relationship with. I'm getting a relationship now. I can talk about music and whatever he's into and girlfriends and that kind of stuff. There's an open line still going. Julian and I will have a relationship in the future.

Yoko: I have love for all things that are beautiful to me. Every day, every moment their beauty excites me and makes me feel thankful and alive. If you have a good feeling about something, that's love. From the time I am up in the morning to late at night when I go to sleep, I feel love for almost everything I see. Artists are all like that. But still I'm a lucky girl!

All of us are wanting the same thing, and expressing ourselves in our own way. Some with words and some with some action. Listen to your heart. Let it lead you to where you want to go. You don't have to listen to anybody else. All of us being ourselves is the best way to world peace.

Try to learn to love your life more and more. Concentrate your mind on giving, loving and thanking. Each time you give, you are in less pain. Give as much as you can. Find something you can love. Love as much as you can. Thank as much as you can. Give your children love and understanding so they can and will take care of themselves whatever the future may bring.

You should know that life is lonely. You come out alone and you go out alone. If you know that, it will get better. Some people will love you and some won't. That's life. If you know that, it's a pretty good life. Every day when I wake up in the morning or when I go to sleep at night, I say, 'I love you', 'I forgive you' and 'I accept you as you are'. It's a good affirmation. I am learning to forgive and love myself. Everything I did in the past is making me what I am today. So that wasn't so bad. When I can totally love myself, I know that I will be in total peace. I'm getting there.

So carry your love and live well. Love what you love and that will give you the wisdom you need. Don't be side-tracked by your fear of what is happening outside of you. If you keep your life in love, things will change. We have to love ourselves as we are, as we are what we have created. To love the result of your creation – that is not vanity. That is called joy. Each time you give what you created with love to the world, it comes back to you tenfold. So don't be afraid – give!

When you send love to your loved one, you are not just sending love to the special person in your life, you are sending your love to yourself, our planet and the universe automatically. All you can do is to do what you can do. So relax a little. Send healthy thoughts, love and give people your warm smile, whenever you bump into them. See what something little like that can do. Start from there.

I want never get
all I got was well

I took my love one out to dinner
I helped her walk across 16 Street
Her tits were growing so much bigger
She looked so beautiful I could weep
well well well

So she could
       get a bite
              to eat.

WELL WELL WELL

Well well well, oh well
Well well well, oh well

I took my loved one out to dinner
So we could get a bite to eat
And though we both had been much thinner
She looked so beautiful I could eat her

Well well well, oh well
Well well well, oh well

I took my loved one to the big field
So we could watch the English sky
We both were nervous feeling dizzy
And neither one of us knew just why

Well well well, oh well
Well well well, oh well
Well well well, oh well
Well well well, oh well
Well well well, oh well
Well well well, oh well
Well well well, oh well
Well well well, oh well
Well well well
Well
Well
Well
Well
Well
Well
Well
Well
Well
Well

Well well well, oh well
Well well well, oh well

We sat and talked of revolution
Just like two liberals in the sun
We talked of woman's revolution
And how the hell we could get things done

Well well well, oh well
Well well well, oh well

I took my loved one to a big field
So we could catch the English sky
We both were nervous feeling guilty
And neither one of us knew just why

Well well well, oh well
Well well well, oh well
Well well well, oh well
Well well well, oh well
Well well well, oh well
Well well well, well
Well well well, well
Well

WELL WELL WELL

John: I've always been politically minded, you know, and against the status quo. It's pretty basic when you're brought up, like I was, to hate and fear the police as a natural enemy and to despise the army as something that takes everybody away and leaves them dead somewhere. I mean, it's just a basic working-class thing, though it begins to wear off when you get older, get a family and get swallowed up in the system. In my case I've never not been political, though religion tended to overshadow it in my acid days, around '65 or '66. And that religion was directly the result of all that superstar shit – religion was an outlet for my repression. I thought, 'Well, there's something else to life, isn't there? This isn't it, surely?'

But I was always political in a way. In the two books I wrote [*In His Own Write* and *A Spaniard in the Works*], even though they were written in a sort of Joycean gobbledegook, there's many knocks at religion and there is a play about a worker and a capitalist. I've been satirizing the system since my childhood. I used to write magazines [*The Daily Howl*] in school and hand them around. I was very conscious of class, they would say with a chip on my shoulder, because I knew what happened to me and I knew about the class repression coming down on us – it was a fact but in the hurricane Beatles world it got left out, I got further away from reality for a time.

Radicalism and everything is in that thing. I want to see the plan. Count me out if it's for violence. Don't expect me to be on the barricades unless it's with flowers. And waving Chairman Mao badges and being a Marxist, or a this-ist or a that-ist, is going to get you shot or locked up. And if that's what you subconsciously really want – to martyr yourselves – I don't buy the martyr bit. I want to know what you're going to do after you've knocked it all down. Can't we use some of it? What's the point of bombing Wall Street? If you want to change the system, change the system. It's no good shooting people.

It seems that all revolutions end up with a personality cult – even the Chinese seem to need a father figure. I expect this happens in Cuba too, with Che and Fidel. In Western-style communism we would have to create an almost imaginary image of themselves as the workers' father figures. All the revolutions have happened when a Fidel or Marx or Lenin or whatever, who were intellectuals, were able to get through to the workers. They got a good pocket of people together and the workers seemed to understand that they were in a repressed state. They haven't woken up here, yet.

They think they are in a wonderful, free-speaking country. They've got cars and tellies and they don't want to think there's anything more to life. They are prepared to let the bosses run them, to see their children fucked up in school. They're dreaming someone else's dream; it's not even their own.

Yoko: No power outside can destroy you. You can destroy yourself by agreeing with them. Nobody can touch you but you. Nobody can deter you, nobody can intimidate you, nobody can stop you, nobody can destroy yourself but you.

John: You can't take power without a struggle. Because when it comes to the nitty gritty, they won't let the people have any power; they'll give all the rights to perform and to dance for them, but no real power.

Yoko: The thing is, even after the revolution, if people don't have any trust in themselves, they'll get new problems.

John: After the revolution you have the problem of keeping things going, of sorting out all the different views. It's quite natural that revolutionaries should have different solutions, that they should split into different groups and then reform, that's the dialectic, isn't it? But at the same time they need to be united against the enemy, to solidify a new order.

Yoko: That's why it will be different when the younger generation takes over.

John: I think it wouldn't take much to get the youth here really going. You'd have to give them free rein to attack the local councils or to destroy the school authorities, like the students who break up the repression in the universities. It's already happening, though people have got to get together more.

And the women are very important too; we can't have a revolution that doesn't involve and liberate women. It's so subtle the way you're taught male superiority. It took me quite a long time to realize that my maleness was cutting off certain areas for Yoko. She's a red-hot liberationist and was quick to show me where I was going wrong, even though it seemed to me that I was just acting naturally. That's why I'm always interested to know how people who claim to be radical treat women. How can you talk about 'Power To The People' unless you realize 'The People' is both sexes.

Yoko: You can't love someone unless you are in an equal position with them. A lot of women have to cling to men

John & Yoko having fun at home; Kenwood, St George's Hill, Weybridge, Surrey, November 1968.
Overleaf: John & Yoko relaxing in the Sun Room, Kenwood, St George's Hill, Weybridge, Surrey, November 1968.

John & Yoko in love at home; Kenwood, St George's Hill,
Weybridge, Surrey, December 1968.

out of fear or insecurity, and that's not love. Basically, that's why women hate men.

John: And vice versa.

Yoko: So if you have a slave around the house how can you expect to make a revolution outside it? The problem for women is that if we try to be free, then we naturally become lonely, because so many women are willing to become slaves, and men usually prefer that. So you always have to take the chance: 'Am I going to lose my man?' It's very sad.

John: Of course, Yoko was well into liberation before I met her. She'd had to fight her way through a man's world – the art world is completely dominated by men – so she was full of revolutionary zeal when we met. There was never any question about it: we had to have a 50/50 relationship or there was no relationship, I was quick to learn.

Yoko inspired me and created all this creation in me. It wasn't her that inspired the songs. She inspired me. I was a working-class macho guy that didn't know any better. Yoko taught me about women. I was used to being served, like Elvis and a lot of the stars were. And Yoko didn't buy that. She didn't give a shit about Beatles – 'What the fuck are the Beatles? I'm Yoko Ono! Treat me as me.' That was the battle. She came out with 'Woman Is the N****r of the World' in 1968 as the title of an article she wrote for *Nova* magazine. Because things were like they were, I took the title and wrote the song.

I had never considered it before. From the day I met her, she demanded equal time, equal space, equal rights. I didn't know what she was talking about. I said, 'What do you want, a contract? You can have whatever you want, but don't expect anything from me or for me to change in any way. Don't impinge in my space.' 'Well,' she said, 'the answer to that is I can't be here. Because there is no space where you are. Everything revolves around you. And I can't breathe in that atmosphere. I'm an artist, I'm not some female you picked up backstage.'

Well, I found out. And I'm thankful to her for the education. I was used to a situation where the newspaper was there for me to read, and after I'd read it, somebody else could have it. It didn't occur to me that somebody else might want to look at it first. I think that's what kills people like Presley and others of that ilk. So-called stars who die in public and lots of people who die privately. The king is always killed by his courtiers, not by his enemies. The king is overfed, over-drugged, over-indulged, anything to keep the king tied to his throne. Most people in that position never wake up. They either die mentally or physically or both. And what Yoko did for me, apart from liberating me to be a feminist, was to liberate me from that situation. And that's how the Beatles ended. Not because Yoko split the Beatles, but because she showed me what it was to be Elvis Beatle and to be surrounded by sycophants and slaves who were only interested in keeping the situation as it was. And that's a kind of death.

She said to me, 'You've got no clothes on.' Nobody had dared tell me that before. Nobody dared tell Elvis Presley that, and I doubt if anybody ever dared to tell Mick Jagger, Paul McCartney or Bob Dylan that they had no clothes on. I didn't accept it at first. 'But I am clothed! Everything is perfect! You're crazy! Nobody tells me – I'm God! I'm King John of England! Nobody tells me nothing!' Because nobody had. She told me, 'You absolutely have no clothes on, and that man whispering in your ear is Machiavelli.' 'But he's been with me for twenty years!' 'Then he's been screwing you for twenty years.' 'Really?' I couldn't face any of that. She still tells me the truth. It's still painful.

Yoko: John was a brilliant writer, a brilliant artist and a brilliant man, who believed in being truthful. More people should get down to being truthful to themselves. That is the most adventurous thing anybody can do. You may not know it at the time, but truth is setting you free. In the end it is the power of the people that will change the world. And it will. So, let's not get discouraged. Keep communicating the truth to the world as much as we can. Peaceful and truthful protests are the only way, because nothing else works. Don't ask how. Just do it in the way you can.

The leaders of each country are being controlled by the military. They should come out and say that. If we know the truth, it doesn't necessarily mean we can end guns and wars right away, but knowing the truth will do something to our brains, and it will know what to do. That's a start. Without knowing the truth of what we are doing politically, we can never create a peaceful world.

Integrity, sincerity and true dedication to their vocation. These are the character traits needed in present politicians.

Be true to yourself. Always.

<u>look at me</u>. (pre jando!).

look at me
who am I supposed to bo?
who am I supposed tobe?
look at me
what am I supposed to be
what am I supposed tobe
look at me   oh my love - oh my love.

here I am
what am I supposed to do
what am I supposed to do
here I am
what can I do for you
what can I do for you
here I am -- oh my love - oh my lon

  look at me, oh please look at me mylove
~~littlethenkwhatever~~ here I am oh my love ~~oh my love~~

who am I
nobody knows but me
who am I   you
nobody else can see
just ~~and~~ you and me.
who are we. oh my love

LOOK AT ME

Look at me
Who am I supposed to be?
Who am I supposed to be?

Look at me
What am I supposed to be?
What am I supposed to be?
Look at me

Oh, my love
Oh, my love

Here I am
What am I supposed to do?
What am I supposed to do?

Here I am
What can I do for you?
What can I do for you?
Here I am

Oh, my love
Oh, my love

Look at me
Oh, please look at me, my love
Here I am
Oh, my love

Who am I?
Nobody knows but me
Nobody knows but me

Who am I?
Nobody else can see
Just you and me
Who are we?

Oh, my love
Oh, my love

LOOK AT ME

John: A couple of tracks, which one would suppose were written under therapy, like 'Look At Me', were written pre-Janov, about a year before therapy. But the theme was the same: 'Look at me', 'Who am I?', all that jazz. So that's why I stuck it on that album. But actually it had come from beforehand.

Yoko: That was probably something that came from the fact that he really wanted his mother to look at him, but the song itself was about 'look at me' to the world.

John: The two years before I met Yoko, I think the others were going through the same thing – of real big depression – after Maharishi, and Brian dying. It wasn't really to do with Maharishi, it was just that period. I was really going through a 'What's it all about? This songwriting is nothing. It's pointless and I'm no good, I'm not talented and I'm shit and I couldn't do anything but be a Beatle and what am I going to do about it?' And it lasted nearly two years and I was still in it during *Sgt. Pepper*.

When we first did the acid bit, the religion, and all of that, it was our ego that was interfering with our relationship together as the Beatles. We suddenly saw each other back to when we were fifteen. We saw each other at that age, what we were back then, and what we've developed into. And then it was all reading the different books, the Leary handouts talking about ego, and we all got into the bit where we thought ego was bad. I had a tremendous ego that got me where I was, but I spent two years killing it stone dead. And it took me two years to get it back again.

It was terrifying, because I'm a naturally nervous and paranoid person, and without an ego, I was nothing. It was terrifying. I just leaned on Paul or one of the other Beatles who hadn't destroyed themselves as much as me. I just thought, 'Get rid of the ego and I'll just be the B-side of the record and I'll let Paul run the other out. I won't be the guy back in school who was pushing and started the group. I'll be someone else.'

I was just coming out of it before I met Yoko. India helped a lot, three months out there. If I hadn't come back and met Yoko, I would have been swamped by this whole scene. I tend to lose it all again and think I can't do anything. But then she came along, and I thought, 'Oh, great, I like your drawings, I like everything.' So she built me up again.

Yoko: I don't know. I was unconscious of it. That's what I think was really great about us, because I'm an egoist, too. I'm a big ego!

John: I had to get an ego to counteract hers, or it would have been impossible. It's all right leaning on a group of guys, because they play it very subtle, but she had to have a sparring partner.

I dropped LSD for I don't know how long. It went on for years, I must have had a thousand trips. I used to just eat it all the time. I had many bad trips. I stopped taking it because of that; I just couldn't stand it. Then I started taking it again just before I met Yoko. I got a message on acid that you should destroy your ego, and I did. I was reading that stupid book of Leary's [*The Psychedelic Experience*]. Leary was the one going round saying, 'take it, take it, take it!' And we followed his instructions in his 'how to take a trip' book. I did it just like he said in the book, and then I wrote 'Tomorrow Never Knows', which was almost the first acid song: 'Lay down all thoughts, surrender to the void', and all that shit, which Leary had pinched from *The Tibetan Book of the Dead*. We were going through a whole game that everybody went through. And I destroyed myself.

I went to India with Maharishi and he was saying: 'Ego is good as long as you look after it.' And I had really destroyed it and I was so paranoid and weak, I didn't believe I could do anything. I let Paul do what he wanted and say, let them all just do what they wanted. And I just was nothing, I was shit.

I was trying to build it back up again and get confidence in myself and we met Derek Taylor again after a long time. Derek did a good job building my ego one weekend at his house, reminding me who I am and what I had done and what I could do, and he and a couple of friends [Pete Shotton and Neil Aspinall] did that for me. They sort of said: 'You're great! You are what you are!' and all that.

Pete Shotton: John, Neil Aspinall and I accepted Derek Taylor's invitation to stay overnight at his temporary home in the countryside, a fabulous Japanese-style retreat owned by Peter Asher, which was situated by a magnificent lake, miles away from the nearest village. The original pretext for this journey was that Derek very much wished to play us the debut album by the heretofore unknown Harry Nilsson.

Richard DiLello: In England, the press were much squarer than in America. Yoko hit them hard because she was uncompromising and clearly not interested in representational art in any way, shape or form. Hers were all new, flexible, intellectual concepts which Fleet Street was utterly incapable of understanding.

Yoko photographed by John Reader for *Time-Life* with still images from her film, *Film No. 5 ('Smile')*, 1968, starring John, 26 July 1968.

Below: John's drawings based on the film, 1968.
Opposite: stills from Yoko's film, *Film No. 5* (*'Smile'*),
filmed with a high-speed camera at home; Kenwood,
St George's Hill, Weybridge, Surrey, November 1968.

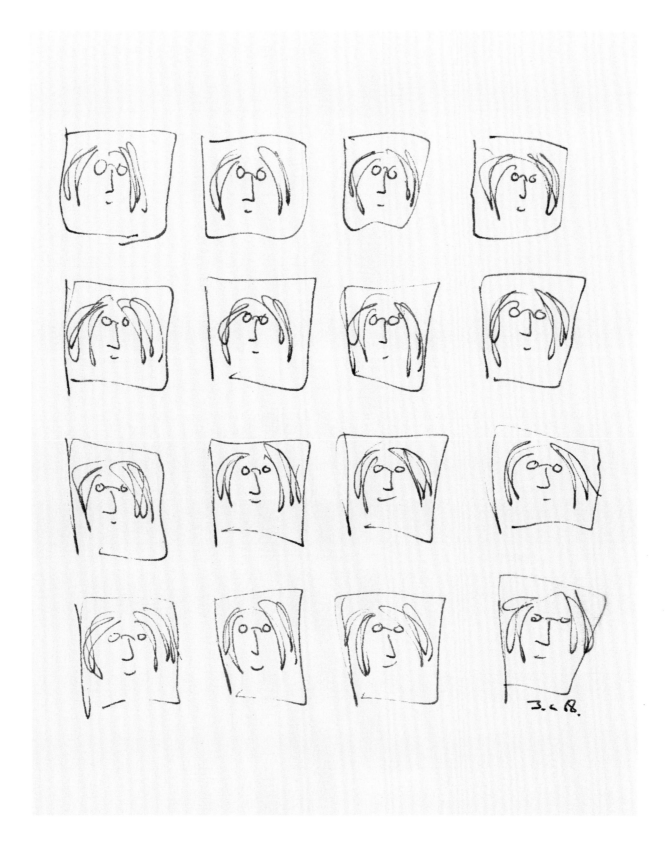

Above: Sgt. Derek W. Taylor RAEC (Royal Army
Education Corps) in his white wicker peacock chair
in the press office; Apple Corps, 3 Savile Row, London,
January 1969.

Below: Dennis O' Dell (Apple Films), Paul McCartney,
Alex Mardas (Apple Electronics), Brian Lewis (Apple Films),
Ron Kass (Apple Music), Neil Aspinall, John, Derek Taylor
(Press); Apple Corps, 3 Savile Row, London 1968.

After Derek's kids had been packed away to bed, we all dropped some acid and smoked a few joints, listening over and over to Harry's wonderful record. At one point, John and I went rowing on the lake, which was beautifully illuminated with spotlights; all the while, the Nilsson LP continued to blare from extension speakers placed outside on the lawn.

When it started to rain, we returned to the house where Derek promptly handed John yet another piece of LSD. 'This one's really special,' he said. 'Split it with Pete.' Not hearing those last four words, John proceeded to swallow the whole thing – much to the horror of Derek, who subsequently beckoned me into another room. 'Listen, Pete,' he whispered, 'that's fantastically strong stuff. John is going to go off on one hell of a trip. We'd better stick close by him.'

The following morning, John admitted to having seen Derek and me slip out of the room after he'd swallowed the LSD. 'I really shit myself when I saw that,' he told me, 'and I began to get very paranoid about what I'd just eaten.'

He grew even more paranoid as the acid took effect, and Derek Taylor ended up sitting by him till well after daybreak. In an attempt to rebuild John's shattered ego, he persuaded him to recount his entire life story, from early childhood onwards. Derek even went through every Lennon/ McCartney song, line by line, to demonstrate to John the extraordinary scope of his contribution to the Beatles' music. By the time John and I finally left, John's spirits had been lifted considerably.

John: Derek tripped me out at his house after he'd got back from LA. He said, 'You're all right.' And he pointed out which songs I'd written, and said, 'You wrote this, and you said this, and you are intelligent, don't be frightened.'

Derek Taylor: We played a great many Beatles records that night and John found his ego again, he wrote and said later. The children woke early next morning and saw him slowly unfolding from a crucifixion stance on the floor, cross-legged and cross-armed and crying like a man, thin as a twig, straggly long hair all over the place.

John: The next week Yoko came down to Derek's. That was it then, I just blew out and it all came back to me like I was back to age sixteen and all the rest of it had been wiped out. It was like going to a psychiatrist. I remember everything. I've got to believe I'm a genius. I've got to believe that I'm great to do anything. It's my mantra. She filled me completely to realize that I was me and it's all right. And that was it. I started fighting again and being a loud-mouth again and saying, 'Well, I can do this', and 'Fuck you', and 'This is what I want', and 'Don't put me down. I did this.'

She came and opened the door a little bit: 'I love you for what you are'. And I respected her genius. For her to love me was the answer then. She wouldn't have loved a dummy which I'd begun to think I was. That helped – the accumulation. I was just out of it then. Of course, she goes through the same thing where I can help her the same, once I'd got over my intellectual reverse snobbery about avant-garde.

So when she's in trouble I can do the same for her, so it's a good combination. Why shouldn't I be a poet, a film-maker, a dancer, an actor? Let's do it all while the going's good.

That's it, really. It's a freedom, it's a relief because you can never escape from the hell on earth, there's no escape from that. Even two people who are as lucky as us two, that have somebody that can be so close on all levels.

Having been through a lot of trips, like macrobiotics, Maharishi, the Bible, I Ching, Yoko brought me out of all of them. The first thing I did was a You Are Here show at the Robert Fraser Gallery. It consisted of a bare gallery and a big white canvas that was round and it just had my writing on it: 'you are here'. You had to go down the stairs and you had to get through all these different charity cans to put money in, like RSPCA, animal and cancer funds, and dogs and people – the room was full of them – and on the left side of the wall was this big, big canvas with 'you are here', a hat to put money in for the artist and a jar of teeny white badges to take that said 'you are here'. We filmed them from behind a dark window with the English Candid Camera team, and let balloons off with 'send your message back when you get it', and they'd write to tell me where it came from. I cut the canvas down and it's about three foot now.

A lot of people went to India to find out they were here. Like Leary's friend Richard Alpert (Ram Dass) went to India and saw all the gurus, chasing all over the place, and all the gurus said to him was 'remember, be here now'. That's all them gurus will ever tell you. Remember this moment now. I was talking to George the other day and I forgot to say to him, 'What are you searching for? You are here!'

John: After I first met Yoko, I sort of blasted open in my head. I had a gallery show out of the blue. I had never done anything like that before. I had a show called *You Are Here* and I dedicated it to Yoko.

Yoko: *You Are Here* was John's answer to my 'This Is Not Here' signs (from *Blue Room Event*, 1966).

Below: John Lennon: *You Are Here* (1968), pen on white circular canvas. Opposite and overleaf: the exhibition also included sixty charity collection boxes, a white busker's fedora hat labelled 'FOR THE ARTIST' and a jar full of 'you are here' badges to take away. Exhibition view, Robert Fraser Gallery, 69 Duke Street, London, 1 July 1968.

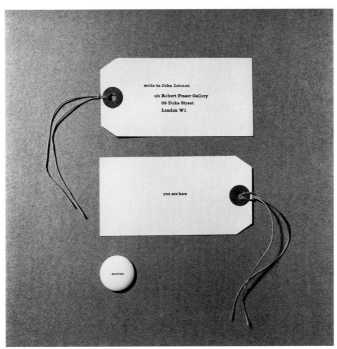

Previous pages: Added at the last minute was a black bicycle from students at Hornsey Art College with a note, 'this exhibit was inadvertently left out' – so John included it. John also added his shoes with a note, 'I take my shoes off to you.' Also at the exhibition, a hidden camera filmed people's reactions to the artworks (overleaf).

Below and opposite: John & Yoko (with Robert Fraser to the left of John) releasing 365 white balloons at the opening of his exhibition. To each balloon was attached a tag encouraging people who found them to 'Write to John Lennon, c/o Robert Fraser Gallery, 69 Duke Street, London.' 1 July 1968.

Overleaf: Stills from the movie of the set-up and opening of John's exhibition, *You Are Here*, 1968. Among those attending are: Richard DiLello inflating balloons, Kevin Harrington, Steve Brendell, Alex Mardas, Robert Fraser, Derek Taylor, Jill Johnston, Jonathan Cott, Victor Spinetti, Paul Nicholas, Peter Blake, Richard Hamilton and many members of the British and International Press. Robert Fraser Gallery, 69 Duke Street, London, 1 July 1968.

GOD.

God is a concept by which we measure our pain
i'll say it again
God is a concept by which we measure our pain

    i don't believe in magic
    " "   " " iching
                        bible
                        tarot
                        hitler
                        jesus
                        kennedy
                        budda
                        mantra
                        gita
                        yoga
                        kings
                        Elvis
                        Dylan
                        Beatles

i just believe in me
and thats reality.
(Yoko and me).

GOD

God is a concept by which we measure our pain
I'll say it again

God is a concept by which we measure our pain

I don't believe in Magic
I don't believe in I-Ching
I don't believe in Bible
I don't believe in Tarot
I don't believe in Hitler
I don't believe in Jesus
I don't believe in Kennedy
I don't believe in Buddha
I don't believe in Mantra
I don't believe in Gita
I don't believe in Yoga
I don't believe in Kings
I don't believe in Elvis
I don't believe in Zimmerman
I don't believe in Beatles

I just believe in me
Yoko and me
And that's reality

The dream is over
What can I say?
The dream is over
Yesterday

I was the dreamweaver
But now I'm reborn
I was the walrus
But now I'm John

And so dear friends
You just have to carry on

The dream is over

GOD

John: You're born in pain. Pain is what we are in most of the time, and the bigger the pain, the more gods we need.

When I felt it, it was like I was crucified, so I know what they're talking about now. At one time I was so much involved in the religious bullshit that I used to go around calling myself a Christian communist, but as Janov says, religion is legalized madness.

'God' was stuck together from three songs. I had the idea: 'God is a concept by which we measure our pain.' When you have a phrase like that, you just sit down and sing the first tune that comes into your head and the tune is simple, because I like that kind of music. And then I just rolled into it – I Ching and Bible and the first three or four just came out, all these things I didn't believe in. It was like a Christmas card list. I thought, 'Well where do I end? Churchill? Who have I missed out?' It just got out of hand. And Beatles was the final thing because I no longer believe in myth, and Beatles is another myth – I don't believe in it. The dream is over. I'm not just talking about the Beatles, I'm talking about the generation thing. The dream is over. It's over, and we, well I have, anyway, personally, got to get down to so-called reality.

The concept from the Bible, and all of that Judeo-Christian story that we've been living by for 2,000 years, is that God and everything is some other thing outside of ourselves – that continual 'us and them' relationship with God, with children, with animals, with nature, the environment, where we've conquered nature, worshipped God, we deal with children. It's this separation business that I don't believe exists. I don't deal with my left leg any different from my right ear. I deal with the reality of the shape, and where it's placed, and how I look after, or wash different parts of the body, but I don't consider them separate.

Yoko: 'God' is pure energy we draw from when we want to. So much human and animal suffering is caused by religion. Religion is made by men. I believe in a godliness which is inside and also outside us, but which is not being controlled by one particular religion. I believe in the great power above, within and around me. But I do not believe in one god or one religion. I don't believe in a white male God with a beard. Santa Claus is more believable, actually. Your soul is eternal now and after, as your love is. Let's not let a concept of God oppress us. Organized religion is not necessarily a representative of God. They never have been. You are the true representative of peace and love.

John: I believe that thing which joins us together is the thing they call 'God'. Like electricity is the power. I believe there's people nearer and further away to the power source, but I believe God is the omnipresent thing that does join everything together. It's just a powerhouse like electricity and we're all a set of light bulbs. I believe in electricity – even though I can't see it, I can see the light bulbs. I've seen a few people that you feel are a bit nearer to whatever's going on.

I don't need to go to church. I respect churches because of the sacredness that's been put on them over the years by people who do believe. As Donovan once said, 'I go to my own church in my own temple, once a day.' That's where the source is. Christ said, 'The kingdom of heaven is within you.' And the Indians say that and the Zen people say that. We're all God and we're all potentially divine – and potentially evil. We're all Jesus and we're all God and he's inside all of us. As soon you start realizing that potential in everyone, then you can change it. I believe what Jesus actually said – the basic things he laid down about love and goodness, not what people say he said.

I believe in reincarnation, and I believe that each time it's better. It's like one bloody big exam, it goes on and on and on. There's no quick way out, like suicide or anything. You've got to go through it. You can't forget it. I've tried that one. And you can't just do it all in a sort of holy buzz. I've tried that one. And I tried the other one when I was younger – let's smash it, let's just kick it down and then see what happens.

I get millions of different, quite interesting books on religion, philosophy and everything, but most of them have just not quite got to the point. Wilhelm Reich seems to be right on the point to me. He really knows what's happening. My friend Ivan Vaughan sent me *The Murder of Christ* and *Listen, Little Man!* He sent the book about not being a leader just at the time when we were going out on the bed again. So I had to keep not being a leader – refusing to – because many people wanted to crown me. Different movements: 'You will be it, John, and you will lead us to...' like they did with Jesus. So Reich's a good right-hand man to keep reading for doing the game, you know, of not getting tricked into being the king. I don't believe in kings.

Instamatic camera snaps by John & Yoko, including John's
new curly maple Dobro D-50SE 'The Uncle Josh Electric'
guitar, upon which he would write many of the songs
for his *Plastic Ono Band* album; California, May 1970.

Overleaf: John relaxing by and in the pool after
Primal therapy at their rented home adjacent to
the Chartwell Mansion; 841 Nimes Road, Bel Air,
California, summer 1970.

John: I'm very suspicious of psychiatrists. I always thought most psychiatrists need a psychiatrist. They never told you how you were. You lie there, telling them how you are. What's the point of that? It's all symptomatic. It's all right to talk if you're lonely, but you pay a lot of money to talk to a psychiatrist over twenty years. I think Janov used to be one of those psychiatrists at one time, so he knew about it. People would come in and talk and talk and talk for twenty years and never make any impression on the inside of them.

There's a point in yourself beyond talking, and that's where Janov's thing was more advanced than the others. I saw him on TV saying that if people had understood Freud, his Primal therapy would have been developed a long time ago. And there's a lot of truth in that. Some of the claims they were making I just can't agree with, because I was in there and it didn't happen to me. It was worth it because it did help me to go through my childhood and delve into it and find out what made me tick.

Nobody should be in Primal therapy more than two months maximum. You don't have to be in it more than three weeks. You get the message the first week. The only reason you keep going back is because you want another fix. It's easier if you have somebody else help you get there than do it yourself. There is no taking away from the initial scream. That's the one. The rest of it is just like 'all right, hmm, uh huh', you know. But them getting you to the scream is the point. That first scream. That's what you go for.

Yoko: Men never have a chance to cry, because they're always told not to cry or scream. And we women can cry at the drop of a hat. So I wasn't very impressed with it.

John: She came along for the ride. Yeah, I just identified more. And I was the male that had never cried. She could cry. I didn't know how to cry. My defences were so great, the cocky chip-on-the-shoulder, macho, aggressive, rock 'n' roll hero who knows all the answers; the smart quip, sharp talking, king-of-the-world business was actually a terrified guy who didn't know how to cry. Simple.

Now I can cry. That's what I learned from Primal therapy. We were there six months because we had a nice house in LA. We'd go down to the session, have a good cry, come back and swim in the pool. And you'd always feel like after acid or a good joint. You'd be in the pool tingling and everything was fine, and then your defences would all come up again, like the acid would wear off, the joint

wears off. You go back for another fix because it's easier to go down there and do it, rather than to use the method that you're shown, yourself.

Yoko: The urge of crying exists in men too, and that's transformed into anger, which is more acceptable. It's considered a macho image – angry young man, or whatever. I think we have anger, too, but we transform that into a more acceptable form of silence, or crying, or whatever. We're going through some sort of painful experience every day. Instead of feeling the pain, you light a cigarette or something like that and try not to feel the pain because it's too painful. But instead of doing that, we just feel the pain and cry, which is the natural thing to do, instead of repressing it.

John: Somewhere along the line we were switched off, not to feel things like, for instance, crying – men crying and women being very girlish, or whatever it is. Somewhere you have to switch into a role and this therapy gives you back the switch. You locate it and switch back into feeling just as a human being, not as a male or a female, or as a famous person or not famous person. They switch you back to being a baby and therefore you feel as a child does, but it's something we forget because there's so much pressure and pain and whatever it is that is life, everyday life, that we gradually switch off over the years. All the generation gap crap is that the older people are more dead. As the years go by, the pain of living doesn't go away. You have to kill yourself to survive. This allows you to live and survive without killing yourself.

We still have a lot of symptoms of neurosis. It's like the acid. The initial excitement about it was it was a cure for everything because we all saw the light on acid. I met a lot of people that had heavy experiences but acid was not the answer to life. It was an experience or a window to things that would never have been presented to us had we not gone through that period and it's the same with the therapy. It was to me. It was six months of natural acid trip and you can't get away from that experience, no matter who or what put you through it, or how you feel about it. I really still would defend his therapy against the usual therapy. He's a pleasant guy and he was a good Daddy while we were at it.

'God' was all part of dissolving the God trip or father-figure trip. Facing up to reality instead of always looking for some kind of heaven. I've grown up. I don't believe in father figures any more, like God, Kennedy or Hitler.

I'm no longer searching for a guru. I'm no longer searching for anything. There is no search. There's no way to go. There's nothing. This is it.

Yoko: He has this father complex and he's always searching for the father. I didn't have the need for it because I had a father who was like Billy Graham – big and strong and supposed to be great. I saw his hypocrisy and I saw his weak side, so whenever I see something that is supposed to be big, such as gurus, or somebody discovered Primal Scream – supposedly big male figures – I'm very cynical about that. I don't go for them.

John: She fought with Janov all the time. He couldn't deal with her at all.

Yoko: I'm not searching for that father in men. I look for something that is tender and weak, that I feel like I want to help. So I'm not searching for that Big Daddy.

John: A lot of us are looking for father figures. Mine was physically not there. Most people's fathers are mentally not there, or physically and mentally always at the office or busy doing their own thing.

Yoko: People are so frantic about Daddies because Daddies are the ones that are never home and they never got enough of Daddy and somehow there's a distance, so there's a mystery about them and mystique. It was that adoration and yearning for Daddy. Whereas Mummy was always there.

John: Maharishi, Elvis Presley, Robert Mitchum – any male image is a father figure. It's not always derogatory, but when you give them the right to give you the recipe for your life, then you're really under the Freud's 'another Daddy' – that was a biggie.

All the leaders are substitute fathers – the Daddy that looks like the Daddies in the commercials. He's got the nice grey hair and right teeth and the parting's on the right side. We choose the Daddy, we take him out of the dog pound of Daddies, which is the political arena, put him on a platform, and start punishing and screaming at the Daddy because Daddy can't do miracles. Daddy doesn't heal us. We don't feel better, so then we'd move the Daddy in four years and we get a new Daddy with a different colour hair, or a variation on a theme. And they keep talking about all these Daddies, 'Well that Daddy was a good Daddy.' All the dead Daddies are the good Daddies.

Everybody's got their -isms and -asms, bagisms, 'Give Peace A Chance' this-ism, that-ism, -ism, -ism, -ism. It's always some big guy in the sky. And if they're dead, they're really good. Then they're perfect when they're dead.

I got over that through living with Yoko. She'd say, 'Do you want another Daddy? OK, we'll go and visit this one,' until I turned around and said, 'OK, enough with the Daddies.'

Yoko: Because I know he dreams about that.

John: You see? She'll come along for the trip. Janov was one. Not to take away from the fact that I enjoyed my scream.

The very fact that he came to us because we were famous took away from his therapy right away. He treated us differently from his other patients, although he spent the six months telling all the other patients that he doesn't treat us any different, until one day I got the courage to say to Daddy, 'Well you fucking well came all the way to England because that would have been a big scoop' – the same as Maharishi blew his cool, too.

What happens to the Daddies that get famous people is the famous people either succumb completely to the Daddy and then they promote the Daddy, or the Daddy blows their cool because they can't contain that eagerness for power and glory. It always shows itself. It showed itself in Maharishi; it showed itself in Janov. At first I was bitter about Maharishi being human and a little bitter about Janov being human. Well I'm not bitter about them being human. They're human, and I'm only thinking what a dummy I am. Although I meditate and I cry. So I cannot deny it.

I still think that Janov's therapy is great but I don't want to make it into a big Maharishi thing. I would never have gone to a psychotherapist if there hadn't been this promise of this scream. The scream was what got to me – this liberated scream – and it was fantastic. Yoko used to do her own Primal on stage, and Janov hated that. The fact that she said, 'I was screaming on stage.'

It did help me, although Janov himself is nothing special. You could go to any of the groups that are doing it now. They all know how to do it. It's just a method. You don't have to worship Newton because an apple fell on his head. We've got gravity. We know about it.

Instamatic camera prints of Yoko with a Gibson J-45 acoustic guitar; 841 Nimes Road, Bel Air, California, May 1970.

The Complete Yoko Ono Word Poem Game (1970), made by John for Yoko by cutting the portrait photo of himself (that was included with the album *The Beatles*) into 134 pieces and writing a single word on the back of each piece, for Yoko to randomly pick and read, reminiscent of the cut-up technique popularized by William Burroughs. John gave it to Yoko in an envelope reading, 'the complete yoko ono word poem game. (for yoko's with heads full of problems). to yoko with love from john, tuesday july 28, 1970. L.A.'

choose count cloud sun you closet seaweed sing
whistle feet perfume find day mummy smell hot
play night spring mirror carry afternoon wall
wish imagine daydream julian hand sad
happy tube feel dance dawn weight them pass
swim two stars kiss stone tell water breathe
bottom wind elevator laugh morning sea
autumn grass moon flower forget hold mist
ma float jump one grapefruit paper escalater
toilet draw sound cut me eat disapear air
fuck shake warm house rain shoes paint
daddy smoke listen mrs tree yoko sweep
fold kyoko write shout head cry cold half
light neace hope promise clock rowboat piss sky
remember hair winter street half fly watch hide
rabbit love think wash stream evening whisper
send mountain we boil snow summer bird understand
see ask shit lift color dream touch us ono

Chocolate Ice Cream Plate Piece (1970). Artwork by John dedicated to Yoko, created using a ceramic plate and chocolate ice cream. Written in the ice cream is 'John to Yoko 1970', and in black ink on the rim of the plate 'the chocolate ice cream plate piece to Yoko from John July 1970 J.L. USA and I love you'.

John: There have only been two great albums that I listened to all the way through when I was about sixteen. One was Carl Perkins's first or second, I can't remember which. And one was Elvis's first. Those are the only ones on which I really enjoyed every track. This fella I knew called Don Beatty showed me the name Elvis Presley in the *New Musical Express* and said he was great. It was 'Heartbreak Hotel'. I thought it sounded a bit phoney: 'Heart-break Hotel'. The music papers were saying that Presley was fantastic, and at first I expected someone like Perry Como or Sinatra. 'Heartbreak Hotel' seemed a corny title and his name seemed strange in those days.

I first heard it on Radio Luxembourg. He turned out to be fantastic. I could hardly make out what was being said. It was just the experience of hearing it and having my hair stand on end. We'd never heard American voices singing like that. They'd always sung like Sinatra or enunciated very well. Suddenly there's this hillbilly hiccoughing on tape echo and all this bluesy background going on. And we didn't know what the hell Presley was singing about, or Little Richard or Chuck Berry. It took a long time to work out what was going on. To us, it just sounded like a noise that was great. I remember rushing home with the record and saying, 'He sounds like Frankie Laine and Johnnie Ray and Tennessee Ernie Ford!'

I'm an Elvis fan because it was Elvis who really got me out of Liverpool. Once I heard it and got into it, that was life. There was no other thing. I thought of nothing else but rock 'n' roll, apart from sex and food and money, but that's all the same thing, really. One of the main reasons to get on stage is it's the quickest way of making contact. We went to see those movies with Elvis or somebody in, when we were still in Liverpool, and everybody'd be waiting to see them, and I'd be waiting there, too, and they'd all scream when he came on the screen. We thought, 'That's a good job.'

Up until Elvis joined the army in 1958, I thought it was beautiful music, and Elvis was for me and my generation what the Beatles were to the Sixties. Elvis really died the day he joined the army. Something happened to him psychologically. That's when they killed him, and the rest was a living death.

When I started, rock 'n' roll itself was the basic revolution to people of my age and situation. We needed something loud and clear to break through all the unfeeling and repression that had been coming down on us kids. We were a bit conscious, to begin with, of being imitation Americans.

But we delved into music and found that it was half white country and western and half black rhythm and blues. Most of the songs came from Europe and Africa, and now they were coming back to us. Many of Dylan's best songs came from Scotland, Ireland and England. It was a sort of cultural exchange. Though I must say the more interesting songs to me were the black ones because they were simpler. They sort of said shake your arse or your prick, which was an innovation, really.

And then there were the field songs, mainly expressing the pain they were in. They couldn't express themselves intellectually, so they had to say in a very few words what was happening to them. And then there was the city blues and a lot of that was about sex and fighting. A lot of this was self-expression but only in the last few years have they expressed themselves completely with Black Power, like Edwin Starr making 'War' records. Before that, many black singers were still labouring under that problem of God. It was often, 'God will save us'. But right through, the blacks were singing about their pain and also about sex, which is why I like it.

We used to stand backstage at Hamburg's Star-Club and watch Little Richard play. He used to read from the Bible backstage and just to hear him talk, we'd sit round and listen. It was Brian Epstein that brought him to Hamburg. I still love him and he's one of the greatest.

I don't believe in Dylan and I don't believe in Tom Jones either in that way. Zimmerman is his name. My name isn't John Beatle. It's John Lennon. I remember in the early meetings with Dylan, he was always saying to me, 'Listen to the words, man', and I said, 'I can't be bothered, I just like listening to the sound of the overall thing'. And then I reversed that and started being a words man. I naturally play with words anyway. I made a conscious effort to be wordy, *à la* Dylan. But now I've relieved myself of that burden and I'm only interested in pure sound. I loved him because he wrote some beautiful stuff. I used to love his so-called protest songs. I see him as another poet, or as competition. You read my books which are written before I heard of Dylan or read Dylan or anybody, it's the same. I didn't come after Elvis and Dylan, I've been around always.

I respect him a lot. I had too many father figures. If I see or meet a great artist, I love them. I go fanatical about them for a short period, and then I get over it. If they wear green socks, I'm liable to wear green socks for a period, too.

John: When I was a Beatle, I thought we were the best group in the goddamn world. And believing that was what made us what we were. Our best work was never recorded. We were performers in Liverpool, Hamburg and round the dance halls. What we generated was fantastic when we played straight rock, and there was nobody to touch us in Britain. As soon as we made it, we made it, but the edges were knocked off. Brian put us in suits and all that, and we made it very, very big. But we sold out. The music was dead before we even went on the theatre tour of Britain. We were feeling shit already, because we had to reduce an hour or two hours' playing – which we were glad about in one way – to twenty minutes, and go on and repeat the same twenty minutes every night.

The Beatles music died then, as musicians. That's why we never improved as musicians – we killed ourselves then to make it. And that was the end of it. George and I are more inclined to say that we always miss the club days because that's when we were playing music. Later on, we became technically efficient recording artists, which was another thing because we were competent people and whatever media you put us in, we can produce something worthwhile.

Performing as a Beatle is much harder than performing as John Lennon & Yoko Ono and the Plastic Ono Band, because you don't have that aura all around you. I saw what happened to Dylan [at the Isle of Wight Festival, 1969]. He gave a reasonable performance. It was late and everybody had waited three days and it was slightly flat. There was nothing wrong with his performance and the audience appreciated it, but they expected Buddha or Jesus to appear.

Now, if you imagine if the four Beatles are going to come on stage, whatever happens, we have such a thing to live up to. Why should the Beatles give more? Didn't they give everything on goddamn earth for ten years? The typical love/hate fan says, 'Thank you for everything you did for us in the Sixties. Will you just give me another go, another chance? One more miracle? Just to convince me. I didn't get enough the first time.'

A lot of people credit the Beatles with changing everything. We were on a wave of change throughout the world, part of the happening of the new youth, when the youth became aware. I don't believe in the Beatles myth – whatever they were supposed to be in everybody's head,

including our own. It was a dream. I don't believe in the dream any more.

My life with the Beatles had become a trap…. I always remember to thank Jesus for the end of my touring days; if I hadn't said that the Beatles were 'bigger than Jesus' and upset the very Christian Ku Klux Klan, well, Lord, I might still be up there with all the other performing fleas! God bless America. Thank you, Jesus.

There was this Japanese monk. He was in love with this big golden temple and he was so in love with it, he burnt it down so that it would never deteriorate. That's what I did with the Beatles. I wanted to kill it while it was on top. Remember, I did say 'I'm not going to be singing "She Loves You" at thirty'.

When I wrote 'the dream is over' I was trying to say to the Beatles thing, 'get off my back'. I was also trying to tell the other people to stop looking at me because I wasn't going to do it for them any more because I didn't even know what the hell I was doing in my own life. When I said 'the dream is over', I had made the physical break from the Beatles, but mentally there was still this big thing on my back about what people expected of me. It was like this invisible ghost. The dream is over. I've got to get down to reality. The 'good old days' is garbage.

People are still attached and possessing the Beatles and the Sixties dream and what I was saying is: that dream is over. Carrying the Beatles and the Sixties around for the rest of your life – to live in that dream is the twilight zone of continual not living in the 'now'. It's continually escaping from the now. It's all illusion. You make your own dream. That's the Beatles' story, isn't it? That's Yoko's story. That's what I'm saying now. Produce your own dream. If you want to save Peru, go and save Peru. It's quite possible to do anything, but not to put it on leaders and parking meters. Don't expect John Lennon or Yoko Ono or Bob Dylan or Jesus Christ to come and do it for you. You have to do it yourself. That's what the great masters and mistresses have been saying ever since time began. They can point the way, leave signposts and little instructions in various books that are now called 'holy' and worshipped for the cover of the book and not what it says. But the instructions are all there for all to see, have always been and always will be. There's nothing new under the sun. All roads lead to Rome. And people cannot provide it for you. I can't wake you up. You wake you up. I can't cure you. You cure you.

John with Yoko's daughter Kyoko, photographed by Yoko,
by and in the swimming pool; 841 Nimes Road, Bel Air,
California, June 1970.

John & Yoko in the bedroom with a banjo and a bottle
of HP sauce, shortly before their return to Tittenhurst;
841 Nimes Road, Bel Air, California, September 1970.

 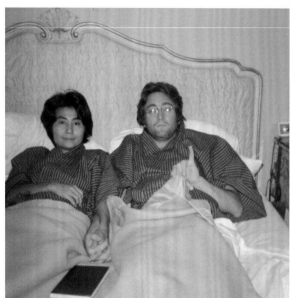

After recording, mixing and releasing their *Plastic Ono Band* albums, John & Yoko take a 'slow boat to Japan', where John will meet Yoko's parents for the first time. They write a postcard to Art and Vivian Janov aboard the *SS Cleveland* from Los Angeles to Yokohama via Honolulu, 20 December 1970–13 January 1971.

PRESIDENT CLEVELAND • PRESIDENT WILSON — Length 610 feet; beam 76 feet; speed 20 knots. These two American President Cruiseliners offer First and Tourist Class service on 43-day Orient Cruises to Hawaii, Japan, Taiwan, Hong Kong and the Philippines. Also 66-day Pacific Circle Cruises, 14-day Mexican Fiesta Cruises and 3-day Party Cruises.

Travel and Ship with the Presidents

Dear ARt + Vivian. PRIMS
We're on our
Way to Japan to
See our Mummy
+ DADDY. Glad you
dig Record, hope you
got BOTH of them.
We passed thru . L.A.
but had no time. love
John + Yoko.

POST CARD

THE JANOVS.
c/o BEN HILL
Beverly Hills Hotel
Garage
9641. Sunset.
Beverly Hills.
California.
U.S.A.

US AIR MAIL 8¢

LITHO IN U.S.A . 7-70 100M ODP-266

<u>my mummy's dead.</u>

my mummy's dead
i can't get it through my head
although it's been so many years
my mummy's dead
it's hard to explain
so much pain
i could never show it
my mummys dead.

to art with love
from John 6/8/70

MY MUMMY'S DEAD

My Mummy's dead
I can't get it through my head
Though it's been so many years
My Mummy's dead

I can't explain
So much pain
I could never show it
My Mummy's dead

MY MUMMY'S DEAD

John: I recently got into haiku in Japan. When you get rid of a whole section of illusion in your mind, you're left with great precision. To me, the best poetry is haiku. All the best paintings are Zen. The less said, the better. I would like to be able to say it without lyrics, but I can't. I'm verbal. It is clarity of expression that I am looking for. I'm just trying to put a clear moment on canvas. The way they paint with Zen is they meditate first, or they get in that frame of mind and then they just do that stroke. The tune was that sort of feeling, almost like a haiku poem.

It helps to say 'my Mummy's dead' rather than 'my mother died' or 'my mother wasn't very good to me'. A lot of us have images of parents that we never get from them. It doesn't exorcise it – bang, gone – but it helps. First of all, you have to allow yourself to realize it.

I never allowed myself to realize that my mother had gone. It's the same if you don't allow yourself to cry, or feel anything. Some things are too painful to feel, so you stop. We have the ability to block feelings and that's what we do most of the time.

These feelings are now coming out of me, feelings that have been there all my life. And they continue to come out. I don't know if every time I pick up a guitar I'm going to sing about my mother. I presume it'll come out some other way now.

Mine is an extreme case. My father and mother split and I never saw my father until I was twenty, nor did I see much more of my mother. But Yoko had her parents there and it was the same.

Yoko: I think anybody who is reading this who is aware of their pain, so much that they're so desperate that they need something, they'll understand it. If they don't understand it, then that means they don't need it so much. We needed it very much so that we understood. It's like if you're hungry and you see food, there's no intellectualism about it, you just grab and eat it. Perhaps one feels more pain when parents are there. I often wish my mother had died so that at least I could get some people's sympathy. But there she was, a perfectly beautiful mother.

John: And Yoko's family were middle-class Japanese but it's all the same repression. Though I think middle-class people have the biggest trauma if they have nice imagey parents, all smiling and dolled up. They are the ones who have the biggest struggle to say, 'Goodbye Mummy, goodbye Daddy'.

The reason Yoko does such far-out stuff is that it's a far-out kind of pain she went through. All art is pain expressing itself. I think all life is, everything we do, but particularly artists – that's why they're always vilified. They're always persecuted because they show pain; they can't help it. They express it in art and the way they live, and people don't like to see that reality that they're suffering.

Janov showed me how to feel my own fear and pain, therefore I can handle it better than I could before, that's all. I'm the same, only there's a channel. It doesn't just remain in me, it goes round and out. I can move a little easier. Once you know how to do it, you know, the secret is to learn how to cry. I don't have to learn how to cry again. I don't believe all that garbage about going back and back and keep digging and digging and digging.

I learned how to cry. It was good for me. It didn't help me not to. It didn't help me behave myself in '74, but I think if I hadn't been there, I might have even been in worse condition. It took me a little time to recover from the Janov experience, which left me bitterer than when I went in, and that did shake me up for a couple of years. In fact, I probably only just recovered from it this year [1975]. It was a bit of a mind blower and it left me faithless. I do have faith now, and have still gained something from the experience of going there.

The difference between us and Janov, as Yoko puts it, is that the past we remember is the past we create now, because of the necessity of the present. I wouldn't have missed it, though. It was very good for me. And I still 'Primal' and it still works.

Yoko: We were on that gig called searching for something you know? When you're searching for something, you tend to narrow your view, to try and head for the mythical nirvana or peace of mind, whatever it is, and we realized you're a bit more relaxed when you're not looking for anything.

John: I just feel like me, whatever that is.

Yoko: He was standing alone, not as part of a group but as John. And he had to really face himself and be honest with himself.

John: I'm not afraid of dying. I'm prepared for death because I don't believe in it. I think it's just getting out of one car and getting into another.

A card for Easter Sunday, 19 April 1957, from John's mother, Julia Lennon, looking forward to his twenty-first birthday, a date she would tragically never see.

Left: 'My Dear Stinker, Wink. Your mum's craby [sic] but she loves you anyhow. See you when your [sic] 21. Lots of love my sweet old feller. Mummy. Judy xxx'.
Right: 'To My Stinker. From Mummy xxxxxx Judy.'

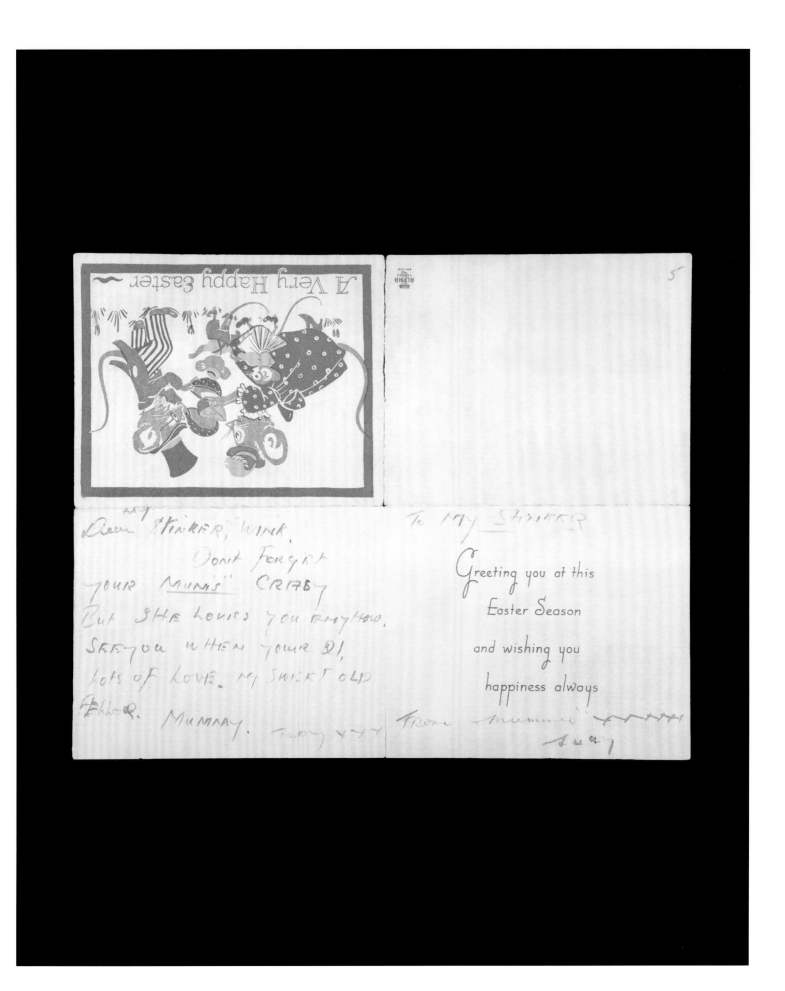

Previous pages: Cover artwork for the twelve-inch vinyl
LPs *John Lennon/Plastic Ono Band* and *Yoko Ono/Plastic
Ono Band* taken by John & Yoko's assistant Dan Richter
on Kodak Safety Film 126 Instamatic square-format
film negative, at their home; Tittenhurst Park, Ascot,
Berkshire, autumn 1970.

Thirty-two one-inch, eight-track tapes in their original boxes, used in the production of the *John Lennon/Plastic Ono Band* album; EMI Studios, 3 Abbey Road, London, recorded 26 September–29 October 1970.

Above: John poses with a chalk board reminding
EMI Studios staff to 'Leave all microphones set
up for John Lennon session', 10 October 1970.
Below: John cutting his thirtieth birthday cake
from Yoko in Studio 3's control room, EMI Studios,
3 Abbey Road, London, 9 October 1970.

JOHN LENNON/PLASTIC ONO BAND

John: The *Plastic Ono Band* album was nice to do and it was minimal. Just my guitar or piano, and bass and drums. I think it's the best thing I've ever done. The poetry on this album is superior to anything I've done because it's not self-conscious. I had the least trouble writing the songs. There's no bullshit. It's realistic and it's true to me.

'In My Life', 'I'm a Loser', 'Help!', 'Strawberry Fields Forever' – they're all personal records. I like first-person music, but because of my hang-ups and many other things, I would only now and then specifically write about me. Now I wrote all about me and that's why I like it. It's me and nobody else.

Yoko: The bones of this particular album were the fact that it's spiritual – expressing people's mind and emotions. We didn't want to kill that with too much production.

Phil McDonald (engineer): Yoko had a lot of input at the start. That's how it really started, just with Yoko being there and John's reassurance that everything was going as he wanted it to go.

Klaus Voormann (bass): John would come into the studio when the session started, run straight to the piano, didn't even say hello to us, just sat on the piano. Yoko would sit next to him and he would play the next song. He would give us the lyrics, written in nice big letters so that we all could see what he was saying. And then we took a pencil and put the chords underneath and he just played it once or twice.

Phil McDonald: Then they'd play a lot of takes to get it perfect. A good sound on the drums, the bass and the guitar, to get the songs across how he wanted them. As you recorded, you put the effects on, so that he could hear it in his earphones in the studio so it would be exactly the same. The drums were done on two tracks, stereo. It was nice to spread and have two tracks to do drums on. Ringo could drum for hours and hours and keep a steady beat. I think he's the only drummer I know who could drum for two or three hours, and you could take 'take one', and 'take sixty', and it would be in the same tempo. Klaus is an excellent bass player. Very steady, very solid – the root of the whole song. Usually we had an amp with a C12 mic, so we'd have a direct feed and an amp feed, and then mix them together onto one track. John playing guitar or piano, very simple. Just a little bit of echo. It wasn't supposed to be a big sound, just back to basics, really.

Yoko: When he was recording with the Beatles, I think there were many times that they all figured they needed more sounds added to John's songs. This time he was just doing it exactly like he wanted.

Richard Lush (engineer): They played in sessions, but as you can hear they're not actually together all the time, perfectly in time. Back then, it was more of a feeling, and if there was a great performance, you went with the performance. Today, people stare at a screen and you can see that the bass isn't in time and you can move it and put it in time. Quite often, this beautiful feeling is lost today because the technology makes you get it perfect. You should do a song with somebody singing along with it at the time. There was a period during the Seventies and Eighties when one put all these tracks down as a backing track and nobody knew where anybody was in the song.

All the Beatles' songs were done with a vocal and all of these were done with John singing. We didn't necessarily keep the vocal, but it gave everybody an idea of what the song was all about. And that comes across on the album. The highlight of this album is the fact that it is real. It's not a piece of manufactured music, it's just great songs played to get a great groove. That's why I like it and I've always liked it.

Phil McDonald: I'd never heard anybody scream and sing like that, or play guitar like that. It was a new sound, a new generation of sound that he wanted himself to do. If you think about punk rock, which came a long way after that, this type of music was going that way. It's like an early part of punk rock.

John: When you are on your own, in charge, you make different decisions; they weren't group decisions. There's a lot of difference between working with a set group and working alone.

Yoko: We were producing and recording it that way and then one day, on John's birthday, Phil Spector walked in. I said, 'Oh my God, I don't want somebody coming here and telling us what to do. I mean it's going so well.' But Phil was so sensitive to the album. He was the one who played that beautiful piano on 'Love'. So I thought 'Oh, he's good' and I just had to shut up and let him do those things.

Klaus Voormann: Phil Spector plays beautiful piano, so quiet and silent. I listened to it and loved it, and I told Phil,

Advertisements placed in *Billboard*, *Cashbox* and *Variety*
magazines as a last resort to attract the attention of absent
co-producer Phil Spector, who was over two weeks late
for work on the *John & Yoko/Plastic Ono Band* album
sessions. He eventually arrived at EMI Studios on
John's birthday, 9 October 1970.

The original one-inch eight-track tape box with an engineer's note recording Phil Spector's arrival to the session in EMI Studio 3 during the recording of 'God' on John's thirtieth birthday, 9 October 1970.

EMITAPE

JOHN LENNON / PHIL SPECTOR   — APPLE —   S6307

Tape No. _EO99926 – 8T_ Identity _JOHN   LENNON_

	Subject	TAKE	START	FINISH	TIME	Remarks
	GOD (THE DREAM IS OVER)	34	00·41	B/D		
		35	1·32	5·30	4·00	
		36	5·31	9·23	3·50	
		37	10·45	14·50	4·00	
		38	15·53	B/D		← PHIL SPECTOR ARRIVES
		39	16·29	20·42	4·10	
		40	20·47	F/S		
		41	21·04	24·22		
	PLEASE RETURN TO TAPE LIBRARY					

TAPE ~~LENGTH~~	STUDIO 3 8T TAPE No. 3m No.2.	ENGINEER RICHARD LUSH – ANDY STEPHENS	TAPE SPEED
		DATE 9TH OCT 1970	15 ips

'You know, your piano playing is great.' You should have heard him doing 'River Deep Mountain High' as a ballad, the way he originally wrote it.

Yoko: He has a fantastic knowledge of technical engineering.

Klaus Voormann: He knows exactly the frequencies the instruments should be in – the bass drum, the bass, the guitars and the voice. Each one has its place. So you leave the spaces for wherever there's space for it. He's just magic.

John: He can make any sound you like, just within seconds. His knowledge is incredible. I learnt a lot from him on this album. Phil lets you present him with a picture you think you want and then he'll take the best shot of it with his camera. The usual trouble is that a person's interpreting all the time on the other side of the board. When he's with you, he's not like an A&R man, he's one of the band.

Klaus Voormann: Phil was so nice, in particular to Yoko. He never said a hard word. And they got on really, really well. It was lots of fun. We were laughing. John & Yoko were completely outraged by the therapy they just experienced, so they were crying a lot, laughing a lot. They were very outgoing. Their whole life had come up because of the Primal Scream thing they had been doing. And it was great to see those two together.

John: Phil's a genius, He's a super energy guy and he came in just at the right moment on the album and inspired us again. There's no bull with him, he can play a control board, he just plays it. He co-produced my album; Yoko and I did Yoko's.

Richard Lush: On all of the sessions, John kept saying to Phil, 'I want it to be simple. I don't want it to go into this huge extravaganza that you're known for.' Lyrically and song-wise it is a very personal album and obviously he felt that he wanted to get that across.

Klaus Voormann: Phil in the control room was already making mixes right there. He knew exactly what he wanted. And whilst he was recording, the machine was running in the back. I think some of those live seven-and-a-half i.p.s. quarter-inch mixes were actually on the record.

Phil McDonald: John didn't really like the sound of his voice. He always wanted to change it, or to take the bottom end out – 'let's make it nasally' – or he'd put his hand to his nose and sing through his nose just to change the sound of his voice because he didn't like listening back to it. That's why he was always having tape echo because that enhanced the voice – you didn't have to listen to him bare. And of course, Mr Spector comes in and he's the echo man himself, there is echo on the echo on the tape echo, just goes on and on and on. I think that's probably why they liked him as well.

Richard Lush: There were normally three things that John liked. He liked double tracking or an Eddie Cochran-type tape delay, or we had a thing John called flanging, where you sent a signal to another tape machine. That was done on about three tracks on the album and he always wanted something to be on it. He wanted it to be different. He didn't want it to be the same every day. If he did one song one day, he said, 'Ah we had flanging yesterday, let's put tape delay back on it today.'

In the song 'God', when he sang 'me, Yoko and me', he wanted the tape echo to come off. He wanted it just to be him on his own, with no effects. I can remember when we mixed it, I had a little mark where the tape delay was, so that I could go back and get the same sound. I must have had it one notch back on where it should have been and Phil Spector said, 'The reverb's different. It's not the same.' I said, 'No of course it is. Look, look it's on the mark.' And we both looked down and it wasn't on the same spot. And John said, 'See, that's why I pay him all this money.'

For 'Working Class Hero', Phil McDonald recorded a version of it and John came to me when I started working on the project and said, 'I've left a verse out and I need to record a verse and put it in. I don't want to do the whole song.' So what we had to do was try and get exactly the same sound, which I didn't do; it was kind of different and he was playing it different and he had a different guitar pick. When we recorded it and edited it together and put the extra verse in, it sounded totally different and I was a bit worried about it – being an engineer you have to get everything right – and he said, 'Oh that, that doesn't matter, the most important thing is that that verse gets in. That's the most important thing.' These days you would spend a long time trying to marry these two things together and back then that wasn't a priority. The priority was for him to be happy and even Spector – it didn't worry him, a person that would get you for having the reverb slightly wrong!

Above: Engineer Richard Lush's track sheet with a hand-drawn studio and microphone plan for EMI Studio 2, 3 Abbey Road, London, on 15 October 1970.

Below: EMI Studios internal memorandums detailing the dates and times booked for the *John & Yoko/Plastic Ono Band* album sessions between 26 September and 8 November 1970.

	STUDIO	NO 2	ARTISTIC DETAILS			DATES – TIMES	ENGINEER
	JOB NO.		JOHN LENNON.			15 OCTOBER 1970 7–12!	RL.

	PURPOSE	MIC.	BOOM–STAND	LINE			MONO	STEREO	4T	8T
1	BASS.	C12	AKGBOOM	A	✓					✓
2	BASS DRM.	D20	T. STAND.	A	✓					
3	—"—	C38A		A	✓	TAPE				815
4	SNARE.	U87	AKG BOOM	A	✓					
5	TOM TOM	U87	—"—	A	✓					
6	—"—	U87	—"—	A	✓					
7	BIG TOM	U87	—"—	A	✓					
8	HIGH HAT	D19C	—"—	A	✓					
9	PIANO	U86	AKGBOOM	B	✓					
10	GUITAR	U87	—"—	A	✓					
11	—"—	—"—	—"—	A	✓					
12	—"—	—"—	—"—	B	✓					
13	VOCAL	U48V	F/E BOOM	B	✓					
14										
15										
16	OSCILLATOR		TRUNK	1						
17										
18										
19	A.D.T	=	CONTROL LINE	1						
20	TAPE ECHO.	=	" "	2 RETURN						
21	PLATE.		" "	3 ECHO SENDS						
22	PLATE.									
23	CHAMBER									
24	CHAMBER.									

ECHO

	1	2	3	4
Send				
Chamb	✓			
Steed				
Plate		✓		
Drum			TAPE	
Top Eq.	10		ECHO	
Bass	600			
RET. (Fader)	23 24 21 22	20		

PLAYBACK

	MONO	STEREO
CUE 1		CANS.
CUE 2		
TELE–PHONES		

OTHER REQUIREMENTS

A62 FOR TAPE ECHO.
A62 LINED UP FOR STEREO REMIX.

REF. NO. 11478

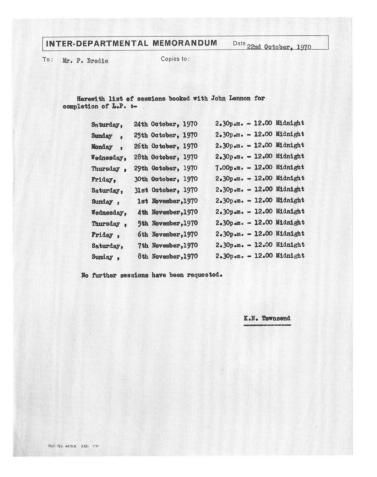

John Lennon. PCS 7124.

Recording Dates 1970

September 26th (8T) Recording
27th Recording + Some Rough remixes
30th " "

October 3rd " "
6th Recording
7th —"— + Remixes "God's Isolation"
9th —"— + Remix "I found out"
10th —"— + Remix @ 7½ ips all titles.
11th Remix @ 7½ ips all titles.
15th Recording + Remix "Working Class Hero."
17th —"— + Remix "Look at Me"
18th —"— + Remix "God' + Look at Me"
19th —"— + Remixes "Mother/Well well well Remember + Love"
24th Remixing
25th Recording + Remix "Working Class Hero."
(Sts)

INTER-DEPARTMENTAL MEMORANDUM   Date 22nd October, 1970

To: Mr. P. Brodie   Copies to:

Herewith list of sessions booked with John Lennon for completion of L.P. :-

Saturday,	24th October, 1970	2.30p.m. – 12.00 Midnight
Sunday ,	25th October, 1970	2.30p.m. – 12.00 Midnight
Monday ,	26th October, 1970	2.30p.m. – 12.00 Midnight
Wednesday,	28th October, 1970	2.30p.m. – 12.00 Midnight
Thursday,	29th October, 1970	7.00p.m. – 12.00 Midnight
Friday,	30th October, 1970	2.30p.m. – 12.00 Midnight
Saturday,	31st October, 1970	2.30p.m. – 12.00 Midnight
Sunday ,	1st November,1970	2.30p.m. – 12.00 Midnight
Wednesday,	4th November,1970	2.30p.m. – 12.00 Midnight
Thursday,	5th November,1970	2.30p.m. – 12.00 Midnight
Friday ,	6th November,1970	2.30p.m. – 12.00 Midnight
Saturday,	7th November,1970	2.30p.m. – 12.00 Midnight
Sunday ,	8th November,1970	2.30p.m. – 12.00 Midnight

No further sessions have been requested.

K.N. Townsend

Ref. No. 4410A EMI CP

John, Ringo Starr and Klaus Voormann recording in EMI
Studio 3 while Yoko and Phil Spector co-produce from
the control room during the Plastic Ono Band sessions.
Illustration by Klaus Voormann.

PHIL

YOKO

Ringo Starr playing drums, London, June 1971.

RINGO STARR / DRUMS

I hadn't played this one for a long time. I just went back to it because of this interview and it's so incredible, the emotion on this record. It is just mind-blowing. The sparseness of the band, the force of John. That's why he's one of the greats. That's how it is. And I think this – you know, not that we had to prove anything – but this record proves it more than most.

He would just sit there and sing them. We would just jam and then we would find out how they would go, and we did 'em. It was very loose, actually, and it being a trio also was a lot of fun.

John is just incredibly great and I think the simplicity of what Klaus and I played with him gave him a great opportunity to, for the first time, really use his voice and his emotion how he wanted. There was no battle going on. He had all the tracks. He wasn't limited to five because Paul would have five, George would have one, I'd have one. So it was all in!

On this record I was mainly a timekeeper. It's very straight. It wasn't difficult at all. Very few fills. There's a few lifting the track occasionally, but my basic job on this record was just holding it down – wherever John wanted to take it.

I can't do anything twice. I've never done a fill the same twice. Because when I do it, it's where I'm at, at that moment. And so if you want to then re-record that track, I'll do a fill in that space but it won't be the same. One time, before this record, one of the other Fabs wanted me to double-track a fill, and that was impossible. I couldn't do it. Because my way of drumming – yeah, I can keep time but where the fill (which I always feel is my art) is, has to do with the surrounding atmosphere at that moment. And so that's what you get. And the atmosphere is always changing; the emotional moment is always changing. So, you know, for 'take three', its basic track is the same, but usually the fill will be different. That's how I play.

The tone of the drums was the tone we'd been using with the Beatles, really. They were very tight. They were very dead. With the old tea towels on top of everything. I would've just got into playing with that sound over the last couple of years.

Klaus Voormann is great. He used to live with me and George Harrison in London. We both really loved the same music. He dug Al Green as much as I did. Klaus is a very thoughtful, Germanic bass player. [laughs] That's a joke! Klaus is very cool. You know if Klaus wasn't a cool bass player, he wouldn't be playing on John's and George's and my records, you know? He is a great lad. He knows, like myself, the track is what we're playing for. And Klaus was behind the track as well. He's not there to show off. We're doing the best we can, for the overall emotion of the piece.

I have no real memory of Phil Spector producing this record at all. I remember he came in, later. But I never felt Phil produced this record, really. The engineer took down what we did and then John would mix it.

'Well Well Well' – what a track. I mean I'm just looking at it now. Ah, great! 'Mother' – I mean, the emotion of 'Mother' is incredible. 'I Found Out' – great drums on 'I Found Out' – that's where they've sort of come up a notch there – it depended on the time; on the minute. That's how it felt we should go. And so I brought in the toms a bit more there. There's no hard-and-fast rule on this record. It's like, 'OK, what time is it? Let's go!' – you know, 'one, two, three, four…' – it was that loose, in such a lot of ways.

He was the best rhythm-cum-lead guitarist because his style of lead was pure – very raw. And he was the rhythm guitar – that's what he was. George was lead, but he would throw in lead bits, and so they always had such passion. Because half the time, I feel he never knew where he was going. And that was the joy – he knew it was an E somewhere, but it was like, 'Oh yeah!'

'Well Well Well' – he just wound everything up. That's how he achieved most of those sounds. Louder was better. Distortion was good. Always wanted a lot of echo on his voice. He had a great voice and when he was singing, he gave all of that. I don't feel personally he was insecure about his voice. Everybody wants to be someone else, to be different. I don't feel it was bringing him down.

'God' – well, isn't that an incredible track? Billy Preston – he's one of the few musicians that never put his hands in the wrong place. Never. I've known him since he was sixteen. He came in on *Let It Be* and then he was on this. It was always a joy when Billy played, because he was just so great.

For me, I can't say enough about this record because there's no downside to it. I think it may have had something to do with the Primal Scream 'cause there's quite a bit of screaming on it. That was the emotional place I feel he was at, at that moment, at that time. It was a very big thing with John. He was going through a hard, heavy time of finding himself, dispelling a lot of his childhood and putting it into a real space, and searching, like the rest of us, for the meaning of life.

Detail from an Instamatic photograph of Ringo Starr,
seated with John & Yoko in the control room during
playback at EMI Studio 3, 3 Abbey Road, London,
October 1970.

I think he was always brave. I could always say that about John. He was always brave. He would put it out there, and the consequences sometimes were very harsh. But he would always put it out there. That's why you could not not love him, you know?

He was an incredible craftsman. He couldn't write you a loving, incredible song, he could write it for himself. But he also got into a space where it wasn't what the words said, it was how the words sounded. That was the important part. Not so much on this, but prior to this, some of his tracks with the Beatles, the words were like gobbledygook in their way, but the sound and the emotion of them carried it through. I don't know if that's clear but that's how I felt.

'Love' – well it was incredible because we all had our wives and our families and we'd go to work and come back and say, 'How was your day?' 'Oh, it was fine, we did a couple of tracks…' and then suddenly Yoko was living in the studio with us. It freaked us out. Freaked me out, anyway. And I asked him, I said, you know, 'What is going on?' He said,

'Well, you know, we're gonna spend every minute together.' So as soon as you knew that, you were cool. And that's what they did. So he never had to go home and say, 'Oh, we did a couple of tracks' or, 'Guess who came for tea?' or whatever. They both knew exactly where they'd been. Which was an incredible thing. John & Yoko were this incredibly close couple. And so, you know, as in the song, 'Hold on Yoko, it's gonna be alright', they supported each other in that love way, musically.

Her record was a lot of fun because it was like a jam. And then she would do her crazy singing on top of it. I never felt with Yoko that there was the verse and the chorus, so we would just jam. John would be the lead musically and we would play and then Yoko would do a [imitates Yoko screaming]. Peace and love, Yoko! [laughs]

It is an incredibly cool record. I wouldn't like to be interviewed on a lot of records [laughs] but this I don't mind, because it's a beautiful record and he was a beautiful man and I'm privileged to feel he was my friend. And Peace and Love!

Postcards sent by John & Yoko to Ringo Starr from Greece, Hawaii, Los Angeles, New York and Tokyo between 1969 and 1971.

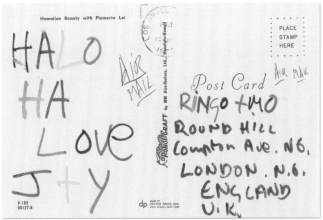

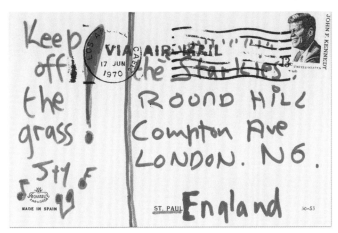

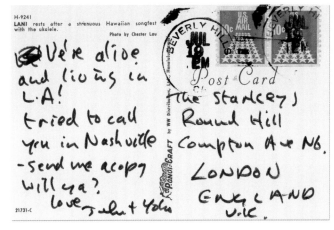

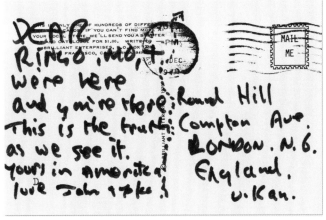

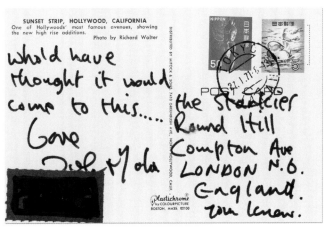

Klaus Voormann playing bass, London, June 1971.

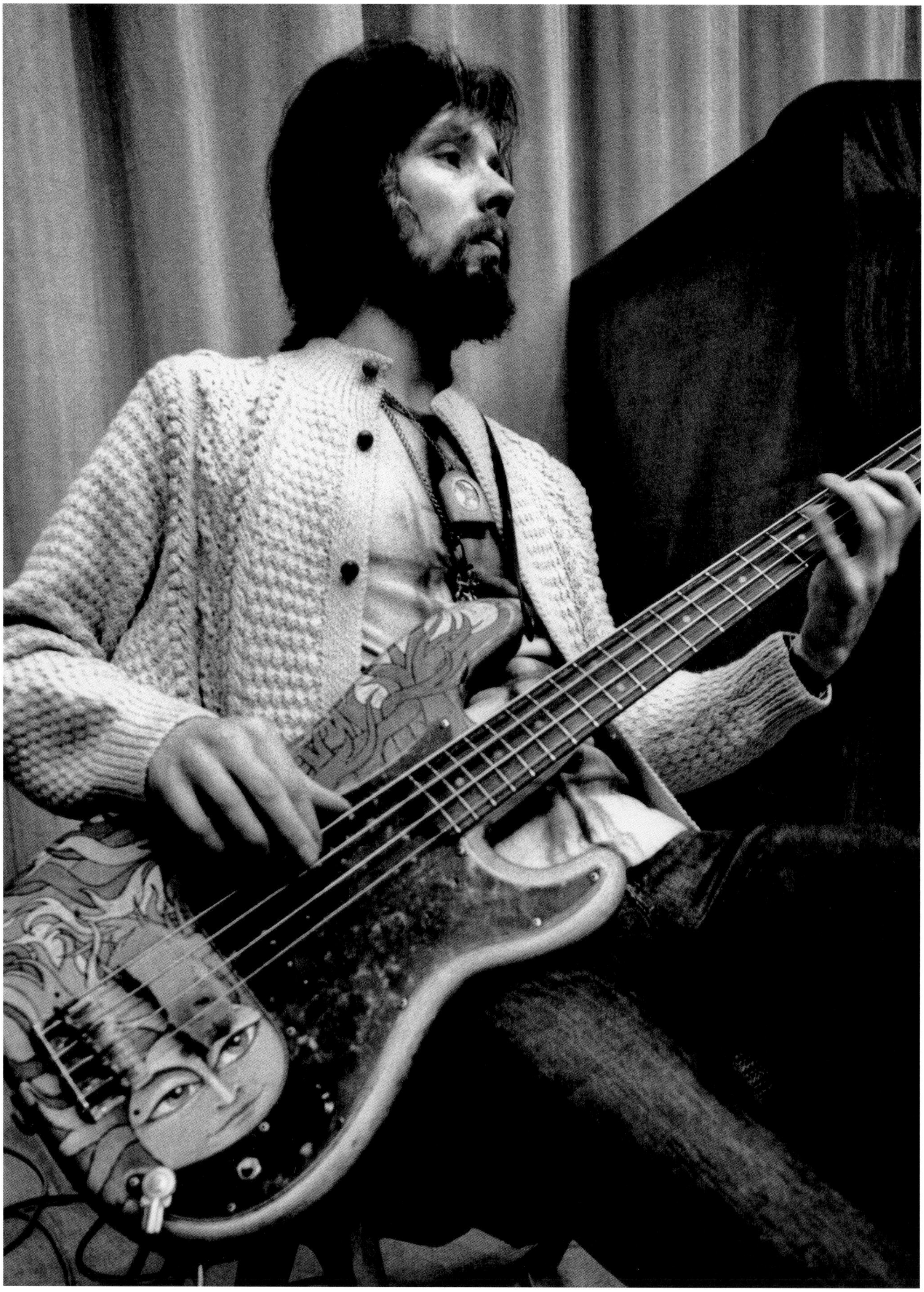

KLAUS VOORMANN / BASS

John had to write those songs. He had to record them onto tape as quickly as possible and keep them as raw as possible. People were supposed to listen to the words, listen to the song and get into the feeling. No big arrangements, no thousand guitars, just three instruments – John, Ringo and myself.

We played live in the studio and the atmosphere of us being together in the studio comes through on the record. You can feel it. This is John's experience. We were all feeling his experience and we put his experience onto tape. Whether it was singing or screaming, it was all natural, all John and only John. That's why I love this album. It's really simple – nothing to it. It didn't matter if there were a few wrong notes, they were the little things that brought it to life. And I was so happy to be in that circle. I already loved John and Ringo. I was starting to get to know Yoko and I really liked her a lot.

Yoko was the start of John finding himself. He still had to deal with the record company. He still had contracts and obligations. He was not yet completely free. Since he had met Yoko, everything was improving for John. He had definitely been very lost. I had several experiences with him where he had been very down, and didn't want to live. He didn't have much joy in his life and he didn't know where he was going to, or what he was doing. He was famous and had everything you could want, but he was very unhappy. Yoko really was the start of him getting better and better.

At the end of 'God', he sang, 'I don't believe in Beatles, I just believe in me' and then he came up to me and said, 'Klaus, should I say, "Yoko and me"?' And I never answered the question. From a feeling point of view, I would have said, 'yes, say "Yoko and me"'. But I could not give him the answer. It had to be him making the decision. It was very nice that he asked me, and he did put it on. It made me very proud.

They were so much in love, it was beautiful. They were sitting on each other's laps, kissing and hugging and showing their emotions, very much into one another. Maybe he overdid it a little, because it was all so fresh to him, but suddenly now, John felt that he was free. It certainly made me feel 'lucky John'. I knew what a bad state of mind he had been in, and this was such a big release.

John was always very direct, honest and interesting, but for a long time he had lost what he was inside. He couldn't put his finger on it. Something had been very wrong for a long time before Yoko came along.

I remember being with him one afternoon, a few years before. It must have been midday or two o'clock in the afternoon. I had gone to his house in Weybridge and he looked like he hadn't slept for five days – really, really bad. I don't know if he was on an acid trip, but he was absent-minded and looked really helpless. We went outside in the garden and he was picking the leaves from a bush. There was already loads of leaves all over the ground and I said, 'John, what are you doing this for? The bush can't help it if you don't feel good.' And then he laughed and said, 'I would just like to not be here, you know?' He just wanted to be away.

Stuart Sutcliffe was John's best friend at art college. He played bass for the Beatles in the early days. He tragically died in Hamburg and when John heard about it, it upset him so much that he had an inappropriate, uncontrollable fit – he couldn't stop manically laughing and he couldn't understand what was happening to him. Inside he was heart-broken, just devastated.

I had seen it happen several times before. In Hamburg he was often uptight and unhappy. He was always making jokes, like all the good clowns do, to cover up for their sadness. In the Star-Club he used to act up – doing the funniest things when the other bands were playing, like going onstage like a stagehand, with a big long board or a cross and knocking everything over. Or he would dress up like an old cleaning lady and clean the microphones and wash people under the arms. Everyone was laughing – they were all having a great time, but John was so uptight, he needed to get something out of his system.

John was always the perfect rhythm guitar player. When we first became friends he showed me how he played, dampening the strings, only playing on two strings, very sparse. Like Ringo has an intuitive talent for the drums, John had the same for the guitar, and he played crazy solos too. He never liked complicated technical soloing, just simple, very down-to-earth rhythm and great sounds.

For the *Plastic Ono Band* album, John used a guitar which was a mixture of a national guitar and an acoustic guitar – half metal, like a banjo, with sound holes which were all chrome looking, and the rest was wood. It had a nasal sound and the one pickup was so close to the strings

John insists to Klaus, Ringo and Yoko that his curly maple Dobro D-50SE 'The Uncle Josh Electric' is 'going to be the only guitar that's going to be played on the LP and that's that' at the start of the recording sessions at EMI Studios, October 1970. Illustration by Klaus Voormann.

that when he played, the strings sometimes stuck to the magnets in the pickup. I was there when he did 'Working Class Hero'. It was two takes cut together, just him in the studio, playing by himself, beautiful.

Whatever John did, it was very important to him to put what he was writing into the way he was singing. That's what makes a good singer. If you listen to 'Mother', he's hoarse when he starts – he had been screaming so much already that he really wrecked his voice in no time. It was natural with John. He couldn't perform any differently. He had to express himself. In a way, he learned it from Yoko but he had done it before, too. The fact that he had to get this despair out of his system meant he had to scream.

John had the gift of being able to express complex ideas very simply, using exactly the right words. Especially when it was about how he felt. He knew he needed to be direct and honest and raw, and that was the exact moment to capture the song. It was a moment in his life. Maybe later he might believe something different, but during that particular period he was going through his whole life and was coming back as a baby, and there he was, saying, 'I'm talking about me. Everything else is not important, I don't believe in it, the dream is over.' It's a perfect statement – exactly the right words. The dream is over.

John loved the Beatles. They were all such close friends and they were all such strong individual personalities. That's what had made them so big. But by 1970, their egos and lives were all pointing in different directions. They were not so much of a unit any more and they all needed to break free.

The way John was doing this was a complete surprise to everyone. I could see it was a release and a relief and I realized he had to go through this process of songwriting, which he loved, but now he was doing it exactly the way he wanted to do it – without the commercial pressures or the expectations connected to being a Beatle.

I think it must have been hard for Ringo to adjust. His old John had gone. Now he had a new John called 'John&Yoko'. Although John was happier, at work he was behaving completely differently to the way he had been before. They were still playing and talking and laughing, but there wasn't so much space for Ringo or the other Beatles in John's life any more.

Ringo is an incredible drummer. He continually comes up with things which nobody else could think of. He can be playing it incredibly straight, but then he will add a little unique beat or sound or fill that you didn't expect – which makes him so beautiful to work with. Often in the studio, drummers listen far too much to what the bassist is playing. They listen so much that they actually lose their own sound. Ringo is always listening, but he doesn't adjust to what I'm playing. He plays his own thing, and that made me so happy and it worked beautifully for all of us.

Billy Preston also knew the Beatles from Hamburg. He got on really well with everybody and had recently played on the *Let It Be* sessions. He was a great session musician and could easily adjust to whoever was in the studio and what they wanted. I think John actually said, 'Come on Billy, do a little of your gospel piano, it's about God.' [laughs] Billy grew up with gospel music and played piano and organ in church. He really believed in God and that's the way he played on the song 'God' – so perfect and beautiful.

Three years earlier, John had written 'All You Need Is Love' for the world – about the gentle, universal love we should all have for one another. And the Beatles played it to 200 million viewers via a global television broadcast.

I believe he wrote 'Love' for himself. At last, he had opened up his innermost places and was experiencing the overwhelming and profound love he had been so desperately looking and longing for, first shared with another person – Yoko – and then, most important of all, a love for himself. He had finally found his own self-worth.

This album was the beginning of John starting to find his way. I remember much later, in the late seventies, being with him at The Dakota and he was teaching me how to cook rice. If you are a person in the limelight, you don't have much time to think about how to cook rice, you just eat it. And there he was, teaching me how to cook rice. He was really happy. He said, 'Klaus, now I don't have any more contractual obligations. I don't have to do a record. I don't want to do a record. I just want to be here and be with my son and be with Yoko and feel good.' He could pick up a guitar and play for fun if he wanted, but he didn't have the pressure of continuously composing new songs for deadlines. And every day he was getting better and better.

Billy Preston playing piano, 1970.

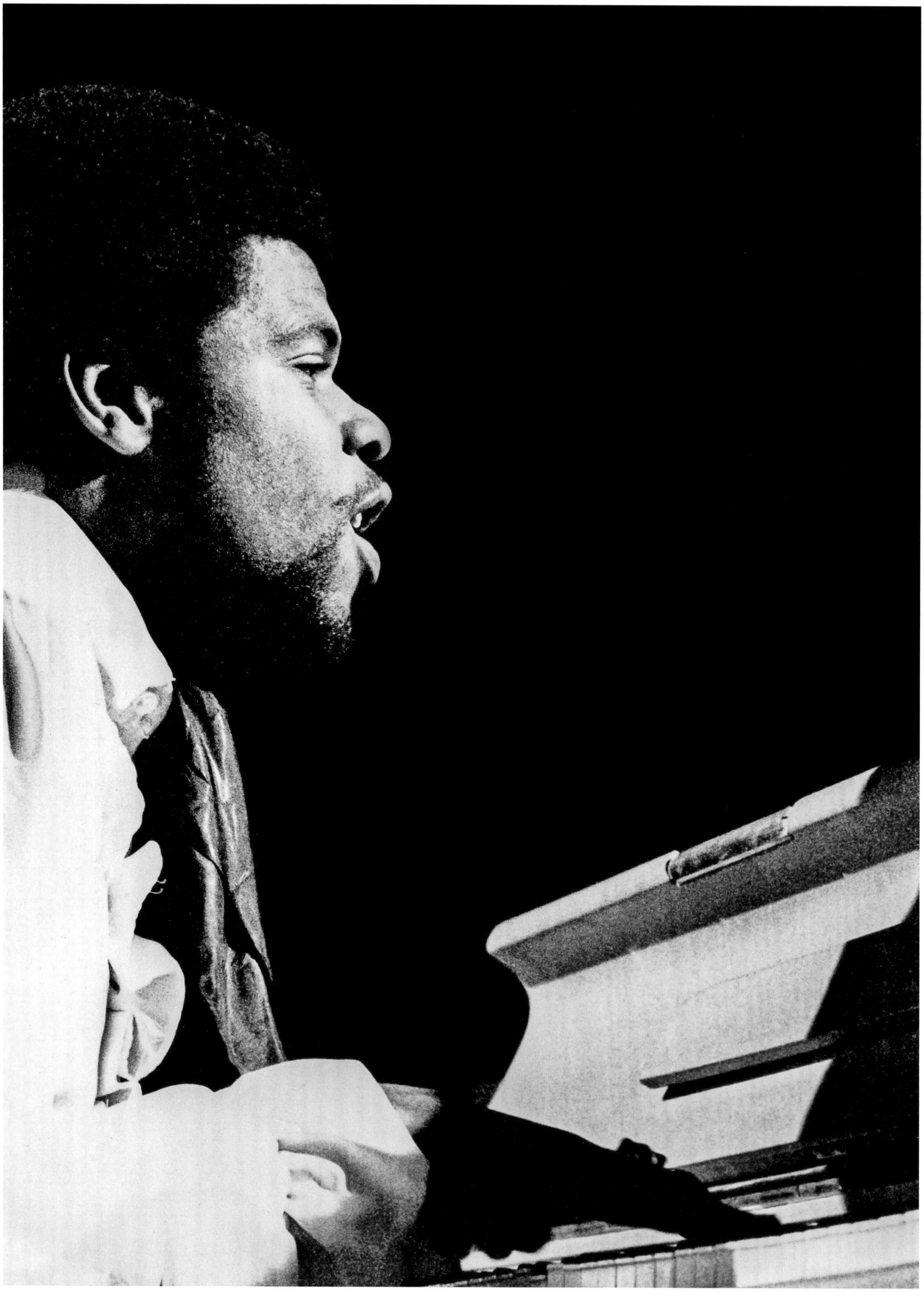

BILLY PRESTON / PIANO

I started playing when I was three years old. My mother is from the church, I was raised in the church and I believe that my talent is a God-given gift, so I can't take too much credit. My older sister played piano and, when I was a baby, I used to sit in my sister's lap and put my hands on top of hers and follow her motions. When I was about six years old, I was playing in church. The first album I ever made was on Sam Cooke's label – Mahalia Jackson – when I was about ten years old.

I wanted to play other types of music and yet do nothing wrong in God's eyes. My mother was very understanding about it. She just told me, 'In all thy ways, acknowledge God.' The church people, a lot of them, said, 'You're gonna go to hell if you play rock 'n' roll.' I had to be strong and look inside and decide that the God I loved couldn't be so narrow-minded. And since he had given me the talent to play all of these things, he would surely agree. God is a personal saviour, he's not the same to everybody.

Ray Charles became my idol at an early age. He had so much feeling, he sang from his heart and he expressed himself so well. His phrasing, the way he touched the piano and the way he moved – everything was just from his soul. I spent three years on the road with him and it was the best experience I ever had. I was just a kid and I learnt so much. The neatness and tautness of his show, the deliverance he had, the emotional communication with an audience, the whole quality of performance.

The first time I played rock 'n' roll was with Little Richard. I saw the excitement he created by performing and it encouraged me to do the same. Until then I had been strictly gospel. Richard was such an entertainer. He would do things I had never seen before, and he really worked hard.

The Beatles were different from all the other bands – their harmonies were great, they looked different, they were my favourite. One night in Hamburg I was standing in the wings watching. My organ was sitting there. George said, 'Come on out and play.' I said, 'Yeah!' But then I thought, 'Well, I'm playing for Little Richard and he's the star and he'll probably fire me and leave me in England', which he did! [laughs]

John was the boss Beatle. He was such a free spirit. He made things happen. It was never a dull moment around John. He was funny, he was so smart and clever. I admired him instantly for his wit and manner. You just knew he was special; genius, I suppose, stood out even then, and even to me, a very naive kid.

While we were in Hamburg on that first tour together, John took the time to teach me how to play the harmonica. The song I learned was 'Love Me Do'. I reciprocated by making sure that he and George, Paul and Ringo ate. They were only the opening act so they didn't get any meals from the promoter. Little Richard, being the big American headliner, got steaks and chops and a fabulous spread nightly, so I made sure that the soon-to-be Fab Four were well fed and watered. John had the great gift to teach and he was most generous with it. I learned so much from working with and around him, lessons I carry with me even today, subtleties that helped me be successful as both a writer and an artist in my own right.

Ringo is another sweetheart. He's such a level guy. He's so easy to get along with and he really cares and looks after everybody in the band. He treats everybody equally and pushes everybody forward. He's a lot of fun to work with.

When I was on Apple [1969–1971], I stayed at George's house and he was beautiful. He's such a spiritual guy. I was playing the organ in their little chapel and one of the Krishna people came in and started chanting. I was playing a gospel song, right? [laughs] and he went on and started chanting 'Hare Krishna!' and we had a service right there! [laughs] In his studio George has a picture of Buddha, a picture of Krishna, a picture of Jesus. I mean, he covers 'em all! [laughs]

I was happy for John. Everybody was happy that he was in love. Everywhere he went, Yoko went. If he crawled under the piano, she went under the piano. It was the closeness there, I was happy for them. Over the years we did become friends. I had a television series *Nightlife* and she was a guest on it in 1986 and she came over and hugged and kissed me and I said 'wow!' so that was nice. She is a nice lady.

John was wonderful. I miss him very much. I don't think that he's gone. His spirit is still here. When he passed, they came to my house and wanted to interview me and I wouldn't answer the door. I couldn't deal with it. He lived a full life and I'm glad that he did find happiness and love in his latter years that he didn't have when he was younger.

Ten original master eight-track tape boxes and one quarter-inch audio tape box containing the master takes of the album *John Lennon/Plastic Ono Band*, recorded at EMI Studios 2 and 3, 3 Abbey Road, 26 September–29 October 1970.

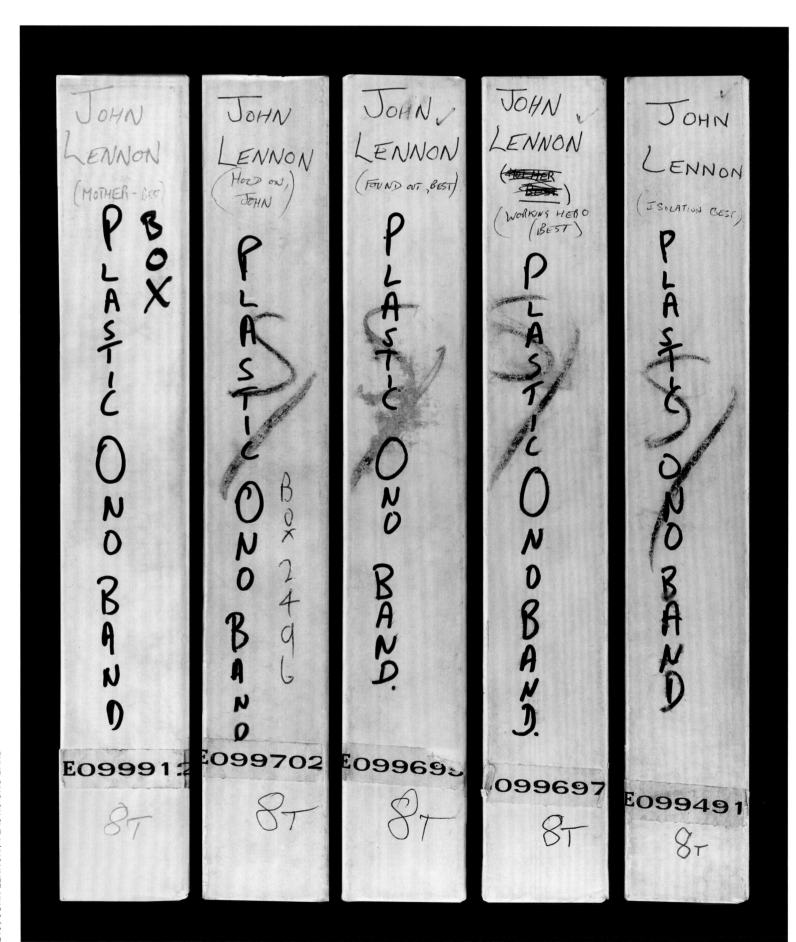

JOHN LENNON (REMEMBER, BEST) PLASTIC ONO BAND BOX 2506

E099928 8T

JOHN LENNON (WELL, WELL BEST) PLASTIC ONO BAND BOX 2496

E099700 8T

JOHN LENNON (LOOK AT ME) PLASTIC ONO BAND BOX 2504

E099906 8T

JOHN LENNON (GOD - BEST) PLASTIC ONO BAND BOX 2505

E099925 8T

TYPE 815/24N

MULTITRACK DIGITAL CUT OUT FOR MASTERS TAPE

BATCH 39140A

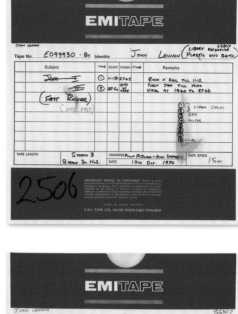
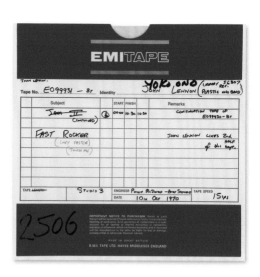

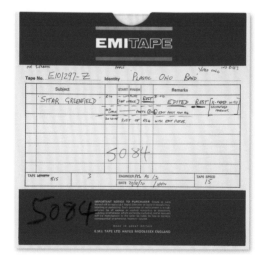

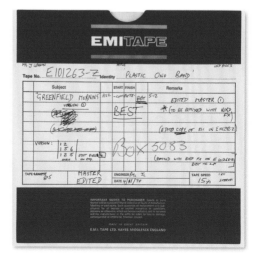
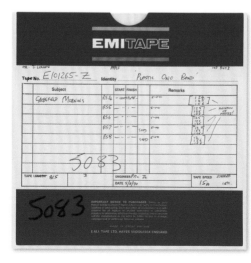

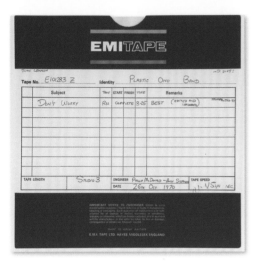

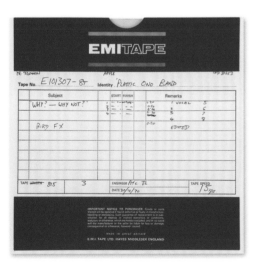
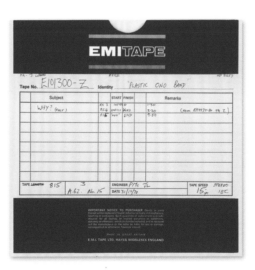

The twenty one-inch eight-track and quarter-inch stereo tapes in their original boxes, used in the production of the album *Yoko Ono/Plastic Ono Band*, EMI Studios 2 and 3, 3 Abbey Road, London, recorded and mixed 10 October–6 November 1970.

Yoko: When a violinist plays, which is incidental: the arm movement or the bow sound? Try arm movement only. If my music seems to require physical silence, that is because it requires concentration to yourself – and this requires inner silence which may lead to outer silence as well. I think of my music more as a practice (gyo) than a music. The only sound that exists to me is the sound of the mind. My works are only to induce music of the mind in people. It is not possible to control a mind-time with a stopwatch or a metronome. In the mind-world, things spread out and go beyond time. There is a wind that never dies.

The sound you play in your mind is different than the sound that comes out. The sounds and music in your mind exist without the physical limitations of the real world. After unblocking one's mind, by dispensing with visual, auditory and kinetic perceptions, what will come out of us? Would there be anything? I wonder. My events are mostly spent in wonderment. I want to wake up this beautiful superpower that each one of us has. You have to find it. And in order to find it, it's good if we create a situation where we participate in artwork or music-work, or something together.

My mother was an established musician in several Japanese instruments, shamisen, and kabuki singing. She played nine instruments. I got training in opera and when I do these vocal things, using the voice as an instrument, a lot of things from my background come out, even if I don't intend it. There are so many ways of using the throat and the vocal cords; you can use different areas, different parts of the body to express different emotions. I got a lot of influence from Berg's operas, like *Lulu*. There's also a lot of Japanese kabuki influence, from the old Japanese way of singing. There's one particular kabuki singing style called hetai, a kind of storytelling form that's almost like chanting and requires you to strain your voice a bit. I also listened to tapes of my voice playing backward and tried to make sounds like that. And I listened to Indian singing, Tibetan singing – all that, mixed.

When I was a very young girl, I was sent to our family summer house in Karuizawa; my mother was in Tokyo. She said, 'Don't ever go to the servants' room because they're talking about things that you shouldn't know.' I was curious, so I sneaked out and there were two teenage servant girls combing their hair and talking to each other saying, 'Did you know that my aunt just had a baby?' 'Oh, really?' And it was just very frightening because she was going like, 'Oh, Oh, Oh, Aaaaahh!' And to give birth is a very painful thing.

And all the servants were going, 'Shut up!' Well, I got scared and I ran away. But that experience stayed with me. That sound I never forgot. And years later, I started to create all sorts of sounds.

I was taught about sounds in a very interesting way at school. So I had a different idea about sounds. Most of my classmates probably did. For instance, I was trying to listen to the clock chiming, and then after it stops, you're supposed to repeat that in your mind to find out how many times it chimed. We were very into music in many different ways to what they usually teach in Japanese or American schools.

When I was going to Sarah Lawrence, I was mainly staying in the music library and listening to Schoenberg and Webern; they thrilled me, really. I was writing songs, throat tones. I was one of these people who didn't care about genre. I didn't stick to anything. It was a 'Who cares?' kind of thing. One time I gave this concert and this guy came in with a shrill voice and told me I shouldn't use a stopwatch in jazz music. Well I didn't like this 'what you are supposed to do or not do in jazz music'. This was not in my dictionary.

While preparing for a show at the Carnegie Recital Hall in 1961, I had an experience that reminded me of the sounds in the summer house. So I thought, 'I'm going to try to recreate that sound of a woman giving birth.' I recorded it and when I went to play it back, I accidentally hit the reverse button. The result was so spooky and weird that I rehearsed it to simulate the backwards sounds. That's how it all started.

At my New York City loft concerts, I was throwing peas from a bag at the people and I had long hair and I was circling my hair and the movement was a sound. Even then, some people were saying that maybe it was too dramatic.

Then there was my *Wall Piece*, which instructed you to hit the wall with your head, and that was called 'too dramatic' as well. But I felt stifled even with that; I was dying to scream, to go back to my voice. And I came to a point where I believed that the idea of avant-garde purity was just as stifling as just doing a rock beat over and over.

I was doing *Music of the Mind* – no sound at all, everybody sitting around, just imagining sounds. I was an avant-garde composer obsessed with the sound of music in my head and in no one else's.

Yoko Ono performing *Voice Piece For Soprano* (1961)
the instruction for which is: 'Scream. 1. against the wind
2. against the wall 3. against the sky. 1961 autumn.'

A selection of musical scores from Yoko's book *Grapefruit*,
first published in 1964: *Secret Piece* (1953), *Voice Piece
For Soprano* (1961); *Bicycle Piece For Orchestra* (1962);
Wall Piece For Orchestra to Yoko Ono (1962); *8 Architecture
Pieces Dedicated to A Phantom Architect* (1965); and
Sense Piece (1968).

SECRET PIECE

Decide on one note that you want to play.
Play it with the following accompaniment:

     The woods from 5 a.m. to 8 a.m.
     in summer.

1953 summer

VOICE PIECE FOR SOPRANO

Scream.
    1. against the wind
    2. against the wall
    3. against the sky

1961 autumn

BICYCLE PIECE FOR ORCHESTRA

Ride bicycles anywhere you can in
the concert hall.
Do not make any noise.

1962 autumn

WALL PIECE FOR ORCHESTRA to Yoko Ono

Hit a wall with your head.

1962 winter

Build a house
(on a hill)
that screams
when the wind blows

Open different windows that make
different screams and make different
air experiences in the rooms

From 8 ARCHITECTURE PIECES DEDICATED
TO A PHANTOM ARCHITECT 1965 SPRING

SENSE PIECE

Common sense prevents you from thinking.
Have less sense and you will make more
sense.

Art is fart. Fart more and you will fart
less.

Screaming is a voice never loud enough
to reach. Scream more and you will scream
less.

1968 spring

I thought, 'Why are women always known for a pretty voice and pretty songs?' Because that's what the world wants. They don't want a woman to sound too strong. We feel we shouldn't scream out. I thought, 'We have to show what women are. We're the birth-givers of the human race. Without us bringing up the new generation, there wouldn't be a human race.' We have this very strong powerful energy in us, but the world wants to think that we are the weaker sex. That's why I want to bring out this thing from me.

I consciously took and morphed my vocalizations from Japanese kabuki and noh. People have told me it is also close to Spanish flamenco. There are unknown areas of sound and experience that people can't really mention in words. Like the stuttering in your mind. I was interested not in the noise you make but the noise that happens when you try not to make it, just that tension going back and forth.

I think that it's more a total experience, and sexuality is part of that, maybe even a large part. I do these sexual sounds, but these sexual sounds could also be someone who is being tortured. I was interested in the animalistic side of the human voice, like the groaning when a woman is having a baby. When I went to Morocco and heard people chanting, I thought it sounded familiar to the stuff I was doing. Deep-rooted memory, human history, part of it, a kind of memory cell in DNA.

It's nice to go into that very, very fine, intricate mixture of sounds and rhythm. It's almost like going into a dream, getting something that doesn't exist in the physical world, unutterable sounds – a kind of metaphysical rhythm. I don't accommodate the audience. I ask the audience to accommodate.

In the avant-garde, I jammed with top musicians like John Cage, David Tudor and La Monte Young in New York; with Ichiyanagi, Mayuzumi, Kobayashi, and Takahashi in Tokyo; and in jazz, with Ornette Coleman and his incredible band: Ed Blackwell, David Izenson and Charlie Haden. I came in from the cold to John's world totally fearless. I didn't know what I was walking into.

I didn't need John then. I was going through a phase when I was the oddball because my thing was less theoretical than most. I was intuitive, so when I followed Ornette, you can obviously hear immediately that Ornette's work is highly intellectualized, sophisticated stuff. I'm howling, and the combination is not a combination really –

it's not merging, it's separate – but I didn't have anybody else to merge with.

John: When she first played me her Albert Hall stuff, I grooved to it. I was saying, all that intellectual jazz going on in the background, I can't stand it, let's do it together, do it this way. Conceptually you think you're going to howl and the musician's going to play but the difference between Ornette Coleman intellectualizing that jazz – which is just to me, intellectual literary crap coming out of a trumpet or whatever he plays – and just playing rock 'n' roll, or just playing the amplifier, is tremendous and that's what happened in Cambridge because it was a small experience.

Yoko: When John and I got together, I was interested in that strong, heavy beat, which I equated with the heartbeat. I thought avant-garde music is mainly for the head. Most male avant-garde composers avoided the voice because it was too animalistic – they were into very cool instrumental things. Cool was in, and by using my voice I was a little uncool in their eyes. The sound of my voice was too human and emotional. I rebelled against that avant-garde tendency and went more animalistic. When I heard the rock beat, I thought, 'Oh this is what I was looking for!' And I never looked back. If you listen to some of my past records, the harsh ones were my signature sounds. I wanted to break the sound barrier with those sounds. The world needed to listen to our scream.

Initially, I wanted to bring my old avant-garde friends to London to make music, while John tried to sell me on his friends. 'You think they're assholes from Liverpool, but they're fucking quick. You got to give them a chance, Yoko. Just explain to them what you want and they'll pick it up like that.'

John was right, of course. They did a brilliant job. Listen to George's sitar on 'Greenfield Morning', to Ringo's drumming on 'Touch Me', Eric Clapton's guitar on 'Don't Worry Kyoko', Klaus Voorman's bass guitar on 'Why' and John's incredible guitar playing throughout. All of these tracks were 'jamprovisations' – jam sessions with no rehearsal, which was what I believed music should be at the time. Performing with Ringo, he was just right there doing it. No hesitation, no strict structure, all improvisation. I don't know how he got it and did it, but he was brilliant. When I started to scream, I think John thought, 'Oh I can do anything!' I would hear his guitar and think, 'Wow, I can answer that.'

Above: Yoko Ono with Peggy Guggenheim and John Cage
in Japan, October 1962.
Below: John Cage, Toshiro Mayuzumi, David Tudor and
Yoko Ono perform John Cage's *Piano Walk* at Tokyo Bunka
Kaikan Hall, Tokyo, as part of the Sogetsu Contemporary
Series, 9 October 1962.

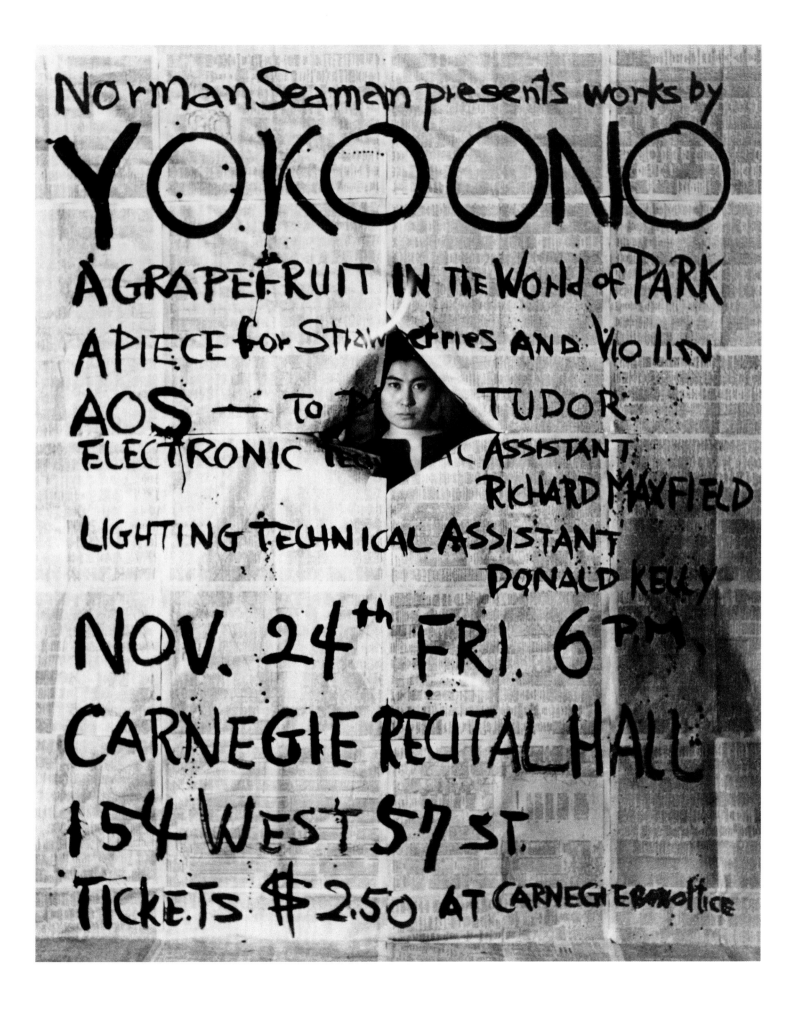

We did some earplay stuff on the board, like adding birds singing and trains passing, but we did not have to correct one drum beat, one guitar note. John and I felt that together we had created a 'New Music', a fusion of avant-garde jazz-rock and East and West.

John: With Yoko's and my album, we're both looking at the same thing from different sides of the table. I call mine a literate version of what we went through in the last year or so and Yoko's is a sort of sound picture, rather than a word picture. Mine is literate, hers is revolutionary. Yoko's was right off, live. We didn't even know we were making it. She did all her tracks in one night. She becomes her voice and you get touched.

Yoko: First of all, John and I were going to make individual LPs, and John started his session first. When he was recording, I was in the control room. Sometimes he had to fool around with his instrument just to get inspired or to get into his music, and I'd be thinking, well, he should be doing his song, not fooling about – that's the feeling you get in the control room – but he just kept jamming and then suddenly I realized how beautiful the jamming was.

He started something very unusual with the guitar so I couldn't help it. I had to join them. John had said 'whenever you feel like joining, join us' and all I have to say is 'no' if I don't want it. In 'Why', he inspired me, and I jumped into the room. John sang, 'Eyugh-eyugh!' He was trying to tell me to get in and join them, and I just joined in.

I liked the idea of improvisation, going somewhere you don't know, just having something vague planned, like doing something that's slow or quiet and the rest of it decided by the wind or whatever. So I went in and started to scream, and then John's guitar was going along frantic.

John: I was dancing around with the guitar in front of her, catching her eye and she was screaming back at me. It was a fantastic scene. There was just the four of us there: Klaus Voormann on the bass and Ringo on the drums, me on the guitar and Yoko on voice and we just knocked it off. It was one of those things that just happened that night. We didn't plan it; the musicians were in a good mood, they were grooving and Yoko was in a good mood. We started 'Why' without her – she was in the control box, it was meant to be my session – and we got into such a good lick and on the beginning of the track I'm shouting, 'Hey! Hey!' – I'm trying to signal her in the control box to come in and start because

it was right for her to start singing with it, but she didn't hear me. She just wandered into the room anyway because she was inspired by the sound; she just came in and grabbed a mic and luckily the engineers got her. Normally when she opens her mouth they're so surprised and they whip down the volume because she blasts the mic to shreds.

Yoko: It was a lot to do with John. It was always in the context of doing his sessions. It was like, 'You're here anyway, why not do Yoko's song?' Most people thought it was terrible. I was aware that I was doing something unique and important. But they thought, 'How dare she?' On 'Why' you hear John saying, 'Were you getting that?' I kept it in because most of the time when we did my stuff, all the engineers picked that time to go to the bathroom. They couldn't stand it. I was very impressed, happy and thankful that John was being extremely cooperative; cooperative for a guy. And especially for a guy who was so successful in the world. He was always into my thing despite the fact that he was attacked for it.

In the avant-garde scene and all that, most of my friends were so intellectual and when we were doing this 'Why' we suddenly realized that John and I had this temperament that we both go mad, really mad. His guitar went really mad and I just started to join in.

I realized that John and I have a very mean streak, it was similar in that sense. There's something about us that's saying, 'Fuck you, I couldn't care less!', and I go mad with my voice and John does it with his guitar. Both of us have that side.

John: I have that side, but it's hard to get it on a two-minute single with a technician like George sitting around.

Yoko: It became a dialogue. We stimulated each other. You don't know who inspired whom, it just goes on.

John: We just did it and ran into the control booth to hear it. We couldn't tell which was her voice and which was the guitar at first, but you can just tell when her voice comes in just after the guitar, you realize one's human and one's steel.

Phil McDonald (engineer): We used to record a lot of jams in those days, straight stereo as well. Because they'd say, 'Well, can we hear that back?' and I'd say, 'What? I didn't record it!' So I used to make sure that I got everything that they did recorded either on the eight-track or on stereo. I used to have a stereo mix on the board; we used to go

Promotional posters from Yoko Ono's early performances. Above left: DIAS (Destruction In Art Symposium) presents Two Evenings with Yoko Ono, The Africa Centre, Covent Garden, London, 28 September 1966. Above right: *Music of the Mind*, Jeanetta Cochrane Theatre, London, 17 November 1966. Below left: Yoko Ono: *Music of the Mind*, The Bluecoat Society of Arts, Liverpool, 26 September 1967. Below right: Yoko Ono at the Savile: *Music of the Mind and the Fog Machine*, 8 December 1967.

Above: Promotional poster for Ornette Coleman's *Emotion Modulation* show where Yoko performed her work 'AOS' with Ornette Coleman, David Izenzon, Charlie Haden and Edward Blackwell at The Royal Albert Hall, London, 29 February 1968.

Below: Yoko's handwritten instructions for the performance of her work 'AOS' to Ornette Coleman and his band at The Royal Albert Hall, London, 29 February 1968.

To Ornette

Do not be concerned about showing many things; simplicity and economy of notes, dynamics and rhythm.
Think of the days when you only had one heart and one penis to give — and one note.
Think of the days when you had to suffer in silence for 10 days of eternity before
you could give, and yet you were afraid of giving because what you were giving was so
true and so total, you knew that you would ~~be~~ suffer a death after that.
Think of the days when you allowed silences in your life for dreaming and thinking of dreaming.
This is no shit. no "mood" or whatever you call it. It's real.
Four of you play like four cats used to chattering with eachother. Forget about eachother.
Forget about what you've learnt or heard in the music academy world or the like, ~~and~~ Be insecure.
  (You should bind one hand and play with one hand if that makes you insecure, or blindfold)
                                                                    for this piece
Section one:
I will call.
don't respond until you are really ready.
respond with same plaintifness — of one note and slight variation.
or you should call to seek for other voices

Section two:
total silence — let's see how long we can hold it, or how long it is necessary.
it is the most tenderest of silences — of making love

Section three:
let's gradually go up — don't go up too quickly. listen to me. I will try to control you from
going up. awkward breaks that are caused by that are part of the music.
and when we are up. stay there until we are completely exhausted and really, so that
the section four will be no fake.
Section four:
very quiet. your exhausted self.
just breath with your instrument
die down.

Yoko. London '68

Above: Yoko and Ornette Coleman, The Arts Lab,
Drury Lane, London, 1968.

Below: Photo of Yoko with Ornette Coleman and his band,
bassists Charlie Haden and David Izenzon and drummer
Ed Blackwell rehearsing 'AOS', used as a promotional
poster for their performance at The Royal Albert Hall,
London, 29 February 1968.

Yoko (voice), John (guitar), John Tchikai (saxophone), John
Stevens (percussion) and Mal Evans (watch) performing
Cambridge 1969 which was recorded during *A Natural Music
Nothing Doing In London Concert*, and released on their
album *Unfinished Music No. 2: Life With The Lions*;
Lady Mitchell Hall, Cambridge, England, 2 March 1969.

straight to stereo so that I could say, 'Oh yes, I've got that, don't worry', which was my safeguard, because it was recording history, in the end.

I think what people didn't realize at the time was that she sang as some classical Japanese singers sing. This screaming that she did was actually part of her culture. To us, it sounded like screaming but to her it was a musical note, and to get this ultimate scream, it could take a while to produce. They weren't ordinary screams, they were yells! Very demonstrative screams, which a lay person would just think there was somebody screaming their head off, but they were actually calculated, and I don't know how the heck she did it, to tell you the truth.

Yoko: When I was a child, I kept having a nightmare about being born in a large space, which scared me. That was the start. That feeling of large space scaring me is still with me. Babies cry; people are just used to shouting and screaming in life in general, so I'm sure they must understand screaming and shouting, but the thing is I think they are too scared to see something.

John: When they hear it, they can't help feeling it. I heard somebody calling in to a programme and it made her skin crawl. It's realism again, it gets to you whether you like it or not, there's no escape from it and that's what people don't like.

Yoko: They can't stand strong emotion. You have to refine the emotion into some pretty music to communicate with them, usually, and I just detest that.

John: If you hear 'Cold Turkey', towards the end of it, I'm getting towards singing, or letting the voice go as much as Yoko does, but not quite. But on 'Well Well Well', I let it go. It's the same as shouting 'Twist And Shout' or 'Tutti Fruitti', only just missing the words. Don't say anything. Because 'tutti fruitti a-wop-bop-a-lula' never said anything, in literary terms. Yoko does the same. She just takes a word or an expression or an idea and works around it. It's like a sax playing it. It's like an instrumental. Yoko's doing with her voice what instrumentalists have done over the past fifty years with their instruments, but she's doing it with her voice. 'Why Not' is today's 'Tutti Frutti'.

Yoko: I realized that modern classical composers, when they went from 4/4 to 4/3, lost the heartbeat. It's as if they left the ground and lived on the fortieth floor. Schoenberg and Webern – Webern's on the top of the Empire State Building.

Our conceptual rhythm got complex, but we still have the body and the beat. Conceptual rhythm I carry on with my voice, which has a very complicated rhythm even in 'Why,' but the bass and the drum is the heartbeat. So the body and the conceptual rhythms go together.

I think we're saying a lot of things in our minds that are too heavy to come out as clean sentences. When I'm embarrassed, I sometimes start to stutter a little bit. And sometimes when I'm trying to say something, I'll begin to stutter. Most of us kill off our real emotions, and on top of them, you have your smooth self – because of our cultured and refined background, we do manage to say something in very smooth sentences, like 'How are you?' But maybe in my mind I'm saying 'How-how-how-how-a-a-a-re-you?' What you're trying to say in your mind is not that specific, it's more like emotional and it's all abstract. When I want to say, 'I'm sorry' in a song, I don't feel like saying, [in a singsong voice] 'I'm sorry, mother', but rather as an emotion should be, [groaning, stuttering] 'I'm so-or-or-orrrry'. A stutterer is someone who's feeling something very genuine, not repressing yourself and talking too smoothly. So in 'Paper Shoes' I say: 'Pa-pa-pa-pa-paper sh-sh-sh-sh-shoooooooes!'

John: Van Gogh's paintings might please you, but you know damn well what shit he went through to do it. The pain is in the painting, but there's still this pleasure and warmth and colour in it. When they brought out abstract art, people were saying, 'He's thrown the paint at the canvas' or, 'Where's the human form in it?' The older you get, the more frustrated you feel. And it gets to a point where you don't have time to utter a lot of intellectual bullshit. If you were drowning you wouldn't say, 'I'd like to be helped because I have just a moment to live.' You'd say, 'Help!' but if you were more desperate, you'd scream out, 'Ayyyiiiieeee!', or something like that. And the desperation of life is really life itself, the core of life, what's really driving us forth. When you're really desperate it's phony to use descriptive and decorative adjectives to express yourself.

Yoko: I never will forget the dawn in the Abbey Road studio when John and I hugged each other after completing the *Yoko Ono/Plastic Ono Band* album. When I was a little girl, I read of Monsieur and Madame Curie discovering radium, with, naturally, the Madame sitting in the driver's seat. That was how I felt. I could not change history. At the time, I was a composer who was stretching her ears to the edge of the boundless universe. We were there and nothing else seemed to matter.

JOHN LENNON/PLASTIC ONO BAND ●

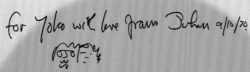

for Yoko with love from John 9/18/70

JOHN LENNON/PLASTIC ONO BAND

Side One

MOTHER
MOTHER, YOU HAD ME BUT I NEVER HAD YOU
I WANTED YOU BUT YOU DIDN'T WANT ME
SO I GOT TO TELL YOU
GOODBYE GOODBYE

FATHER, YOU LEFT ME BUT I NEVER LEFT YOU
I NEEDED YOU BUT YOU DON'T NEED ME
SO I JUST GOT TO TELL YOU
GOODBYE GOODBYE

CHILDREN, DON'T DO WHAT I HAVE DONE
I COULDN'T WALK AND I TRIED TO RUN
SO I GOT TO TELL YOU
GOODBYE GOODBYE

MAMA DON'T GO
DADDY COME HOME

HOLD ON
HOLD ON JOHN, JOHN HOLD ON
IT'S GONNA BE ALRIGHT
YOU GONNA WIN THE FIGHT

HOLD ON YOKO, YOKO HOLD ON
IT'S GONNA BE ALRIGHT
YOU GONNA MAKE THE FLIGHT

WHEN YOU'RE BY YOURSELF
AND THERE'S NO ONE ELSE
YOU JUST TELL YOURSELF
TO HOLD ON

HOLD ON WORLD, WORLD HOLD ON
IT'S GONNA BE ALRIGHT
YOU GONNA SEE THE LIGHT

WHEN YOU'RE ONE
REALLY ONE
YOU GET THINGS DONE
LIKE THEY NEVER BEEN DONE
SO HOLD ON
HOLD ON

I FOUND OUT
I TOLD YOU BEFORE, STAY AWAY FROM MY DOOR
DON'T GIVE ME THAT BROTHER, BROTHER, BROTHER,
BROTHER
THE FREAKS ON THE PHONE WON'T LEAVE ME ALONE
SO DON'T GIVE ME THAT BROTHER, BROTHER, BROTHER,
BROTHER NO!
I FOUND OUT!

NOW THAT I SHOWED YOU WHAT I BEEN THROUGH
DON'T TAKE NOBODY'S WORD WHAT YOU CAN DO
THERE AIN'T NO JESUS GONNA COME FROM THE SKY
NOW THAT I FOUND OUT I KNOW I CAN CRY
I FOUND OUT!

SOME OF YOU SITTING THERE WITH YOUR * IN YOUR
HAND
DON'T GET YOU NOWHERE DON'T MAKE YOU A MAN
I HEARD SOMETHING 'BOUT MY MA AND MY PA
THEY DIDN'T WANT ME SO THEY MADE ME A STAR
I FOUND OUT!

OLD HARE KRISHNA GOT NOTHING ON YOU
JUST KEEP YOU CRAZY WITH NOTHING TO DO
KEEP YOU OCCUPIED WITH PIE IN THE SKY
THERE AIN'T NO GURU WHO CAN SEE THROUGH YOUR EYES
I FOUND OUT!

I SEEN THROUGH JUNKIES I BEEN THROUGH IT ALL
I SEEN RELIGION FROM JESUS TO PAUL
DON'T LET THEM FOOL YOU WITH DOPE AND COCAINE
CAN'T DO YOU NO HARM TO FEEL YOUR OWN PAIN
I FOUND OUT!

WORKING CLASS HERO
AS SOON AS YOU'RE BORN THEY MAKE YOU FEEL SMALL
BY GIVING YOU NO TIME INSTEAD OF IT ALL
TILL THE PAIN IS SO BIG YOU FEEL NOTHING AT ALL
A WORKING CLASS HERO IS SOMETHING TO BE
A WORKING CLASS HERO IS SOMETHING TO BE

THEY HURT YOU AT HOME AND THEY HIT YOU AT SCHOOL
THEY HATE YOU IF YOU'RE CLEVER AND THEY DESPISE
A FOOL
TILL YOU'RE SO * CRAZY YOU CAN'T FOLLOW THEIR
RULES
A WORKING CLASS HERO IS SOMETHING TO BE
A WORKING CLASS HERO IS SOMETHING TO BE

WHEN THEY'VE TORTURED AND SCARED YOU FOR
20 ODD YEARS
THEN THEY EXPECT YOU TO PICK A CAREER
WHEN YOU CAN'T REALLY FUNCTION YOU'RE SO FULL
OF FEAR
A WORKING CLASS HERO IS SOMETHING TO BE
A WORKING CLASS HERO IS SOMETHING TO BE

KEEP YOU DOPED WITH RELIGION AND SEX AND TV
AND YOU THINK YOU'RE SO CLEVER AND CLASSLESS
AND FREE
BUT YOU'RE STILL * PEASANTS AS FAR AS I CAN
SEE
A WORKING CLASS HERO IS SOMETHING TO BE
A WORKING CLASS HERO IS SOMETHING TO BE

THERE'S ROOM AT THE TOP THEY ARE TELLING YOU STILL
BUT FIRST YOU MUST LEARN HOW TO SMILE AS YOU KILL
IF YOU WANT TO BE LIKE THE FOLKS ON THE HILL
A WORKING CLASS HERO IS SOMETHING TO BE

YES, A WORKING CLASS HERO IS SOMETHING TO BE
IF YOU WANT TO BE A HERO WELL JUST FOLLOW ME
IF YOU WANT TO BE A HERO WELL JUST FOLLOW ME

ISOLATION
PEOPLE SAY WE GOT IT MADE
DON'T THEY KNOW WE'RE SO AFRAID
ISOLATION
WE'RE AFRAID TO BE ALONE
EVERYBODY GOT TO HAVE A HOME
ISOLATION

JUST A BOY AND A LITTLE GIRL
TRYING TO CHANGE THE WHOLE WIDE WORLD
ISOLATION
THE WORLD IS JUST A LITTLE TOWN
EVERYBODY TRYING TO PUT US DOWN
ISOLATION

I DON'T EXPECT YOU TO UNDERSTAND
AFTER YOU CAUSED SO MUCH PAIN
BUT THEN AGAIN YOU'RE NOT TO BLAME
YOU'RE JUST A HUMAN, A VICTIM OF THE INSANE

WE'RE AFRAID OF EVERYONE
AFRAID OF THE SUN
ISOLATION
THE SUN WILL NEVER DISAPPEAR
BUT THE WORLD MAY NOT HAVE MANY YEARS
ISOLATION

* omitted at the insistence of E.M.I.

JOHN LENNON: GUITAR PIANO* VOCALS
YOKO ONO: WIND
RINGO STARR: DRUMS
KLAUS VOORMANN: BASS

Side Two

REMEMBER
REMEMBER WHEN YOU WERE YOUNG
HOW THE HERO WAS NEVER HUNG
ALWAYS GOT AWAY
REMEMBER HOW THE MAN
USED TO LEAVE YOU EMPTY HANDED
ALWAYS, ALWAYS LET YOU DOWN
IF YOU EVER CHANGE YOUR MIND
ABOUT LEAVING IT ALL BEHIND
REMEMBER, REMEMBER, TODAY

DON'T YOU WORRY
'BOUT WHAT YOU'VE DONE
DON'T FEEL SORRY
'BOUT THE WAY IT'S GONE

REMEMBER WHEN YOU WERE SMALL
HOW PEOPLE SEEMED SO TALL
ALWAYS HAD THEIR WAY
REMEMBER YOUR MA AND PA
JUST WISHING FOR MORE STARDOM
ALWAYS, ALWAYS PLAYING A PART
IF YOU EVER FEEL SO SAD
AND THE WHOLE WORLD IS DRIVING YOU MAD
REMEMBER, REMEMBER, TODAY

LOOK AT ME
LOOK AT ME
WHO AM I SUPPOSED TO BE?
WHO AM I SUPPOSED TO BE?
LOOK AT ME
WHAT AM I SUPPOSED TO BE?
WHAT AM I SUPPOSED TO BE?
LOOK AT ME
OH MY LOVE OH MY LOVE

LOVE
LOVE IS REAL, REAL IS LOVE
LOVE IS FEELING, FEELING LOVE
LOVE IS WANTING TO BE LOVED

LOVE IS TOUCH, TOUCH IS LOVE
LOVE IS REACHING, REACHING LOVE
LOVE IS ASKING TO BE LOVED

LOVE IS YOU
YOU AND ME
LOVE IS KNOWING
WE CAN BE

LOVE IS FREE, FREE IS LOVE
LOVE IS LIVING, LIVING LOVE
LOVE IS NEEDING TO BE LOVED

WELL WELL WELL
I TOOK MY LOVED ONE OUT TO DINNER
SO WE COULD GET A BITE TO EAT
AND THOUGH WE BOTH HAD BEEN MUCH THINNER
SHE LOOKED SO BEAUTIFUL I COULD EAT HER
WELL WELL WELL OH WELL

WE SAT AND TALKED OF REVOLUTION
JUST LIKE TWO LIBERALS IN THE SUN
WE TALKED OF WOMEN'S LIBERATION
AND HOW THE HELL WE COULD GET THINGS DONE
WELL WELL WELL OH WELL

I TOOK MY LOVED ONE TO A BIG FIELD
SO WE COULD WATCH THE ENGLISH SKY
WE BOTH WERE NERVOUS FEELING GUILTY
AND NEITHER ONE OF US KNEW JUST WHY
WELL WELL WELL OH WELL

HERE I AM
WHAT AM I SUPPOSED TO DO?
WHAT AM I SUPPOSED TO DO?
HERE I AM
WHAT CAN I DO FOR YOU?
WHAT CAN I DO FOR YOU?
HERE I AM
OH MY LOVE OH MY LOVE

LOOK AT ME OH PLEASE LOOK AT ME, MY LOVE
HERE I AM—OH MY LOVE

WHO AM I?
NOBODY KNOWS BUT ME
NOBODY KNOWS BUT ME
WHO AM I?
NOBODY ELSE CAN SEE
JUST YOU AND ME
WHO ARE WE?
OH MY LOVE OH MY LOVE

GOD
GOD IS A CONCEPT
BY WHICH WE MEASURE
OUR PAIN
I'LL SAY IT AGAIN
GOD IS A CONCEPT
BY WHICH WE MEASURE
OUR PAIN
I DON'T BELIEVE IN MAGIC
I DON'T BELIEVE IN I-CHING
I DON'T BELIEVE IN BIBLE
I DON'T BELIEVE IN TAROT
I DON'T BELIEVE IN HITLER
I DON'T BELIEVE IN JESUS
I DON'T BELIEVE IN KENNEDY
I DON'T BELIEVE IN BUDDHA
I DON'T BELIEVE IN MANTRA
I DON'T BELIEVE IN GITA
I DON'T BELIEVE IN YOGA
I DON'T BELIEVE IN KINGS
I DON'T BELIEVE IN ELVIS
I DON'T BELIEVE IN ZIMMERMAN
I DON'T BELIEVE IN BEATLES
I JUST BELIEVE IN ME
YOKO AND ME
AND THAT'S REALITY

THE DREAM IS OVER
WHAT CAN I SAY?
THE DREAM IS OVER
YESTERDAY
I WAS THE DREAMWEAVER
BUT NOW I'M REBORN
I WAS THE WALRUS
BUT NOW I'M JOHN
AND SO DEAR FRIENDS
YOU JUST HAVE TO CARRY ON
THE DREAM IS OVER

MY MUMMY'S DEAD
MY MUMMY'S DEAD
I CAN'T GET IT THROUGH MY HEAD
THOUGH IT'S BEEN SO MANY YEARS
MY MUMMY'S DEAD
IT'S HARD TO EXPLAIN
SO MUCH PAIN
I COULD NEVER SHOW IT
MY MUMMY'S DEAD

All songs written by John Lennon

PRODUCED: JOHN AND YOKO AND PHIL SPECTOR
ENGINEERS: PHIL MACDONALD, RICHARD LUSH, JOHN LICKIE, ANDY STEVENS AND EDDIE
COVER PHOTOGRAPH: DAN RICHTER
SLEEVE DESIGN: JOHN AND YOKO
TEA AND SYMPATHY: MAL EVANS

*BILLY PRESTON ON 'GOD' AND PHIL SPECTOR ON 'LOVE'

Reproduced by permission of
Northern Songs Ltd.

‡Reproduction rights also claimed
by Maclen (Music) Ltd.

An Apple Record
An EMI recording

This page: John Lennon's sketches.
Above: *A Family Tree*, 1976; centre: *Subtle Woffell*, 1968; below: *I Sat Belonely*, 1964.

I Sat Belonely
by John Lennon, 1964

I sat belonely down a tree,
humbled fat and small.
A little lady sing to me
I couldn't see at all.

I'm looking up and at the sky,
to find such wondrous voice.
Puzzly puzzle, wonder why,
I hear but I have no choice.

'Speak up, come forth, you ravel me',
I potty menthol shout.
'I know you hiddy by this tree'.
But still she won't come out.

Such sofly singing lulled me sleep,
an hour or two or so
I wakeny slow and took a peep
and still no lady show.

Then suddy on a little twig
I thought I see a sight,
A tiny little tiny pig,
that sing with all it's might

'I thought you were a lady',
I giggle, – well I may,
To my surprise the lady,
got up – and flew away.

Opposite: Alternative shots from the *Plastic Ono Band* album covers photo session; Tittenhurst Park, Ascot, autumn 1970.

Previous pages: The *John Lennon/Plastic Ono Band* album cover, label and inner artworks. Above left: album cover, based on a drawing by John; below left: Apple Records labels for sides one and two with the track listings for each side; above right: childhood photograph of John, previously used on the cover of the Beatles single, 'Strawberry Fields Forever'; below right: inner sleeve, front and back, designed by John & Yoko, dedicated 'For Yoko with love from John 9/10/70'.

Overleaf: The *Yoko Ono/Plastic Ono Band* album cover, label and inner artworks. Above left: album cover, based on a drawing by John; below left: Apple Records labels for sides one and two with the track listings for each side and the instruction 'PLAY IN THE DARK'; above right: childhood photograph of Yoko, used as the rear cover; below right: inner sleeve, front and back, designed by John & Yoko, dedicated 'For John with love from Yoko 9/10/70'.

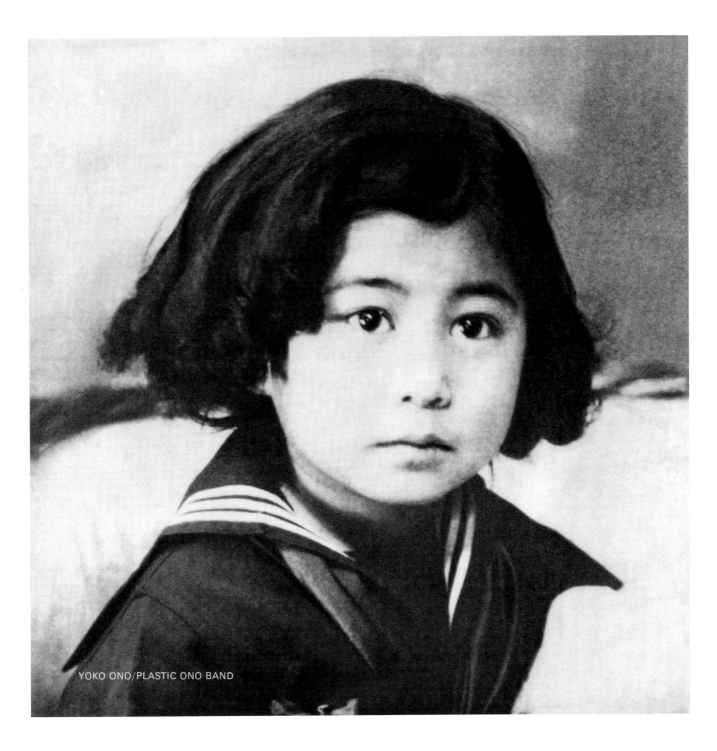

YOKO ONO/PLASTIC ONO BAND

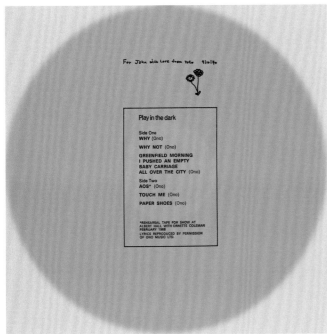

For John with love from Yoko 9/10/90

Play in the dark

Side One
WHY (Ono)

WHY NOT (Ono)

GREENFIELD MORNING
I PUSHED AN EMPTY
BABY CARRIAGE
ALL OVER THE CITY (Ono)

Side Two
AOS* (Ono)

TOUCH ME (Ono)

PAPER SHOES (Ono)

*REHEARSAL TAPE FOR SHOW AT
ALBERT HALL WITH ORNETTE COLEMAN
FEBRUARY 1968
LYRICS REPRODUCED BY PERMISSION
OF ONO MUSIC LTD.

YOKO ONO/PLASTIC ONO BAND

YOKO ONO: VOCALS
JOHN LENNON: GUITAR
RINGO STARR: DRUMS
KLAUS VOORMANN: BASS

ORNETTE COLEMAN: TRUMPET
EDWARD BLACKWELL: DRUMS
DAVID IZENZON: BASS
CHARLES HADEN: BASS

PRODUCED: JOHN AND YOKO
ENGINEERS: PHIL MACDONALD, JOHN LICKIE, ANDY STEVENS AND EDDIE
COVER PHOTOGRAPH: DAN RICHTER
SLEEVE DESIGN: JOHN AND YOKO
SALAD: MAL EVANS
Published by Ono Music

An Apple Record

JANUARY 21, 1971
50c
UK. 3/-

ROLLING STONE

The
Rolling Stone
Interview:
John Lennon
Part One
The
Working
Class
Hero

ANNIE LEIBOVITZ

FEBRUARY 4, 1970 /
50¢   UK. 3/-

ROLLING STONE

The
Rolling Stone
Interview:
John Lennon
Part Two
**Life
With
The
Lions**

John had felt hurt and abandoned for years. If you look at his songwriting as a Beatle in the years that preceded their break-up, you can see he was dealing with the same extremely personal themes of love and loss in songs like 'Julia', but he couldn't fully get to the real depth and pain of those issues and be as brutally honest as he wanted. While still one of the 'Mop-Tops', one of the Beatles, one of four people, he had to be expressing what the group wanted to express. He could get a certain amount through, but to dive deep, to be painful, he had to be on his own. He hated the hypocrisy. There had been a lot of anger and resentment building up.

His developing and deepening relationship with Yoko was opening up his mind, making it obvious to him that there were so many other things going on in the world; so many other points of view and possibilities for art. Having met such an intelligent and trustworthy soulmate, all these ideas and energies started to be released. And then meeting Janov and going through intense Primal Scream therapy gave him the outlet, the methodology and the justification.

It's easy to forget that when John wrote all those songs and when he made all those bold statements to me in the *Rolling Stone* interview – so powerful and so profound – that he was still a young man of only thirty, still discovering the world. Even at thirty we are so hot-tempered and full of passion and only really a step removed from the madness of adolescence.

I was very surprised about how open and candid he was. I had never heard anything like that from any artist, let alone from a Beatle. The Beatles were surrounded by walls of protection and mythology and sanctity. They were almost as revered as the royal family. John had gone along with it like everybody else. They couldn't admit they were fucking a lot of girls, or using lots of drugs or misbehaving behind the scenes, because others would destroy the Beatles myth. Everybody went along with it. When he said that the Beatles were more popular than Jesus, although he believed it, he really was forced by the rest of them to apologise and back down and he hated doing it.

John wanted everything he did to be Number One. He felt it was a great album and was hoping for immediate commercial success. He knew that he had done something very special and it was very personal and very powerful. He knew that releasing an album that was so sparse, simple and painful would be controversial. He knew saying, 'I don't believe in Beatles' would have an effect and he was leading with his chin. He was taking on the world.

It was the first solo album by a Beatle. He knew in the interview with me that he was announcing the break-up of the Beatles, which had never been formally announced. No member of the Beatles had said, 'You know what, it's over.' And so I think he knew he was on the edge of momentous changes in his life and the lives of his mates. I think what also appealed to him was the idea that he was going to bring a change in a point of view and attitude to the entire world through all the Beatles' fans that the fairytale, the dream, or whatever you want to call it, was over. And that's like one of the most important lines on that record – 'the dream is over'. 'God' is a cruel, powerful, sad and poignant song. When I hear it, I still choke up.

My first reaction on listening to the album as a whole was that it was stunning in every way. The singing, the experience, the songs, the writing, what he is saying, what he is saying to the world, what he is saying to the Beatles, what he is saying about himself.

Bob Dylan has written many incendiary albums that are poignant and powerful, but nobody has written as powerful an album about themselves as this, and particularly at his level of popularity. John abandoned all interest in appealing to his popular fanbase. He just said, 'I'm going to tell the truth as I see it and let it all be damned.' The power and strength – that an artist of that quality, imagination and creativity could reach such truths about themselves – was overwhelming.

In the interview, he talked a lot about how he & Yoko had been treated. Her as a second-class citizen, as a woman, as an Asian. I think there was a lot of truth to that and I also think that she was treated as an interloper by his mates. You can be best buddies with someone and then they get married and you don't like the wife. It's very difficult to go and hang out at the weekends if the wives don't like each other. So she got blamed for what he himself wanted to do, which was get out of this teenage thing that he had been involved in all his life, grow up and marry the woman he loved.

On 21 January 1971, we published the first part of the interview, with the title 'Working Class Hero' with John on the cover in bib-and-brace dungarees, his National Health issue round glasses and beard, looking for all the world like a Working Class Hero.

That particular picture was never meant to be the cover. It was just one of the pictures that Annie Leibovitz took during the set-ups. When she brought me the whole shoot

Previous pages: John on two front covers of *Rolling Stone* magazine, photographed by Annie Leibovitz, with edited excerpts of founding editor Jann S. Wenner's interview with John & Yoko on 8 December 1970, published in two parts, 'The Working Class Hero' on 21 January 1971 (left), and 'Life With The Lions' on 4 February 1971 (right).

Above: John in conversation with author Tom Wolfe. Below: Yoko smiling with Jann, photographed by Annie, whilst John & Yoko were filming Yoko's *Film No. 12 ('Up Your Legs Forever')* at West 61st St., New York, 4 December 1970. Jann's handwritten message on the print reads, 'Yoko – Annie took this in 1970! xxx Jann'.

Yoko — Annie took this in 1970! xxx Jann

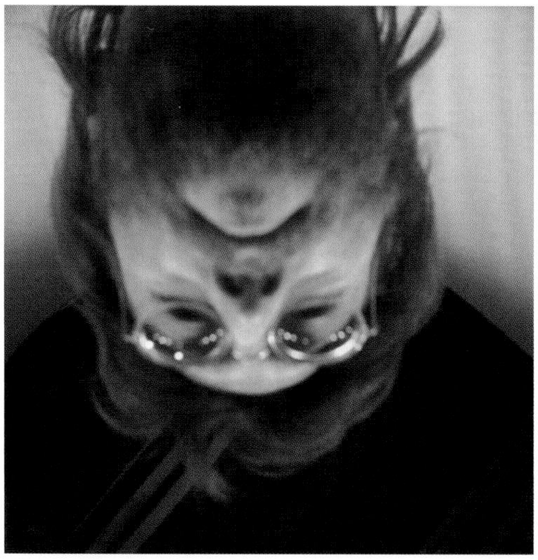
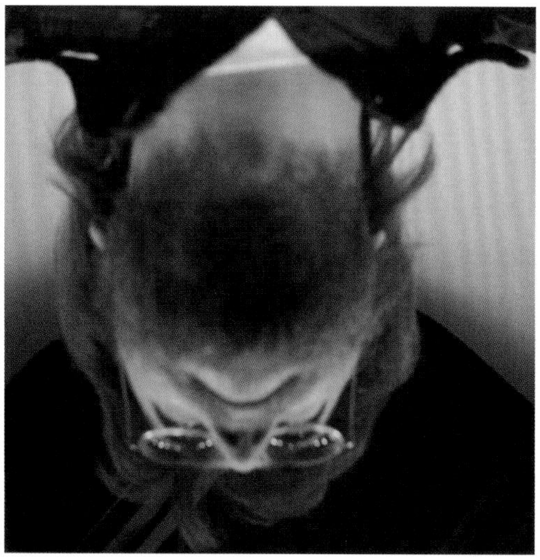
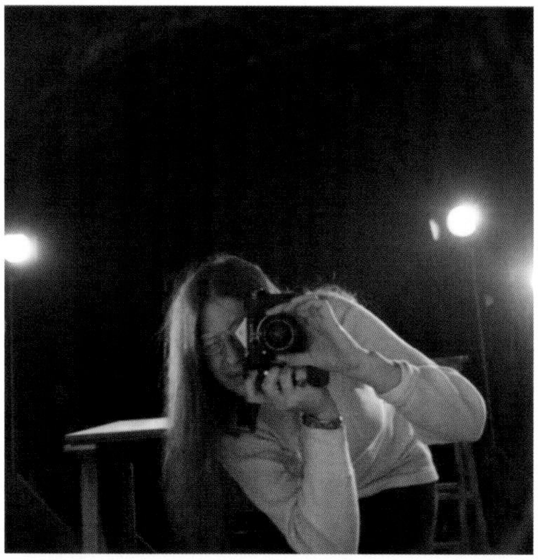
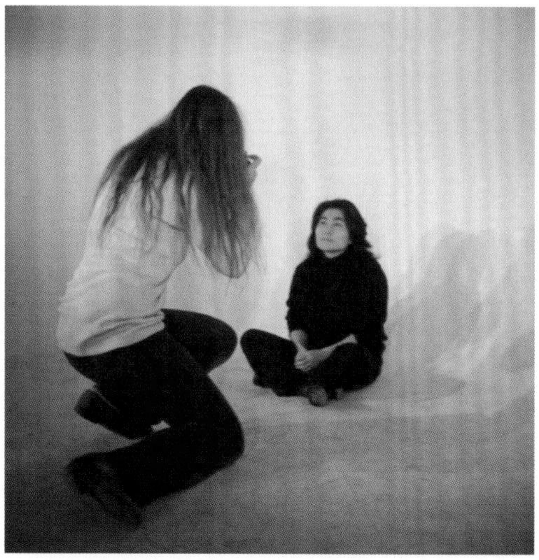
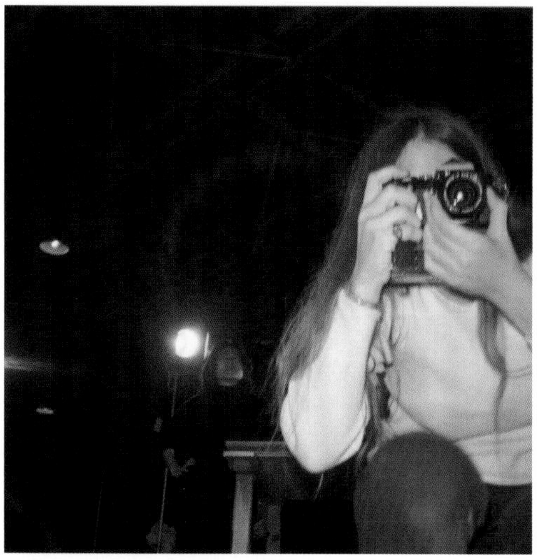
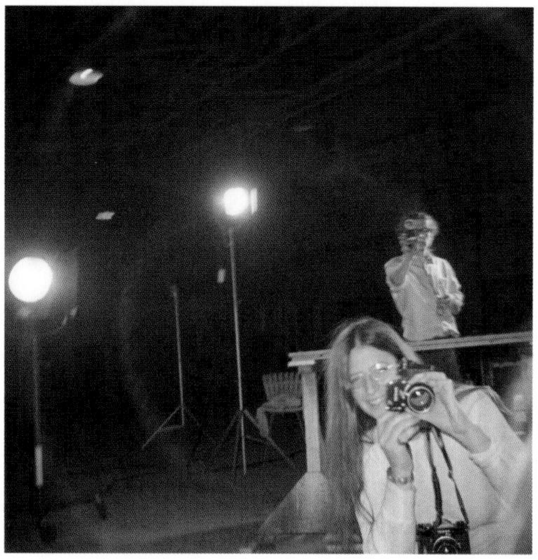
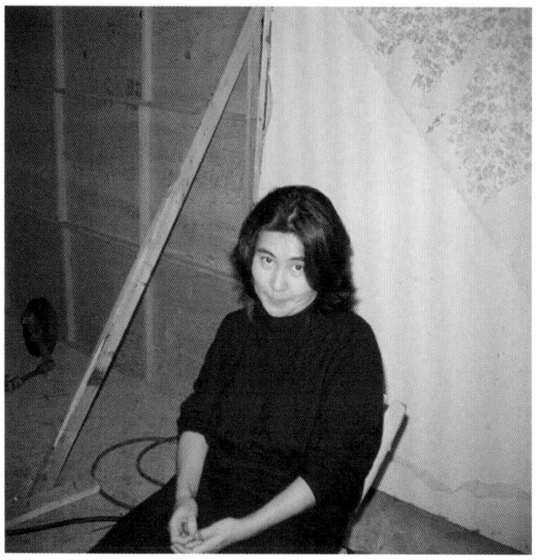
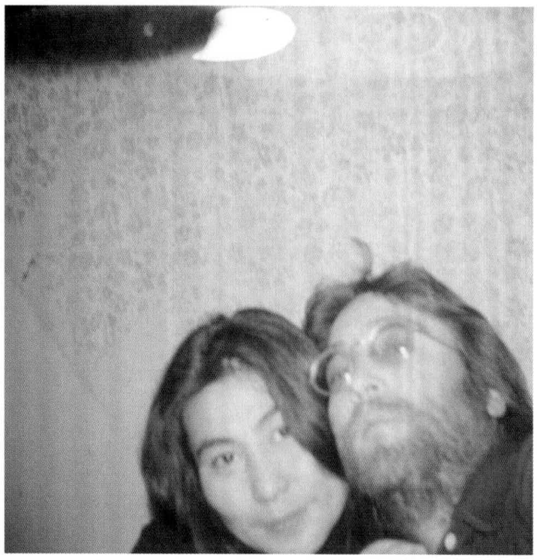

and I saw that image, that was it. There was no question in my mind and it was obvious to everybody. It was the first thing that she shot and he just happened to be looking right at that camera in a very transparent way, not posing, almost as if he wasn't looking at the camera, thinking about something else entirely, just in his own mind.

The interview was a more explicit and more obvious and more detailed statement of the same themes in the album and his intentions. John shot his mouth off so regularly he was usually pleased with all the attention. But as much as he thought he knew this would provoke some reaction, I don't think he was prepared for the shock, anger and disappointment it provoked all around the world. 'I don't believe in Beatles' – he said that in print in *Rolling Stone*, and on the album. I think he thought 'Well, you know, some people cry over spilt milk, but basically people will accept it; people be happy for me because I am being liberated.' People were furious. 'The dream is over? How dare you tell me that kind of stuff! I don't believe in Beatles? Excuse me, Mr. Lennon, but I believed in the Beatles for the last ten years and I've got all your records!'

From the fan level up to the more intellectual, people believed in the Beatles as one of the great phenomena of our time, with their powerful unifying music, love and humour. And he just came out and shat on it in his unbalanced and crazy way. I think today he would look back and say, 'Wait a minute, wait a minute, the Beatles was great, really. Boy, what a piece of work, blah, blah, blah', but people were angry at him for doing that. And I think he was genuinely surprised.

Throughout his life, John was always enthusiastically searching for some kind of dream, answer or solution – something that would bring him peace, or bring world peace. He went through enormous numbers of ideas, philosophies and fads. Macrobiotic foods, bags, drugs, Buddhism, Hare Krishna, politics, this group, that thing, Phil Spector, etc. He would eat them up, get really enthusiastic and overboard and then discover that it wasn't all it was cracked up to be and ultimately pull back into a more balanced state. He would retain some of what he'd learned and generally reject most of it. Then he would move on and get unbalanced again with another new discovery of the latest 'thing'.

Before John died, he had made the ultimate discovery. He finally settled down and realized, in a really personal direct sense, the eternal values of love in raising a child and having peace of mind and how much that meant to him. I think he really did find his happiness at the end.

ANNIE LEIBOVITZ / PHOTOGRAPHER

I went to the San Francisco Art Institute thinking I was going to be an art teacher. I was enrolled in the painting programme there and the first semester I had an Art History class and Fred Martin made it quite clear: 'you couldn't become an art teacher until you became an artist'. I still didn't know what that meant. I wasn't such a great painter. I loved life drawing, but at that time the style of painting coming out was very abstract expressionist. It was the Vietnam War, it was the end of the Haight-Ashbury, it was a dark San Francisco period and the abstract painters were angry and painting was very isolating.

The photography department was young and there was a lot of social activity going on and the camera to a young person like myself was like having a friend that would take you out to places, so the following summer I took a workshop in photography. My first camera was a Minolta SRT 101 I bought in Japan. It had a little needle inside and you would line the needle up and when it was in the circle, you knew it was the correct exposure. The school had a dark room. I would go out during the day, take pictures and come back at the end of the day, develop them and have them printed. That night you would be looking at what you did and talking about it. I was never a technical photographer. It was always about content for me. I liked the immediacy of it. There was something really wonderful about the whole process. It just clicked. [laughs]

The school was really based on Robert Franks who was considered the father of 35mm photography in the United States and Henri Cartier-Bresson who represented the same kind of photographer in Europe. They were considered the first photographers who took photography in a way that had never been done before and made it portable. Very portable, very relaxed, very fluid because they had a small camera. And this is how I learned to take pictures.

I started working for *Rolling Stone* a couple of years later, even before I finished school. I was looking to be adopted and found Jann and Jane, and it turned into family for me. It was more than a magazine. It was a way of life. My first cover was one of the photographs from the peace rally – a crowd shot – and they used it as an illustration for revolution in the country at that time.

Rolling Stone instilled in me at a very young age that what I did mattered and was important. I think it's so important to believe in what you're doing and care about what you're doing and I was so lucky to be in a place where I was surrounded by people doing the same thing at a time when our country was so politically charged at that moment in the early Seventies.

I'd heard rumours in the office that Jann was going to New York and he was going to do the *Rolling Stone* interview with John Lennon and I sort of volunteered myself and asked if I could go. I said I would stay with friends and I would fly youth fare, which I think was $75 to go cross-country. I talked him into taking me and it was really an experience that would set the tone for how I would work with well-known people.

I really didn't know how to direct anyone to do anything. John & Yoko were just very straightforward and normal and honest and caring and cooperative and they helped me. They really set the standard for me. It was such a great experience because he was one of the Beatles. He immediately set me at ease and taught me this wonderful lesson about just being yourself and playing it as straight as you can. It stuck with me forever, and ever since, I expect the same from everyone and from myself – just to be yourself.

I had two cameras. One had the 35mm lens on it and one had a little longer lens, the 105mm, which had a built-in light meter. I was taking a light meter reading and he just lifted his head and looked straight at me and I clicked the picture at the same time. The hardest thing to do is a single person image, because then it's me and that person relating. I wasn't really ready for that kind of photograph to be so straightforward – a person looking straight back at me like that.

When we got back to San Francisco, Jann chose that picture for the cover. I was heartbroken because I really liked the more wide angle lens that showed more of where they were and the environment. I grew to like that picture. It took me years to like it. That kind of picture felt to me very standard; it felt very normal. I've always liked environmental pictures that pull back a bit and you see more.

I learned very early on that something that wouldn't seem like it was anything would be something. And I enjoy that aspect of it so much. I never like to presume something about a story or a person until I got there. In order to get the best possible pictures, one had to become part of what was going on, and then you're there and no one pays you any mind and then you can take the pictures you want to take.

John in denim dungarees with his Kodak Instamatic camera. One of many portraits by Annie Leibovitz for *Rolling Stone* magazine, 4 December 1970.

Overleaf: John & Yoko resting during the filming of *FLY*. John is holding his sitka spruce-top, mahogany-sided CF Martin 5-18 parlour guitar; Dan Seymour's loft, 184 Bowery, New York, 14 December 1970.

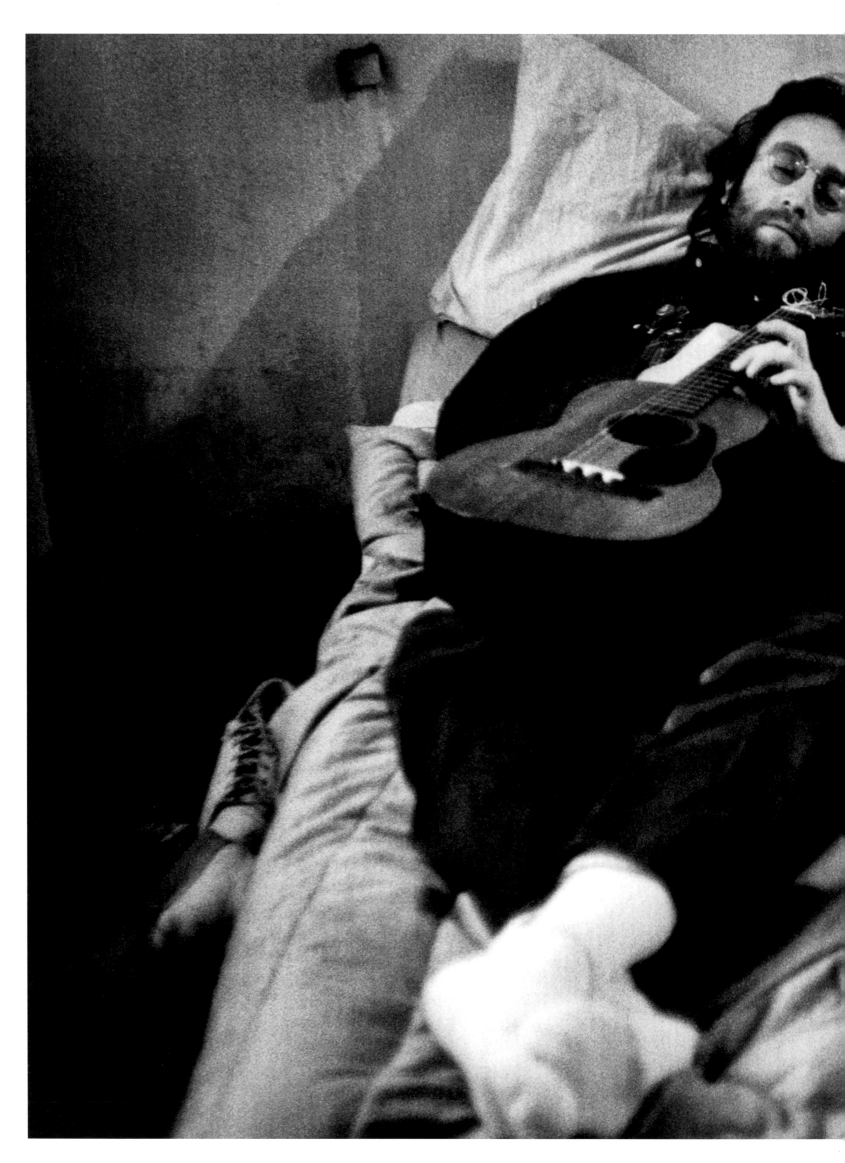

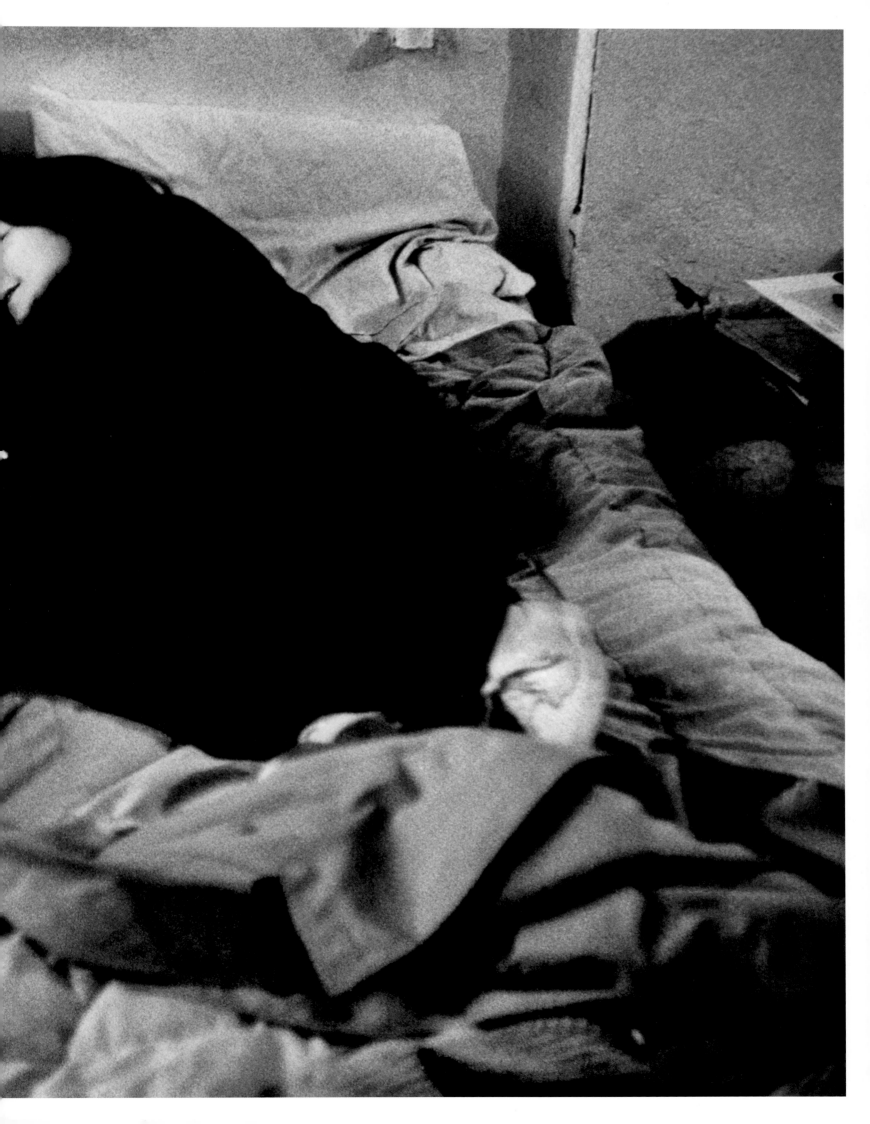

遅き日や谺聞ゆる京の隅　　The slow day;
Echoes heard
In a corner of Kyoto.

John: This is how I feel now.

After their 'slow boat to Japan', John quotes his new favourite haiku poet Yosa Buson to journalist Junichi Yano who interviews and photographs John & Yoko for *Asahi Graphic* magazine wearing kimonos (opposite), striking Kaiun no Kane (The Bell of Better Fortune) and giving alms to a Buddhist monk (below) at Enryakuji Temple, Kyoto, 18 January 1971.

John & Yoko recording an interview with Kenji Mizuhara,
Apple Label Manager for Japan, which was subsequently
released on a '33 Compact' seven-inch single in a limited run
of 1,000 to the first people who replied to a postcard included
with the initial Japanese releases of John & Yoko's *Plastic
Ono Band* albums; Imperial Hotel, Tokyo, 25 January 1971.

During John & Yoko's first Japanese vacation together, Yoko took him to visit the Imperial Shrine of Yasukuni (a Shinto-style shrine commemorating the Japanese war dead) in Chiyoda, Tokyo, 14 January 1971. Photographed for *Shukan Myojo* magazine, 21 January 1971.

「ヨーコはママに会いに、ボクはお寺を見にきたんだ。それだけさ」いたずらをみつけられた子どものように困まった顔のジョン・レノン(30)。3年前に結婚した洋子夫人(37)と船でお忍びの来日(1月14日、東京の靖国神社)
撮影／本誌・望月和夫

REFERENCES

13
Yoko Ono Lennon, 2020; contains an excerpt of: Essay: Yoko Ono, 'On Plastic Ono Band', 1971

16–17
Essays: Yoko Ono, 'On Plastic Ono Band', 1971; John Lennon, 'Plastic Ono Band', 1970

22–25
Audio Interview: David Sheff, 10–28 September 1980; BBC Radio, 6 December 1980; Jody Denberg, 2010

Online Interview: John Rieber, johnrieber.com, 2016

Print Interviews: Ian McGillis, *Montreal Gazette*, 2017; Michael Cragg, *Guardian*, 2013; Tariq Ali and Robin Blackburn, *Ramparts*, 1971

Television Interviews: *Speaking Freely*, First Amendment Center, 2001; Tom Snyder, *The Tomorrow Show*, NBC, 1976

Video Interview: Dave Sidaway, *Montreal Gazette*, 2017

23
Lyrics: 'The Ballad of John & Yoko'. Written by John Lennon and Paul McCartney © 1969 Sony/ATV Music Publishing LLC

26–27
Lyrics: 'Give Peace A Chance'. Written by John Lennon © 1968 Sony/ATV Music Publishing LLC

33
Essays: Derek Taylor, 'What Is The Plastic Ono Band?', *Disc and Music Echo*, 1969; John Peel, *Disc and Music Echo*, 1969 (in response to the previous)

36–42
Audio Interviews: BBC Radio, 6 December 1980; Barry Miles, Zapple, 23–24 September 1969; (Alan White, Klaus Voormann): Simon Hilton, 2016–2020

Audio recording: Plastic Ono Band, *Live Peace In Toronto 1969*, 1969

Essay: Mal Evans, *The Beatles Book*, 1969

Film Interview: *24 Hours: The World of John and Yoko* (raw camera footage), BBC/Lenono, 3 December 1969

Online Interview: Harvey Kubernik, Cave Hollywood, 2013

Print Interviews: Alan Smith, *New Musical Express*, 20 September 1969; Ritchie Yorke, *Detroit Free Press*, 3 October 1969

Book: Keith Badman, *The Beatles: The Dream Is Over, Off The Record 2*, Omnibus Press, 2002

Video Interview (Klaus Voormann): raw camera footage courtesy of Yoko Ono, 2005

50–51
Lyrics: 'Cold Turkey'. Written by John Lennon © 1969 Lenono Music

52–55
Audio Interviews: BBC Radio, 6 December 1980; David Sheff, 10–28 September 1980; Jann S. Wenner, 8 December 1970; Robbie Dale (The Admiral), 23 October 1969

Book: Peter Brown and Steven Gaines, *The Love You Make*, Pan Books, 1984

Film Interviews: Gloria Emerson, *24 Hours: The World of John and Yoko* (raw camera footage), BBC/Lenono, 3 December 1969; Marshall McLuhan, *CBC Weekend*, CBC, 19 December 1969

Letter: John Lennon, to Her Majesty Queen Elizabeth II, Bag Productions, 25 November 1969

Print Interviews: Carol Clerk, *Uncut*, January 1998; Glenn Plaskin, *Chicago Tribune*, 6 May 1990; Tim Teeman, *The Daily Beast*, 13 October 2015; Carol Clerk, *Uncut*, September 2003; Ritchie Yorke, *John, Yoko and Year One*, 28 June 1970

57
Letter: John Lennon, to Her Majesty Queen Elizabeth II, Bag Productions, 25 November 1969

59
Audio Interviews: BBC Radio, 6 December 1980; Jann S. Wenner, 8 December 1970; Jonathan Cott, 5 December 1980; (Alan White): Simon Hilton, 12 September 2019

Film Interview: Alan Smith, *24 Hours: The World of John and Yoko* (raw camera footage), BBC/Lenono, 3 December 1969

Print Interviews: Alan Smith, *NME*, 20 December 1969; Richard Robinson, *Hit Parader*, August 1970

Audio Interview: Emperor Rosko, Midday Spin Radio, 15 February 1970

64–65
Lyrics: 'Instant Karma! (We All Shine On)'. Written by John Lennon © 1970 Lenono Music

67
Audio Interview: Jann S. Wenner, 8 December 1970

69–72
Audio Interview: BBC Radio, 6 December 1980; David Sheff, 10–28 September 1980; Howard Smith, 12 December 1970; Jann S. Wenner, 8 December 1970; (Alan White): Simon Hilton, 12 September 2019

Book: *Beatles Anthology*, Apple Corps, Cassell and Co., 2000

Essays: Yoko Ono, Facebook and Twitter Q&As, imaginepeace.com, 2009–2016

Film Interview (Klaus Voormann): Matthew Longfellow, *Classic Albums: John Lennon/Plastic Ono Band* (raw camera footage), Eagle Rock Entertainment, 2008

Online: B.P. Fallon, bpfallon.com, 9 October 2015; Nick Deriso, Something Else!, 3 November 2011

Print Interview (Andy Stephens): *Uncut*, 2016

Audio Interview: Emperor Rosko, BBC Radio, February 1970

Video Interview (Billy Preston): Q&A, Beatlefest, 1966

75
Poem: Michael X, 'One Flower', 1969

78
Essays: Yoko Ono, Facebook and Twitter Q&As, imaginepeace.com, 2009–2016

84–93
Film Interview (Arthur Janov): Matthew Longfellow, *Classic Albums: John Lennon/Plastic Ono Band* (raw camera footage), Eagle Rock Entertainment, 2008

Print Interview (Arthur Janov): John Harris, *Mojo*, 2000

Video Interviews (Arthur Janov): raw camera footage courtesy of Yoko Ono, 2005; What is Primal Therapy?, Primal Institute, 2008

98–99
Lyrics: 'Mother'. Written by John Lennon © 1970 Lenono Music

100–103
Audio Interviews: Barry Miles, Zapple, 23–24 September 1969; David Sheff, 10–28 September 1980; Elliot Mintz, 1976; Kenny Everett, Radio Monte Carlo, 27 March 1971; Scott Muni, WNEW–FM, 13 February 1975; John Lennon diary tape, 5 September 1979; Lenono, 1977

Essay: Alfred Lennon, 1975

Film Interview: Barbara Graustark, *Yoko Ono: Then And Now*, Sekhmet, 1984

Print Interviews: Hunter Davies, 1978;

Alan Smith, *New Musical Express*, 1963; Robert Hilburn, *LA Times*, 1980

TV Interview: Mike Douglas, *Mike Douglas Show*, Westinghouse, 20 January 1972

109
Letter: John Lennon, to Alfred Lennon, 1 September 1967

110–111
Lyrics: 'Hold On'. Written by John Lennon © 1970 Lenono Music

112–120
Audio Interviews: David Sheff, 10–28 September 1980; Jann S. Wenner, 8 December 1970; Kenny Everett, Radio Monte Carlo, 27 March 1971; Maurice Hindle, Daniel Wiles and Bob Cross, 2 December 1968

Essays: Yoko Ono, Facebook and Twitter Q&As, imaginepeace.com, 2009–2016

Letter: John Lennon, to Simon, 1977

Lyrics: 'Early 1970' written by Richard Starkey © 1971 Startling Music Ltd.

114–115
Letter: John Lennon, to Christine Marsh, spring 1968

118
Letter: John Lennon, to Mr. Miller, spring 1968

119
Letter: John Lennon, to Mr. Bulla, spring 1968

121
Essays: Yoko Ono, 'Dance Report – On Hiding', 'Dance Report – On Facing', *Thirteen Day Dance Festival*, September and October 1967

122–123
Lyrics: 'I Found Out'. Written by John Lennon © 1970 Lenono Music

124–127
Audio Interviews: Barry Miles, Zapple, 23–24 September 1969; David Sheff, 10–28 September 1980; Howard Smith, 12 December 1970; Jann S. Wenner, 8 December 1970; Kenny Everett, 27 March 1971; Press Conference, Amsterdam, 1969; Tariq Ali & Tony Blackburn, *Red Mole*, 21 January 1971

Audio recording: John Lennon diary tape, 5 September 1979

Film Interview (George Harrison): *Beatles Anthology*, Apple Corps, 1990s

130–131
Lyrics: 'Working Class Hero'. Written by John Lennon © 1970 Lenono Music

132–140
Audio Interviews: BBC, 6 December 1980; Howard Smith, 6 December 1980, 5 January 1972, 23 January 1972; Jann S. Wenner, 8 December 1970; Jonathan Cott, 5 December 1980; Kenny Everett, Radio Monte Carlo, 27 March 1971; Paul Drew, RKO, April 1975; Tariq Ali & Tony Blackburn, *Red Mole*, 21 January 1971

Film Interviews: CBC TV, 1969; 'Bed-In', Lenono, May 1969; Press Conference, Chicago, 11 August 1966; Press Conference, Toronto, 17 August, 1966; Press Conference, Memphis, 19 August 1966; Press Conference, New York, 22 August, 1966; Press Conference, Tokyo, 30 June 1966

Print Interviews: Maureen Cleave, *Evening Standard*, 4 March 1966; Ray Connolly, *The Sunday Times Magazine*, 6 September 2009

133
Book: Mark Lewisohn, *The Beatles Tune In*, Little Brown, 2013

139
Print Interviews: Maureen Cleave, *Evening Standard*

142
Film Interview: CBC TV, 1969

144–145
Lyrics: 'Isolation'. Written by John Lennon © 1970 Lenono Music

146–154
Audio Interviews: BBC, 6 December 1980; David Sheff, 10–28 September 1980; Jann S. Wenner, 8 December 1970; Kenny Everett, Radio Monte Carlo, 27 March 1971

Online Interview: Taylor Norman, *Citizens of Humanity*, 25 January 2016

Print Interviews: Barbara Graustark, *Newsweek*, 29 September 1980; Fiona Sturges, the *Independent*, 1 September 2013

Book: Keith Badman, *The Beatles: The Dream Is Over, Off The Record 2*, Omnibus Press, 2002

156
Audio Interview (Nic Knowland): Simon Hilton, 2016

158–159
Lyrics: 'Remember'. Written by John Lennon © 1970 Lenono Music

170–171
Lyrics: 'Love'. Written by John Lennon © 1970 Lenono Music

172–179
Lyrics: 'The Ballad of John & Yoko'. Written by John Lennon and Paul McCartney © 1969 Sony/ATV Music Publishing LLC

Audio Interviews: Barry Miles, Zapple, 23–24 September 1969; Howard Smith, 12 December 1970; Jann S. Wenner, 8 December 1970; Jonathan Cott, 13 December 1970; Press Conference, Amsterdam, 1969

Book: *Beatles Anthology*, Apple Corps, Cassell & Co., 2000

Essays: Yoko Ono, Facebook and Twitter Q&As, imaginepeace.com, 2009–2016

Print Interviews: Barbara Graustark, *Newsweek*, 29 September 1980; Robert Goldman, *National Lampoon*, September 1970

Video Interview: raw camera footage courtesy of Yoko Ono, 2005

Print Interview: Betty Rollin, *Look*, 18 March 1969

180–181
Lyrics: 'Well Well Well'. Written by John Lennon © 1970 Lenono Music

188–189
Lyrics: 'Look At Me'. Written by John Lennon © 1970 Lenono Music., with additional handwritten note from John: 'pre Janov!'

196
Audio Interviews: Jonas Mekas, 18 and 21 December 1970

Essays: Yoko Ono, Facebook and Twitter Q&As, imaginepeace.com, 2009–2016

201
Television Interview: David Frost, *Frost On Saturday*, ITV, 1968

204–205
Lyrics: 'God'. Written by John Lennon © 1970 Lenono Music

206–216
Audio Interviews: David Sheff, 10–28 September 1980; David Wigg, *Scene and Heard*, BBC, 8 May 1969; Elliot Mintz, 2 April 1973; Howard Smith, 17 December 1969, 12 December 1970, 9 September 1971, 23 January 1972;

Jann S. Wenner, 8 December 1970; Maurice Hindle, Daniel Wiles and Bob Cross, Kenwood, 2 December 1968; Barry Miles, Zapple, 23–24 September 1969; Press Conference, Tokyo, 4 October 1977; Tariq Ali and Robin Blackburn, *Red Mole*, 21 January 1971

Book: *Beatles Anthology*, Apple Corps, Cassell & Co., 2000

Essays: John Lennon, 'The Ballad of John & Yoko', 1969, published in *Skywriting By Word of Mouth*, Pan Books, 1986; Yoko Ono, Facebook and Twitter Q&As, imaginepeace.com, 2009–2016

Print Interviews: Alan Smith, *New Musical Express*, 7 August 1971; Alan Smith, *Hit Parader*, February 1972; Barbara Graustark, *Newsweek*, 29 September 1980; Leonard Gross, *Look*, 1966; Robert Hilburn, *LA Times*, 1980

Audio Interview: Gilles Gougeon, Radio-Québec, 1969

Television Interviews: Jean-François Vallée, *Un Jour Futur*, 18 March 1975; Tom Snyder, *The Tomorrow Show*, 8 April 1975

Video Interview: Chuck Collins, *Underground News*, 26 July 1972

212–213
Essay (cut-up): John Lennon, 'The Complete Yoko Ono Word Poem Game', 28 July 1970

219
Postcard: John & Yoko, to Arthur and Vivian Janov, December 1970

220–221
Lyrics: 'My Mummy's Dead'. Written by John Lennon © 1970 Lenono Music. With additional handwritten note: 'to Art with love from John 6/8/70', part of a portfolio of typed and handwritten lyrics given to Arthur and Vivian Janov by John & Yoko when they left California to return home to England

222
Audio Interviews: David Wigg, BBC, 1969; David Sheff, 10–28 September 1980; Howard Smith, 12 December 1970

Book: *Beatles Anthology*, Apple Corps, Cassell and Co., 2000

Print Interviews: *Disc*, 1975; *Hit Parader*, 1972; Tariq Ali and Robin Blackburn, *Ramparts*, 1971; Tariq Ali and Robin Blackburn, *Red Mole*, 1971

223
Card: Julia Lennon, to John Lennon, 'Dear Stinker, wink', Easter Sunday 19 April 1957

229–232
Audio Interviews: BBC Radio, 6 December 1980; Howard Smith, 12 December, 1970; Jann S. Wenner, 8 December 1970; Simon Hilton, 2012–2020

Film Interviews (Klaus Voormann, Phil McDonald, Richard Lush): Matthew Longfellow, *Classic Albums: John Lennon/Plastic Ono Band* (raw camera footage), Eagle Rock Entertainment, 2008

237–238
Film Interview: Matthew Longfellow, *Classic Albums: John Lennon/Plastic Ono Band* (raw camera footage), Eagle Rock Entertainment, 2008

Reviewed and approved by Ringo Starr, April 2020

239
Postcards: John & Yoko, to Ringo and Maureen Starr, 1969–1971

241–242
Audio Interviews (Klaus Voormann): Simon Hilton, 2016–2018

Film Interview (Klaus Voormann): Matthew Longfellow, *Classic Albums: John Lennon/Plastic Ono Band* (raw camera footage), Eagle Rock Entertainment, 2008

Reviewed and approved by Klaus Voormann, April 2020

244
Book: Billy Preston, *Memories of John Lennon*, edited by Yoko Ono, HarperCollins, 2005

Print Interviews (Billy Preston): John Abbey, *Blues and Soul*, 1979; Mike Boehm, *LA Times*, 1990

Television Interviews (Billy Preston): Dick Clark, *American Bandstand*, 1981; Jools Holland, *Later With Jools Holland*, 2005

Video Interview (Billy Preston): Midem festival, 1972

Video Interview (Billy Preston): Q&A, Beatlefest, 1966

250–261
Audio Interviews: Simon Hilton, 2016–2020; Barry Miles, Zapple, 23–24 September 1969; Howard Smith, 12 December 1970; Kenny Everett, 27 March 1971

Essays: Yoko Ono, 'To The Wesleyan People', 1966; Yoko Ono, 'London Jam', *Onobox*, 1997; Yoko Ono, Facebook and Twitter Q&As, imaginepeace.com, 2009–2016

Film Interview (Phil McDonald): Matthew Longfellow, *Classic Albums: John Lennon/Plastic Ono Band* (raw camera footage), Eagle Rock Entertainment, 2008

Online Interview: Titania Kumeh, *Mother Jones*, 22 February 2010

Print Interviews: Helen Brown, *Telegraph*, 2017; Henry Edwards, *Crawdaddy*, 29 August 1971; Alexis Petridis, *Guardian*, 2016; Jonathan Cott, *Rolling Stone*, 1971; Joy Press, *Wire*, 1996; Miya Masaoka, *San Francisco Bay Guardian*, 1997; Robert Palmer, *Rolling Stone*, 1981

258
Essay: Yoko Ono, 'To Ornette', February 1968

264
Poem: John Lennon, 'I Sat Belonely', from *In His Own Write*, Jonathan Cape/Simon & Schuster, 1964

270–273
Film Interview: Matthew Longfellow, *Classic Albums: John Lennon/Plastic Ono Band* (raw camera footage), Eagle Rock Entertainment, 2008

Reviewed and approved by Jann S. Wenner, April 2020

274
Film and video Interviews: *A Conversation with Annie Leibovitz at John F. Kennedy Presidential Library and Museum*, Boston MA, WGBH Forum, 2011; Annie Leibovitz Q&A session, Elliott Bay Book Company, Seattle WA, Gluechonk, 2011; Barbara Leibovitz, *American Masters*, Adirondack Pictures, Eagle Rock Entertainment, Thirteen/WNET, 2007; Cannes Lions 60, Adlip, 2013; Eileen Prose, *Good Day!*, WCVB, 1991; Enrique Cerna, *Conversations at KCTS9*, 2009, Seattle WA; Rebecca Frayn, *The South Bank Show*, Middlemarch Films/LWT, 1993

Print Interview: *San Diego Union-Tribune*, November 23, 2003

Reviewed and approved by Annie Leibovitz, April 2020

278
Haiku: *Yosa Buson* (1716–1784)

Print Interview: Junichi Yano, *Asahi Graphic*, 1971

SOURCES OF ILLUSTRATIONS

INDEX

Illustrations are in **bold**.

INDEX

ACKNOWLEDGMENTS

A dream you dream alone is only a dream;
A dream you dream together is reality.
y.o.

Producer and Creative Direction: Yoko Ono Lennon

Editor: Simon Hilton

Publishing Coordinator: Tristan de Lancey

Thames & Hudson: Jane Laing, Phoebe Lindsley and Sadie Butler

Weldon Owen International: Raoul Goff and Roger Shaw

Lenono Photo Archive: Karla Merrifield and Sari Henry

Lenono Art Archive: Connor Monahan, Marcia Bassett,
Michael Sirianni and Nick Lalla

Lenono Audio Archive: Rob Stevens

Special thanks to Paul Hicks, Matthew Cocker and Cary Anning at
Abbey Road Studios

Lenono Film Archive: Simon Hilton

Studio One: Helen Barden, Sibyl Bender and Bob Deeb

Legal: Jonas Herbsman

Design: Daniel Streat at Visual Fields

Initial photo restoration and Photoshop: Simon Hilton and Sam Gannon

Additional research: Sam Gannon, Beth Walsh, Ben Baker, Akiko Ono
Amelia Peters, Grace Whitrick-Davyd, Patrick McKechnie, Simon Prentis,

Film footage transfers: Dave Northrop, Bruce W Goldstein

Special thanks:
Sean Ono Lennon, Julian Lennon, Kyoko Ono, Jonas Herbsman, Olivia
and Dhani Harrison, Ringo and Barbara Starr, Klaus and Christine Voormann,
Alan and Gigi White, Eric Clapton, Jann S. Wenner, Annie Leibovitz, Karen
Mulligan, Paul Hicks, Dan and Jill Richter, Sandrine Garnier-Marten and
the Janov Family Trust, Michael Cadwallader, Stanley Parkes, Richard and
Candace DiLello, Nic Knowland, Toni Myers, Phil McDonald, Richard Lush,
Andy Stephens, John Leckie, Eddie Klein, Petula Clark, Tommy Smothers,
Vanessa Taylor, Kim Fowley, Gary Evans, Julie Rossow, B. P. Fallon, Pete
Shotton, the Estates of Timothy Leary, Billy Preston and Ornette Coleman,
Jon Hendricks, Sandra Carli Karlsson; Jonathan Clyde and Aaron Bremner
at Apple Corps; Geoff Kempin, Peter Worsley, Melissa Morton-Hicks and
Matthew Longfellow at Eagle Rock Entertainment; Orla Lee Fisher, Guy
Hayden and Mike Heatley at Universal Music; Jo Cosbert, Allan Rouse,
Peter Shukat, Amanda Keeley, Martin Darvill, Anna Hilton Rinsler, Diana
Hilton, Lucienne Powell, Florencia Belén Pérez Figueroa, Andre Ribuoli
at Ribuoli Digital; John Waite and Tony Window at Metro Images

Websites:
johnlennon.com
imaginepeace.com
plasticonoband.com

First published in USA and Canada in 2020 by Weldon Owen International
1150 Brickyard Cove Road, Point Richmond, California 94801, USA

Published by arrangement with Thames & Hudson Ltd, London

John & Yoko / Plastic Ono Band © 2020 Yoko Ono Lennon
Text © 2020 Yoko Ono Lennon

For image copyright information, see p.284

ISBN 978-1-68188-589-6

Printed and bound in China by C&C Offset Printing Co. Ltd

weldonowen.com

Page 1: *John Lennon/Plastic Ono Band* cover photo taken by John & Yoko's assistant Dan Richter at their home, Tittenhurst Park, Ascot, Autumn 1970.

Page 2: 'People For Peace': John & Yoko during the filming of two performances of 'Instant Karma! (We All Shine On)' for BBC TV show *Top Of The Pops*, Studio 8, BBC Television Centre, London, 11 February 1970.

Pages 4 & 5: The *Plastic Ono Band*: sculptures by John Lennon & Yoko Ono, consisting of Perspex columns made by Charles Melling and electronic equipment fitted by 'Magic' Alex Mardas and David Goodwin at Apple Electronics, London 1968.

Pages 6 & 7: Following their marriage, in a gesture of feminist equality, John added Ono to his name by deed poll at the same place where, just two months

before, the Beatles had performed their final concert, on the roof of the Apple offices, 3 Savile Row, London, 22 April 1969.

Pages 8 & 9: John & Yoko in the garden, Tittenhurst Park, Ascot, Berkshire, 4 December 1969.

Page 10: John & Yoko in front of John's artwork *You Are Here* at the exhibition opening, Robert Fraser Gallery, London, 1 July 1968.

Overleaf: John Lennon & Yoko Ono – *War Is Over! If You Want It Love and Peace from John & Yoko*, 1969/1971.

Front Cover: Composite of portrait photographs of John & Yoko, February 1970. Courtesy Yoko Ono Lennon.

Back Cover: The *Plastic Ono Band* Perspex sculpture, photographed by Iain Macmillan © Yoko Ono Lennon.

WAR IS OVER!

IF YOU WANT IT

Love and Peace from John & Yoko